The Technical Interview Guide to Investment Banking

The Wiley Finance series contains books written specifically for finance and investment professionals as well as sophisticated individual investors and their financial advisors. Book topics range from portfolio management to e-commerce, risk management, financial engineering, valuation and financial instrument analysis, as well as much more. For a list of available titles, visit our Web site at www.WileyFinance.com.

Founded in 1807, John Wiley & Sons is the oldest independent publishing company in the United States. With offices in North America, Europe, Australia and Asia, Wiley is globally committed to developing and marketing print and electronic products and services for our customers' professional and personal knowledge and understanding.

The Technical Interview Guide to Investment Banking

PAUL PIGNATARO

WILEY

Published by John Wiley & Sons, Inc., Hoboken, New Jersey.
Published simultaneously in Canada.

For general information on our other products and services or for technical support, please contact our Customer Care Department within the United States at (800) 762–2974, outside the United States at (317) 572–3993 or fax (317) 572–4002.

Wiley publishes in a variety of print and electronic formats and by print-on-demand. Some material included with standard print versions of this book may not be included in e-books or in print-on-demand. If this book refers to media such as a CD or DVD that is not included in the version you purchased, you may download this material at http://booksupport.wiley.com. For more information about Wiley products, visit www.wiley.com.

Library of Congress Cataloging-in-Publication Data is available:

ISBN 978–1–119–16139–4 (Hardcover)
ISBN 978–1–119–16141–7 (ePDF)
ISBN 978–1–119–16140–0 (ePub)

Cover Design: Wiley
Cover Image: © Mikhail Zahranichny/Shutterstock

Printed in the United States of America
10 9 8 7 6 5 4 3 2 1

This book is dedicated to every investor in the pursuit of enhancing wealth—those who have gained, and those who have lost—this continuous struggle has confounded the minds of many. This book should be one small tool to help further this endeavor; and if successful, the seed planted will contribute to a future of more informed investors and smarter markets.

Contents

Preface

Investment banks perform two major functions. First, they act as intermediaries between investors, or suppliers of capital, and entities that request capital such as corporations. Second, investment banks advise corporations on mergers, acquisitions, restructurings, and other major corporate actions.

Jobs within the investment banking industry vary widely; some roles can be very lucrative and as a result be highly sought after and competitive.

This book seeks to give any student or professional interested in the investment banking industry the technical tools to ace an investment banking interview. Having worked in the investment banking industry, I will give my personal perspective on what the investment banking interview process is like. I will provide advice and strategy on how to best navigate such an interview process. The book will contain a series of standard investment banking and interview preparation questions that increase in difficulty. We will also go through a series of case studies important for later-stage investment banking and private equity interviews. This book is the ideal go-to guide for anyone who is looking to break into the industry.

HOW THIS BOOK IS STRUCTURED

This book is divided into five parts:

1. Introduction to Investment Banking
2. Core Financial Statements
3. Valuation
4. Mergers and Acquisitions
5. Leveraged Buyouts

Each part will aim to give a brief overview of the core concepts: enough to better your knowledge for investment banking interviews or just a refresher. After each overview, chapters will contain interview questions and answers in increasing difficulty. These questions and answers do not capture every single possible topic, but will cover the most common. The most important thing to remember is you will never know exactly what will be asked in an interview, or how a particular question or scenario will be posed; but if you have the proper conceptual understanding of the core topics, you will be able to handle a multitude of questions asked on each topic.

If you need a stronger technical understanding or an actual modeling overview of each topic, I would recommend reading my other books, which dive deeper into each topic and provide steps for building a model from scratch:

Financial Modeling—*Financial Modeling and Valuation: A Practical Guide to Investment Banking and Private Equity*

Valuation—*Financial Modeling and Valuation: A Practical Guide to Investment Banking and Private Equity*

Mergers and Acquisitions—*Mergers, Acquisitions, Divestitures, and Restructurings: A Practical Guide to Investment Banking and Private Equity*

Leveraged Buyouts—*Leveraged Buyouts: A Practical Guide to Investment Banking and Private Equity*

Introduction

An investment bank is large, complex, and has many facets. In order to best understand the investment banking interview process, it is important to first give an overview of the major investment banking departments operating within an investment bank and the major roles within each department. This will help a job seeker identify and better understand the roles sought after in an investment bank and the most popular areas of interest for job applicants. Note this is just a high-level overview; you will always find more departments as you dig deeper, and each bank may slightly vary.

It is first important to highlight the difference between an investment bank and a commercial bank. An investment bank underwrites securities and performs advisory services while a commercial bank accepts and manages deposits for businesses and individuals.

In 1933 the United States issued the Glass-Steagall Act that prohibited banks from performing both "investment banking" and "commercial banking." This act was set up in response to the Stock Market Crash of 1929 in order to prevent banks from betting on the market at the expense of depositors. This act was repealed, however, in 1999.

OVERVIEW OF MAJOR DIVISIONS

The following chart highlights the major banking divisions I will explore. Again this is not meant to be a complete overview, but just the key areas. These descriptions are meant to be a very brief overview just to give you enough of an idea to differentiate between divisions for interview purposes. Going into complete detail of these roles and what they entail is grounds for another book. Please refer to the chart on the next page for reference.

Senior Management

At the top of the pyramid we have senior management. Senior management includes the CEO, CFO, and others who run the entire firm.

Investment Banking

Investment Banking is a group within the investment bank itself. The investment banking group is typically broken up into Coverage, Mergers and Acquisitions, and Capital Markets.

Coverage

This core investment banking department is divided into industry groups: Energy, Technology, Media, and Healthcare are good examples. The role of these groups is to go to

Structure of an Investment Bank

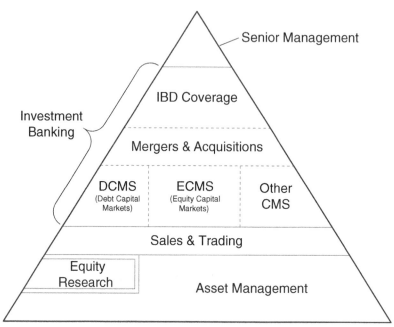

clients within the particular industry and sell investment banking products—products aimed to drive growth in the client's business. These products are most likely Mergers and Acquisitions (M&A) and Underwriting. So if you were a managing director within one of these groups, you would be responsible for "covering" several companies within the industry group. The role would be to sell some M&A or Underwriting business to said client. Most often presentations (pitchbooks) are created as a tool to help "pitch" or sell business. An analyst would be responsible for researching the data for slides that would populate the presentations. These slides may require some analyses such as financial modeling, valuation, in addition to market research. The pitchbook would at its core provide an overview of the market environment, maybe a valuation of the client, and would hope to sell an M&A or Underwriting product. An analyst would also be responsible for drafting memoranda, setting up conference calls, and other process-oriented tasks. If the client expresses further interest in one of the products mentioned, then the coverage team would coordinate with the respective product team. For example, if the client expressed interest in raising equity (a subset of underwriting), then the coverage team would coordinate with the equity capital markets team to further the potential transaction.

Mergers and Acquisitions

Mergers and Acquisitions is probably the most sought after group (from a junior perspective) within the Investment Banking department primarily because it's the most model intensive. The goal of the Mergers and Acquisitions group is to aid in advising clients on the potential merger or acquisition of another asset or corporate entity. Mergers and acquisitions is a general definition that often also applies to divestitures and other types of restructurings, although some banks separate restructurings as another group. If a client is interested in acquiring or divesting all of or some part of their business, the

M&A team is assigned to work on the transactions. The analyst will be responsible for modeling the financial impacts of the transaction in addition to drafting memoranda, setting up conference calls, and other process-oriented tasks. But it is the M&A modeling exposure that is typically most desirable for a junior analyst. This technical knowhow opens doors to other career paths such as private equity and hedge funds. My book, *Mergers, Acquisitions, Divestitures, and Other Restructurings*, walks step-by-step through the technical analyses.

Note: Some industries have unique enough account nuances that when more complex M&A modeling is needed, that industry coverage group performs their own "in-house" M&A as opposed to pairing with the more generalist M&A group. I'm mentioning this because often during the recruiting process the M&A group is in the most demand. It's wise to express interest in a less popular group (maybe Energy, for example) to alleviate competition. However, people often think that only in the M&A group will one get serious consideration for the larger private equity firms or hedge funds as the more sophisticated modeling often happens in the M&A group. So a strategic angle is to express interest in a less popular group that also happens to do its own M&A. This not only gives you that highly sought-after M&A exposure, but will give you exposure to the coverage process, which is important. It also gives you uniquely nuanced accounting skills of a specific industry, which may come in handy later in one's career. This is a good networking and positioning strategy I recommend utilizing.

Capital Markets

Capital Markets is typically subdivided into Equity, Debt, and Convertible. Each of these groups aids in the process of raising capital or trading securities for a client, be it equity, debt, convertible securities, or other types of securities respectively. So if the preceding client, for example, had expressed interest in raising equity, the coverage team would pair up with the equity capital markets team. The equity capital markets team would advise the client on the types of equity securities that could be raised based on various market conditions. They would advise on how much equity could be raised given the nature of the markets and a recommended type of security to get most value for their equity. Obviously it's the expertise of the managing directors in this equity capital markets group that would be able to provide this guidance. This takes years of experience and a strong understanding of the markets. Investment banks depend on these managing directors to give good guidance based on market conditions and further be able to follow up with their recommendation when it comes time to actually issue said securities. The results of their guidance would most likely also go into a section of the pitchbook presentation. This section would contain an overview of the equity markets, maybe the last few equity transactions and pricing information, and of course the managing directors' recommendation. The same idea would apply to debts, convertible securities, or other securities, if the client had been interested in those respective securities. In these groups the analyst would be responsible for populating the presentation slides (among other duties), which entails data mining, market research, and some modeling and analysis. But again the modeling would not be as intensive as in the M&A group. Actually it's sometimes known that the capital markets groups are the least intensive. This can be a benefit for those who want to get into the investment banking industry but are not interested in working 100 hours or more. On the other hand, the less intensive groups don't always get the attention of the premium private equity and hedge funds.

Sales and Trading

The Sales and Trading department is outside of the Investment Banking department. Salespeople and traders are responsible for the selling and trading of investment securities. So, for example, if the preceding client was in fact interested in raising equity as per the advice of the equity capital markets managing director, the sales and trading team would be responsible for the execution of said security. The sales process begins with calling potentially interested investors and other institutions about securities such as hedge funds and mutual funds. A list of interested buyers would be maintained in a process called "bookrunning." A firm would want their books to be oversold, meaning they have more potential buyers than needed, which better guarantees a complete execution of the security when it becomes time. When the time comes to sell the equity, trading begins. Nowadays this is done via computers as opposed to the yelling and screaming you may see in the news. An analyst in the sales and trading group would likely maintain records of trades and the portfolio positions. They could also be responsible for calling potential investors and over time executing the trades. Hours are generally limited to market open and close in addition to some early morning meetings and possibly some after-market analysis, but certainly not the 100 hours or more demanded in the investment banking groups.

Equity Research

The Equity Research department is responsible for providing written reports demonstrating the expected valuation of a stock based on the opinion of the Wall Street "analyst." These reports are sold to clients and funds among others who are interested in the analyst's stock expectations. Here's another confusing note of convention: An equity research analyst is often referred to as the managing director responsible for the entire report and its opinions. This differs from the idea of an analyst being the junior person on a team. This is confusing, but the norm. The Equity Research department is also divided into sectors, just as the coverage group is (i.e., Energy, Technology, Healthcare). As a junior analyst, one would be responsible for constructing and updating models resulting in stock valuations. Working in the Equity Research department is strong as it entails modeling and valuation. However, it is important to note that often the type of modeling performed is not as robust as the investment banking type of modeling. On the other hand, another positive in the Equity Research department is that one would get specific knowledge of an industry, which can come in handy later in one's career. The hours in the Equity Research department are significantly less than in investment banking. Weekends are generally free, and a junior analyst is often out by 7 at the latest (except for the quarterly and annual earning seasons when all models need to be updated based on company performance results).

Asset Management

Asset management helps manage the client's assets and investments in certain securities. Clients typically include high-net-worth individuals in addition to other institutions. Asset managers diversify a client's portfolio by investing across different asset classes, including equity, fixed income, and derivatives.

STANDARD HIERARCHY

It is important to understand the general hierarchy within an investment banking group. The roles and duties in investment banks can vary from firm to firm, but the general hierarchy follows.

Analyst

The analyst is the most junior level in the investment banking industry. Note the difference between "analyst" in terms of hierarchy and an equity research analyst as defined within the equity research overview discussed earlier. Most often, an investment bank would hire an analyst for two years. Often an analyst is allowed to stay for a third year before exploring other options. If an analyst does stay for a third year, it is recommended to do so in a different group to expand network and gain more skills. After two or three years, an analyst may be able to get promoted to the *associate* level, or be required to go to business school and get an MBA before getting a promotion. Sometimes, however, an analyst moves on to venture capital or private equity or leaves the industry altogether.

The key roles of an analyst entail financial modeling, updating presentations, drafting memoranda, facilitating research, performing due diligence, and setting up meetings.

Associate

An associate is one step above the analyst. Associates are responsible for the technicals and memoranda in a transaction. They are responsible for the quality of output of presentations, the data and flow of key memoranda, and the execution of deal process. Associates manage the analysts and aid in quality control of their work. An associate role will typically last three to four years before getting promoted to vice president. There is a major distinction here between the role of an associate and the role of a vice president, which often becomes a big hurdle for budding vice presidents. Analysts and associates have largely technical roles, responsible for the underlying data, materials, and process of transactions. Once transitioned to VP, one is more responsible for structuring and selling the deal—a more client-focused role. Often very technical candidates are great analysts and associates but are not personable or articulate enough to be good vice presidents. This causes a roadblock for many junior bankers.

Vice President

Typically, the vice president, although still responsible for technicals and execution, starts to gain exposure to the management process, including more direct interaction with the client. The duration of service varies vastly from firm to firm. I've seen vice presidents stay in their role for many years or get promoted after three to five years. It completely depends on the firm, their staffing needs, and the state of the markets.

Director

The director is also another vague role. Some firms refer to this role as executive director or president, and the specifics vary. Directors typically shadow managing directors and are being groomed to be the next key contact to a client. The move from director to managing director is typically not as structured a time as from analyst to associate. It depends on the state of the particular investment banking group.

Managing Director

The managing director is the key client relationship holder. The managing director is responsible for advising the client on particular M&A or underwriting products. The success of the managing director's role is often determined by how many products can be sold to the clients covered by the managing director.

This brief overview of the major divisions and roles within an investment bank is solely to provide a very high-level overview. More specifics on the investment banking recruiting process and interview preparation follow.

About the Author

Paul Pignataro is an entrepreneur specializing in finance education. He has built and successfully run several startups in the education and technology industries. He also has over 14 years of experience in investment banking and private equity in business mergers and acquisitions (M&A), restructurings, asset divestitures, asset acquisitions, and debt and equity transactions in the oil, gas, power and utilities, Internet and technology, real estate, defense, travel, banking, and service industries.

Mr. Pignataro most recently founded New York School of Finance, which evolved from AnEx Training, a multimillion-dollar finance education business, providing finance education to banks, firms, and universities throughout the world.

The New York School of Finance is a semester-long program, based in New York and geared toward helping business students from top-tier and lower-tier business schools to prepare for jobs at the top firms on Wall Street.

At AnEx Training, Mr. Pignataro continues to participate on the training team, actively providing training at bulge bracket banks and for M&A teams at corporations, and has personally trained personnel at funds catering to high-net-worth individuals worth billions of dollars. AnEx continues to train at over 50 locations worldwide, and Mr. Pignataro travels extensively on a monthly basis to do trainings at sovereign funds and investment banks overseas.

Prior to his entrepreneurial endeavors, Mr. Pignataro worked at TH Lee Putnam Ventures, a $1 billion private equity firm affiliated with buyout giant Thomas H. Lee Partners. Before that, he was at Morgan Stanley, where he worked on various transactions in the technology, energy, transportation, and business services industries. Some of the transactions included the $33.3 billion merger of BP Amoco and ARCO, the $7.6 billion sale of American Water Works to RWE (a German water company), the sale of two subsidiaries of Citizens Communications (a $3.0 billion communications company), and the sale of a $100 million propane distribution subsidiary of a $3 billion electric utility.

Mr. Pignataro is the author of *Financial Modeling and Valuation: A Practical Guide to Investment Banking and Private Equity* (John Wiley & Sons, 2013). He graduated from New York University with a bachelor's degree in mathematics and computer science.

One

Introduction to Investment Banking

As someone who was not a business student, breaking into the investment banking industry was a challenging and competitive task. Lucky enough to get an offer in the investment banking industry at Morgan Stanley, I was at one time part of their recruiting team. Seeing the recruiting process from the recruiter's side was helpful and interesting, and I had always thought if I understood what the process was truly like *before* going through the interview process, I would have been much more competitive. This is the very perspective that I will provide in this part.

CHAPTER 1

Investment Banking Recruiting

As a first-year analyst at Morgan Stanley, I had volunteered to be part of the NYU recruiting team. The recruiting team consisted of bankers from various levels including the most junior analyst through the senior managing director. In our NYU group, there were several of us first-year analysts (mostly junior) on the team, maybe one or two associates, and a vice president who was in charge of the recruiting process on behalf of the school. The interviewing process for senior undergraduate students for full-time jobs upon graduation would begin in late August or early September. Everyone on the NYU recruiting team at Morgan Stanley would coordinate a day in our schedules to meet and go through all resumes submitted. *Every* submitted resume was, in fact, sent to us and reviewed. We would have a binder of all submitted resumes and would sift through them one by one as a group. It was during this meeting where we would select candidates we felt were appropriate for a first-round interview. We would hope to get 40 to 50 candidates to interview. In my experience, we narrowed down candidates based on three different categories:

1. Students who had prior bulge bracket internships
2. Students who had M&A and other relevant experience
3. Students who we felt may be good analysts

So let me explain these categories. For category 1, we would automatically select anyone who had previously interned in the investment banking group at a bulge bracket bank. But this candidate needed to have received a job offer after that particular internship. If not, there needs to be a good explanation. Some firms actually choose not to give follow-on offers to any intern. That's an acceptable explanation. But if a firm has given out offers to select interns but not the particular candidate in question, then that would give us pause for concern. For category 2, knowing we wouldn't find 40 to 50 candidates just by filtering down to those with bulge bracket internships/offers, we would also select candidates who had relevant experience either at a smaller bank or investment firm or in other types of firms where the candidate may have had investment banking related exposure (i.e., financial modeling and valuation). Again we are looking for students who will interview well and will be good analysts. So students who interned at mid-market or boutique banks in the M&A division would be selected, for example, or even candidates who interned in the equity research division of a bank. Even though equity research is not a key investment banking department, the role does require some financial modeling and valuation skills that can be transferrable. Finally, for category 3, we would select anyone else who we felt could interview well and be a good analyst. This is vague—on purpose. As we sat in our group flipping through resumes, if we came across someone we had recognized, we could identify that candidate and include their resume in the "to be interviewed" pile. This is a very important category, which relates to the need for everyone looking to get into the investment banking industry to make themselves known. My strong advice here is to find out who is on the recruiting team from your school and begin an initiative to get in front of them and let them know that you would be a good candidate. If you were not lucky enough to get a bulge bracket or relevant internship, this is your chance to have someone on the recruiting team call your name when the time comes. This is where networking is key.

NETWORKING AND INTERVIEWING

Networking comes in many forms, so in this part I will just focus on a few major helpful tips for getting into the investment banking industry. Now that you have a general view of how the process can go internally, you see the importance of getting in front of the right person and making yourself known. If you are a senior at a university looking for first-year analyst roles, the best person to get in front of are college alums who just got hired. As the bulge bracket hiring season begins early in the fall, recently graduated students who got hired into these banks typically go through a training program in the summer. So by early fall they are just beginning their full-time role and are still eager and excited about their position. Get in front of those analysts before the job duties become so overwhelming that they no longer have time to reciprocate.

Getting in Front of Key People

I'm often asked who the best person in HR is to reach out to. It's important to note that most investment banking groups actually appoint an analyst, associate, or vice president to manage the groups' daily operations—including hiring. This particular person is a banker who liaises with HR to determine staffing needs. A candidate needs to find out who that person is. So, for example, if a candidate applies for an investment banking position online, that resume typically gets sent to the HR department and is sorted among potentially thousands of others. To enhance your chances of getting selected, find an actual analyst or associate working in the group you are applying for and reach out to them. LinkedIn is an excellent resource for this. So if you submit your resume for a position in Mergers and Acquisitions at Credit Suisse, for example, use the LinkedIn search bar to find who is actually working in that group and send them an InMail. InMails are more powerful that just connecting with that person, as an InMail typically goes directly into their inbox.

When I was a first-year analyst, I would get a flood of emails from students who wanted to break into the investment banking industry. In the beginning, I was eager and excited to respond to everyone. Over time, as work took over, and conversations with students became repetitive, I started to filter whom I responded to. I was still very interested in recruiting good analysts, but I wanted to be sure I was speaking to someone who was really serious and would interview well if I brought them into the firm for an interview. So it is very important that candidates prove in some way that they know what they are getting themselves into either through experience or extensive knowledge about the industry. "Breaking into the industry" could mean the candidate read about banking in a blog and knows they can make a lot of money but doesn't really understand the function and roles of a banker. Or it could mean someone is seriously qualified but just hasn't gotten the right opportunity to interview. We look for the latter, and it's very important that you demonstrate right away that you are someone who truly knows what you are getting yourself into and understands what an investment banking job entails. So having a prior internship and the relevant skills matters. In addition, how candidates present themselves is most important and will be discussed.

The Two Most Important Investment Banking Interview Questions

Whether it's an initial phone call or a first-round interview, I would easily determine a candidate's qualifications by asking the candidate to introduce himself ("Tell me about yourself") and then asking another simple, yet key question: "Why do you want to get into investment banking?" I will explain what the recruiter is typically looking for next.

You will never know exactly what someone will ask in an interview, but there are certain topics that almost always get covered. No matter how the call or interview is introduced, you will most likely be expected to explain why you want to work in this type of field and explain who you are. The answers to these questions are simple, yet they demonstrate intent. Believe it or not, I have easily narrowed down 50 candidates to 15 by asking these two simple questions. Often, even students at the top business schools just haven't prepared themselves in a concise way to answer these questions effectively. "Tell me about yourself" is your "elevator pitch" of yourself. It's what you are about. The perspective is very important. I will explain.

Tell Me About Yourself Candidates often confuse the questions "Tell me about yourself" and "Walk me through your resume" as one and the same. In fact, they are the opposite from a timeline perspective. "Tell me about yourself" is a story of who you are—what you are *about*. It should be an overview of pivotal moments in your life beginning with when and where you are from through to why you are speaking to the recruiter today, and they all need to connect in some way. "Tell me about yourself" is a 60- to 90-second elevator pitch of you explaining why you should be chosen for the job. The answer to this question not only demonstrates intent, but preparedness and presentation.

You should always begin by introducing yourself by simply stating your name and where you are from. Keep it simple. Then focus on where you attended college or university and why your specific major was chosen. This should lay out some groundwork toward the career of choice. If the major is not related to career of choice, then you must be prepared to explain what situation occurred that led you to change course. It would be ideal if there were some transferable skills from major to career that can be highlighted to help explain the transition. *Briefly* give an overview of past internships by simply stating the nature of the role and why it applies to overall goals. Remember the important component here is *why*. Many people rattle off their history but do not explain why they've chosen their specific major or internship. Finally, you should conclude with why you want to work in the current field. This very general framework is summarized as:

1. Where you are from?
2. Why did you choose your university and major?
3. Tie together your past experiences in a way that explains why you want to work in the field.
4. Conclude with the answer to why you want to work in investment banking, which we will explain further.

Thinking about this general framework will help keep focus. All too often candidates start discussing aspects of their life that are not relevant and will lose the recruiter. Other aspects of a candidate's life that are possibly relevant and interesting can be thrown in during the discussion but do it after the initial pitch. The answer to this question makes an important first impression and will set the tone of the rest of the interview. If it is not concise, it may reflect poorly. Also, I do not recommend going into the actual day-to-day duties in each internship or experience described; just provide an overall description and how the experience fits into the overall story. Details can be saved for later questions, like "Walk me through your resume." Again, "Tell me about yourself" should be an overarching story of who you are and how you fit into this role. I will explain more in the next section.

Explanation of Past Experience   Candidates often have trouble simplifying their past experiences. Often their explanations are too long-winded and lose focus on the overall story. As mentioned earlier, it's important to focus solely on an overview of what the role was and why the role was chosen. And this should ultimately explain how choosing that role fits into the candidate's overall career goals. If a candidate is pursuing an investment banking career and they have prior investment banking internships, the story is clear and direct. But often candidates have had several varying experiences or are trying to make a transition. One needs to be careful in explaining these past experiences as part of the story. If a candidate has a lot of varying experiences on their resume, a recruiter can rightfully be concerned that the position they are interviewing for may also be just another of the many. Most recruiters want to know this job is a serious step in a candidate's career and will potentially be a long-term one. The candidate needs to demonstrate that. A candidate needs to treat each and every past experience as a small step toward their ultimate goal as opposed to "random" short stints. If one can explain each experience as building toward their ultimate goal, this will help give a recruiter comfort in the seriousness of their candidacy.

For example, let's say we have a candidate looking to enter the investment banking industry. This particular candidate, however, did not have prior investment banking experience. They had an internship in accounting at "Big 4" accounting firm Ernst & Young. A recruiter would most likely question the accounting internship to see if the candidate is actually interested in investment banking. Now, we all know investment banking is a highly competitive industry, so how the Ernst & Young experience is presented is very important. If a candidate loosely explains this past experience, and maybe even others, without making a connection into the banking industry, the recruiter may see this as a sign of lack of focus. How would a recruiter know that the candidate's investment banking interest is not another short-term one like the candidate's interest in accounting? Recruiters do not like this impression of candidates bouncing around from role to role and industry to industry. This is where tying together everything in the story comes to play. I also strongly recommend that you keep your explanation positive; don't focus on any negative aspects of the internship. I often hear candidates explain, "I didn't like the people," or "Accounting wasn't for me." Find positive transferable skills that make the recruiter believe the accounting was a steppingstone toward the ultimate goal of getting into the investment banking industry, something more like this: "My experience at Ernst & Young provided me with the strong basics of practical accounting. I strongly believe the corporate accounting and due diligence skills learned during my internship could be directly applicable toward analyzing and valuing companies in M&A and underwriting transactions. This would best prepare me for a full-time analyst role within the investment banking industry." You could also add something like "Although Ernst & Young wasn't my number-one choice, it was the best offer I was able to receive at the time as the investment banking industry is a highly competitive one."

So this method can be applied for most past experiences. Keep explaining how each prior role was a step to the next and all toward the ultimate goal of investment banking. You are building a story and making an impression.

Explanation of Irrelevant Experience Sometimes past internships are not relevant at all. What if the candidate had other internships that were, for example, in marketing or sales prior to Ernst & Young? Or what if the experience was even more distant, like working at a coffee shop? First of all, you don't have to put *every* experience on your resume, especially if you have had so many jobs or internships that your resume extends to a second page. Keep the resume to one page and drop the oldest experiences, especially if they are irrelevant. So if this candidate had worked at a coffee shop, let's say as a freshman in high school before all other internships, it's okay to not include it. In my opinion it's okay to eliminate prior experiences if they are far in the past and not relevant. As for the sales and marketing internship, the candidate can include them but simply talk over them so as to not make them a focus of the goal and story. For example, the candidate can add, "While at university, I took various internships until I finally received something I thought would help me build toward my ultimate investment banking pursuit." The candidate can then continue to speak about their Ernst & Young experience. The key focus here is that it is unlikely that a candidate is going to get an investment banking internship before their junior and senior years. First, not every firm hires freshmen and sophomores, and the ones that do have very limited spots. So the more a candidate can turn their junior and senior experiences into a positive and continue to demonstrate their ultimate goal, the more presentable they will be and the more successful a candidate they will become.

Why Do You Want to Get into Investment Banking? Again you never know what a recruiter is going to ask in an interview but be assured they will want to know why you want to work in the field. Even if this question is not asked outright, it should be part of your overall story: "Tell me about yourself." "Why do you want to do investment banking?" is a staple, and believe it or not, it is not always answered adequately. The wrong way to answer the question is to focus on the money. "I want to be a dealmaker" is another poor answer. These answers are superficial and don't focus on the specifics of why investment banking exists and what it does to provide value. Often I hear answers like "I want to work with smart people," "I want to be in a competitive environment," or "I want to be challenged." Although these are possible true answers, these answers can apply for many different fields—consulting, equity research, even a nonprofit. The answer to why you want to do investment banking needs to be specific and focus on what investment banking is and how it provides value. It also needs to mention to whom it provides value. So, to better understand what a good answer is, it is important to understand that investment banking is two things: (1) mergers and acquisitions (M&A) and (2) underwriting. mergers and acquisitions is the process of buying and selling business. Underwriting is the process behind raising capital. Both are initiatives utilized to hopefully drive external growth in some company. A managing director in an investment banking group would advise the client on some M&A or underwriting opportunity. This opportunity should aim to be of value in driving growth in the client.

A good answer should have a personal "hook," something like "I want to work in the investment banking industry because I want to understand the process and strategy behind M&A and underwriting, both processes that drive value in business." This is completely different from the general "working with smart people in a competitive environment" type of answer and certainly sets a candidate apart from his or her peers.

Hook So, as mentioned earlier, it's important to have a story, an "elevator pitch" of yourself, from when and where you were born all the way to today—why you are sitting in front of the recruiter. This pitch is complete with the addition of a hook. This is a story, ideally from your past, that ties all these components together. The hook both completes and personalizes the story. The hook should in some way lead into your answer to why you are choosing investment banking. Some examples of hooks deal with a rooted passion in stock investing, or maybe a company that you started when you were young. Another great example of a hook is an experience with a family business—maybe one that was failing. The hook is designed to extract a rooted passion that seeded your interest in the field.

Think about what your hook should be. This hook will apply to not only your story but cover letters and networking emails. So let's say this candidate who worked previously at Ernst & Young was a young entrepreneur and started a company selling crafts years ago. This could have been a very early step toward exploring a career in business. Now trace from the time of this hook toward the other necessary pieces included in the story and find a way to apply this original experience to each, connecting them all. So maybe this candidate did, in fact, decide to study finance because he or she found potential interest in the career through trying to start a company. But how would this ultimately lead all the way toward an interest in investment banking? How can an entrepreneurial experience be banking related? Well, remember investment banking is at its core M&A and securities underwriting—initiatives that drive growth in business. Maybe the candidate faced a major growth hurdle in the startup company that required the need to raise money. That could be an angle. Underwriting is the process of raising capital by issuing securities. If you can connect your hook to investment banking in this way and apply the earlier components, you will have a complete story, maybe something like this:

"I was born in Malaysia and ever since I was young thought of myself as an entrepreneur. At an early age I started a crafts company that sparked my interest in business. Unfortunately, I hit a few hurdles with my business due to lack of funding. Despite that setback, the experience led me to pursue a business degree in the U.S. While studying at my university, I researched and explored several career paths and realized investment banking is at its core the process behind growing businesses through M&A and underwriting. Maybe if I had these skills previously I would have been able to grow my business. So I decided to pursue this field as a career. Because the investment banking industry is very competitive, especially for a junior-level internship, I settled for a summer role at Ernst & Young. Although not ideal, it strengthened my accounting from a practitioner's perspective and gave me exposure to the due diligence process, which are both applicable to investment banking. Now I am here to apply my passion for growing businesses through M&A and underwriting, and my knowledge of accounting and the due diligence process learned at Ernst & Young toward a career in the investment banking industry."

That's a good answer. Answering this question appropriately gives the recruiter the impression you were meant for this job in some way. Few candidates are that thorough in their answer, so this will set the candidate well apart from the competition.

Once you've crafted an ideal story for yourself, it's time to get up to speed technically. There are many guides out there that focus on the myriad additional behavioral questions one should prepare for. This book is designed to be a technical preparation guide. So having presented my perspective on the most important behavioral questions above, I will now move on to the technical.

Two

Financial Statements

Most first-round interviews from a technical perspective will cover the topics of financial statements and valuation. Anyone interviewing for investment banking should know at least how major financial statements are created and how they flow into one another and cover the core methods of valuation. We will review them here, and then give common technical questions.

CHAPTER 2

Financial Statements Overview

It is important to know six major statements in financial modeling:

1. Income statement
2. Cash flow statement
3. Balance sheet
4. Depreciation schedule
5. Working capital schedule
6. Debt schedule

THE INCOME STATEMENT

The income statement measures a company's profit (or loss) over a specific period of time. A business is generally required to report and record the sales it generates for tax purposes. And, of course, taxes on sales made can be reduced by the expenses incurred while generating those sales. Although there are specific rules that govern when and how those expense reductions can be utilized, there is still a general concept:

$$\text{Profit} = \text{Revenue} - \text{Expenses}$$

A company is taxed on profit. So:

$$\text{Net Income} = \text{Profit} - \text{Tax}$$

However, income statements have grown to be quite complex. The multifaceted categories of expenses can vary from company to company. As analysts, we need to identify major categories within the income statement in order to facilitate proper analysis. For this reason, one should always categorize income statement line items into nine major categories:

1. Revenue (sales)
2. Cost of goods sold (COGS)
3. Operating expenses
4. Other income
5. Depreciation and amortization
6. Interest

7. Taxes
8. Nonrecurring and extraordinary items
9. Distributions

No matter how convoluted an income statement is, a good analyst would categorize each reported income statement line item into one of these nine groupings. This will allow the analyst to easily understand the major categories that drive profitability in an income statement and can further allow him or her to compare the profitability of several different companies—an analysis very important in determining relative valuation. We will briefly recap the line items.

REVENUE

Revenue is the sales or gross income a company has made during a specific operating period. It is important to note that when and how revenue is recognized can vary from company to company and may be different from the actual cash received. Revenue is recognized when "realized and earned," which is typically when the products sold have been transferred or once the service has been rendered.

COST OF GOODS SOLD

Cost of goods sold (COGS) is the direct costs attributable to the production of the goods sold by a company. These are the costs most directly associated with the revenue. COGS is typically the cost of the materials used in creating the products sold, although some other direct costs could be included as well.

Gross Profit

Gross profit is not one of the nine categories listed, as it is a totaling item. Gross profit is the revenue less the cost of goods sold. It is often helpful to determine the net value of the revenue after the cost of goods sold is removed. One common metric analyzed is gross profit margin, which is the gross profit divided by the revenue.

A business that sells cars, for example, may have manufacturing costs. Let's say we sell each car for $20,000, and we manufacture the cars in-house. We have to purchase $5,000 in raw materials to manufacture the car. If we sell one car, $20,000 is our revenue, and $5,000 is the cost of goods sold. That leaves us with $15,000 in gross profit, or a 75 percent gross profit margin. Now let's say in the first quarter of operations we sell 25 cars. That's 25 × $20,000 or $500,000 in revenue. Our cost of goods sold is 25 × $5,000, or $125,000, which leaves us with $375,000 in gross profit.

Car Co.	1Q 2015
Revenue	$500,000.0
COGS	125,000.0
Gross Profit	375,000.0
% Gross Profit Margin	75%

OPERATING EXPENSES

Operating expenses are expenses incurred by a company as a result of performing its normal business operations. These are the relatively indirect expenses related to generating the company's revenue and supporting its operations. Operating expenses can be broken down into several other major subcategories. The most common categories are:

- *Selling, general, and administrative (SG&A).* These are all selling expenses and all general and administrative expenses of a company. Examples are employee salaries and rents.
- *Advertising and marketing.* These are expenses relating to any advertising or marketing initiatives of the company. Examples are print advertising and Google Adwords.
- *Research and development (R&D).* These are expenses relating to furthering the development of the company's products or services.

Let's say in our car business we have employees who were paid $75,000 in total in the first quarter. We also had rents to pay of $2,500, and we ran an advertising initiative that cost us $7,500. Finally, let's assume we employed some R&D efforts to continue to improve the design of our car that cost roughly $5,000 in the quarter. Using the previous example, our simple income statement looks like this:

Car Co.	1Q 2015
Revenue	$500,000.0
COGS	125,000.0
Gross Profit	375,000.0
% Gross Profit Margin	*75%*
Operating Expenses	
SG&A	77,500.0
Advertising	7,500.0
R&D	5,000.0
Total Operating Expenses	90,000.0

OTHER INCOME

Companies can generate income that is not core to their business. As this income is taxable, it is recorded on the income statement. However, since it is not core to business operations, it is not considered revenue. Let's take the example of the car company. A car company's core business is producing and selling cars. However, many car companies also generate income in another way: financing. If a car company offers its customers the ability to finance the payments on a car, those payments come with interest. The car company receives that interest. That interest is taxable and is considered additional income. However, as that income is not core to the business, it is not considered revenue; it is considered "other income."

Another common example of other income is income from noncontrolling interests, also known as income from unconsolidated affiliates. This is income received when one company has a noncontrolling interest investment in another company. So when a company (Company A) invests in another company (Company B) and receives a minority stake in Company B, Company B distributes a portion of its net income to Company A. Company A records those distributions received as "other income."

EBITDA

Earnings before interest, taxes, depreciation, and amortization (EBITDA) is a very important measure among Wall Street analysts. We will see later its many uses as a fundamental metric in valuation and analysis. EBITDA can be calculated as Revenue – COGS – Operating Expenses + Other Income.

It is debatable whether "other income" should be included in EBITDA. There are two sides to the argument.

1. *Other income should be included in EBITDA.* If a company produces other income, it should be represented as part of EBITDA, and other income should be listed above our EBITDA total. The argument here is that other income, although not core to revenue, is still in fact operating and should be represented as part of the company's operations. There are many ways of looking at this. Taking the car example, we can perhaps assume that the financing activities, although not core to revenue, are essential enough to the overall profitability of the company to be considered as part of EBITDA.
2. *Other income should not be included in EBITDA.* If a company produces other income, it should not be represented as part of EBITDA, and other income should be listed below our EBITDA total. The argument here is that although it is a part of the company's profitability, it is not core enough to the operations to be incorporated as part of the company's core profitability.

Determining whether to include other income as EBITDA is not simple and clear-cut. It is important to consider whether the other income is consistent and reoccurring. If it is not, the case can more likely be made that it should not be included in EBITDA. It is also important to consider the purpose of your particular analysis. For example, if you are looking to acquire the entire business, and that business will still be producing that other income even after the acquisition, then maybe it should be represented as part of EBITDA. Or maybe that other income will no longer exist after the acquisition, in which case it should not be included in EBITDA. As another example, if you are trying to compare this business's EBITDA with the EBITDA of other companies, then it is important to consider if the other companies also produce that same other income. If not, then maybe it is better to keep other income out of the EBITDA analysis, to make sure there is a consistent comparison among all of the company EBITDAs.

Different banks and firms may have different views on whether other income should be included in EBITDA. Even different industry groups' departments within the same firm have been found to have different views on this topic. As a good analyst, it is important to come up with one consistent defensible view, and to stick to it. Note that the exclusion of other income from EBITDA may also assume that other income will be excluded from earnings before interest and taxes (EBIT) as well.

Let's assume in our car example the other income will be part of EBITDA.

Car Co.	1Q 2015
Revenue	$500,000.0
COGS	125,000.0
Gross Profit	375,000.0
% Gross Profit Margin	*75%*
Operating Expenses	
SG&A	77,500.0
Advertising	7,500.0
R&D	5,000.0
Total Operating Expenses	90,000.0
Other Income	1,000.0
EBITDA	286,000.0
EBITDA Margin	*57%*

Notice we have also calculated EBITDA margin, which is calculated as EBITDA divided by revenue.

DEPRECIATION AND AMORTIZATION

Depreciation is the accounting for the aging and depletion of fixed assets over a period of time. Amortization is the accounting for the cost basis reduction of intangible assets (intellectual property such as patents, copyrights, and trademarks, for example) over their useful lives. It is important to note that not all intangible assets are subject to amortization.

EBIT

Similar to EBITDA, EBIT is also utilized in valuation. EBIT is EBITDA less depreciation and amortization. So let's assume the example car company has $8,000 in D&A each quarter. So:

Car Co.	1Q 2015
EBITDA	$286,000.0
EBITDA Margin	*57%*
D&A	8,000.0
EBIT	278,000.0
EBIT Margin	*56%*

Notice we have also calculated EBIT margin, which is calculated as EBIT divided by revenue.

INTEREST

Interest is composed of interest expense and interest income. Interest expense is the cost incurred on debt that the company has borrowed. Interest income is commonly the income received from cash held in savings accounts, certificates of deposit, and other investments.

Let's assume the car company has taken out $1 million in loans and incurs 10 percent of interest per year on those loans. So the car company has $100,000 in interest expense per year, or $25,000 per quarter. We can also assume that the company has $50,000 of cash and generates 1 percent of interest income on that cash per year ($500), or $125 per quarter.

Often, the interest expense is netted against the interest income as net interest expense.

EBT

Earnings before taxes (EBT) can be defined as EBIT minus net interest.

Car Co.	1Q 2015
EBIT	$278,000.0
EBIT Margin	*56%*
Interest Expense	25,000.0
Interest Income	125.0
Net Interest Expense	**24,875.0**
EBT	**253,125.0**
EBT Margin	*51%*

Notice we have also calculated EBT margin, which is EBT divided by revenue.

TAXES

Taxes are the financial charges imposed by the government on the company's operations. Taxes are imposed on earnings before taxes as defined previously. In the car example, we can assume the tax rate is 35 percent.

Net Income

Net income is calculated as EBT minus taxes. The complete income statement follows.

Car Co.	1Q 2015
Revenue	$500,000.0
COGS	125,000.0
Gross Profit	**375,000.0**
% Gross Profit Margin	*75%*

Car Co.	1Q 2015
Operating Expenses	
SG&A	77,500.0
Advertising	7,500.0
R&D	5,000.0
Total Operating Expenses	**90,000.0**
Other Income	1,000.0
EBITDA	**286,000.0**
EBITDA Margin	*57%*
D&A	8,000.0
EBIT	**278,000.0**
EBIT Margin	*56%*
Interest Expense	25,000.0
Interest Income	125.0
Net Interest Expense	24,875.0
EBT	**253,125.0**
EBT Margin	*51%*
Tax	88,593.75
Tax Rate (%)	*35%*
Net Income	**164,531.25**

NONRECURRING AND EXTRAORDINARY ITEMS

Nonrecurring and extraordinary items or events are income or expenses that either are one-time or do not pertain to everyday core operations. Gains or losses on sales of assets or from business closures are examples of nonrecurring events. Such nonrecurring or extraordinary events can be scattered about in a generally accepted accounting principles (GAAP) income statement, so it is the job of a good analyst to identify these items and move them to the bottom of the income statement in order to have EBITDA, EBIT, and net income line items that represent everyday, continuous operations. We call this "clean" EBITDA, EBIT, and net income. However, we do not want to eliminate those nonrecurring or extraordinary items completely, so we move them to the section at the bottom of the income statement. From here on out we will refer to both nonrecurring and extraordinary items simply as "nonrecurring items" to simplify.

DISTRIBUTIONS

Distributions are broadly defined as payments to equity holders. These payments can be in the form of dividends or noncontrolling interest payments, to name the two major types of distributions.

Noncontrolling interest is the portion of the company or the company's subsidiary that is owned by another outside person or entity. If another entity (Entity A) owns a noncontrolling interest in the company (Entity B), Entity B must distribute a portion of Entity B's earnings to Entity A.

Net Income (as Reported)

Because we have recommended moving some nonrecurring line items into a separate section, the net income listed in the previous example is effectively an adjusted net income, which is most useful for analysis, valuation, and comparison. However, it is important to still represent a complete net income with all adjustments included to match the original given net income. So it is recommended to have a second net income line, defined as net income minus nonrecurring events minus distributions, as a sanity check.

SHARES

A company's shares outstanding reported on the income statement can be reported as basic or diluted. The basic share count is a count of the number of shares outstanding in the market. The diluted share count is the number of shares outstanding in the market plus any shares that would be considered outstanding today if all option and warrant holders who are in-the-money decided to exercise on their securities. The diluted share count is best thought of as a what-if scenario. If all the option and warrant holders who could exercise would, how many shares would be outstanding now?

Earnings per Share (EPS)

Earnings per share (EPS) is defined as the net income divided by the number of shares outstanding. A company typically reports a basic EPS and a diluted EPS, divided by basic shares or diluted shares, respectively. It is important to note that each company may have a different definition of what exactly to include in net income when calculating EPS. In other words, is net income before or after noncontrolling interest payments? Or before or after dividends? For investors, it is common to use net income before dividends have been paid but after noncontrolling interest investors have been paid. However, we recommend backing into the company's EPS historically to identify the exact formula it is using.

$$\text{Basic EPS} = \text{Net Income/Basic Shares}$$

$$\text{Diluted EPS} = \text{Net Income/Diluted Shares}$$

THE CASH FLOW STATEMENT

The cash flow statement is a measure of how much cash a company has produced or spent over a period of time. Although an income statement shows profitability, that profit may or may not result in actual cash gain. This is because many income statement items that are recorded do not necessarily result in an effect on cash. For example, when a sale is made, a customer can pay in cash or on credit. If a company has $10 million in sales and all customers have paid in cash, then the company has actually generated $10 million in cash. But if a company has $10 million in sales on credit, then although the revenue has been recorded on the income statement, cash has not been received. The cash flow statement aims to determine how much cash the company actually generated, which is broken out into three segments:

1. Cash from operating activities
2. Cash from investing activities
3. Cash from financing activities

The sum of all the cash generated (or spent) from operating activities, from investing activities, and from financing activities results in the total amount of cash spent or received in a given period.

CASH FLOW FROM OPERATING ACTIVITIES

Cash flow from operating activities is a representation of how much cash has been generated from net income or profit. We explained earlier how revenue could be received in cash or on credit. As revenue is a source of income, if a portion of that revenue is on credit, we need to make an adjustment to net income based on how much of that revenue is actually cash. Similarly, expenses recorded on the income statement could be cash expenses (they have been paid) or noncash expenses (they have not been paid). Let's take a billing invoice on an operating expense such as office supplies as an example. Once the invoice is received (a bill we have to pay), we would need to record this on the income statement, even if we had not actually paid that bill yet. Having this expense on our income statement would bring our profitability down. But when looking at cash available, that bill should not be included, as we have not paid it. So, for cash flow from operations, we would add that expense back to the net income, effectively reversing the expense effects.

Example:

Income Statement	
Revenue (collected in cash)	$10,000,000.0
SG&A (invoice we did not pay)	2,000,000.0
Net Income	8,000,000.0
Cash Flow	
Net Income	$8,000,000.0
Add back SG&A	2,000,000.0
Cash from Operations	10,000,000.0

This should make logical sense. We've collected $10 million in cash from our sales; we received an invoice of $2 million, but we did not pay that invoice. The invoice is expensed properly on the income statement, but we do not want to include that in our cash analysis, as it did not yet affect our cash. So, we add that expense back to the net income. The cash from operations rightfully shows that we still have $10 million in cash.

Now, let's say of the $10 million in revenue, only $8 million was cash sales, and $2 million was sold on credit. The income statement looks exactly the same, but the cash flow statement is different. If we had collected only $8 million of that $10 million of revenue in cash, then we would need to subtract the $2 million of revenue we did not collect from the net income. So:

Income Statement	
Revenue (only $8MM collected in cash)	$10,000,000.0
SG&A (invoice we did not pay)	2,000,000.0
Net Income	8,000,000.0

(continued)

Income Statement	
Cash Flow	
Net Income	$8,000,000.0
Subtract revenue we did not collect in cash	(2,000,000.0)
Add back SG&A we did not pay	2,000,000.0
Cash from Operations	**8,000,000.0**

This analysis may seem trivial, but it is important to understand the methodology as we apply this to more complex income statements. In general, cash from operating activities is generated by taking net income and removing all the noncash items.

Or, in its most fundamental form, cash from operations as demonstrated is:

Net Income + Expenses we did not pay − Revenue we did not receive

But it gets slightly more complex. To understand this completely, let's take a look at all of the components of an income statement and determine which items can be considered cash and which are noncash.

Revenue

As we had explained previously, if revenue is received on credit, this would be removed from net income. The portion of revenue received on credit is called "accounts receivable."

Cost of Goods Sold

Cost of goods sold (COGS) is the inventory costs related to the item sold. If it costs $50 to make a chair, for example, and we sell that chair for $100, then for each chair sold, we will record a $50 expense related to the manufacturing cost of the product; this is cost of goods sold. However, we must also reduce our inventory balance by $50 for each chair sold. A reduction in inventory results in a positive cash inflow in the cash from operations section on the cash flow statement. We will illustrate examples of this in the next section.

Operating Expenses

As explained previously with the $2 million invoice, if an expense received had not been paid, this would be added back to net income. The portion of operating expenses that has not been paid is called "accrued expenses."

Depreciation

Depreciation is an expense that is never actually paid. As described earlier, it is accounting for the aging of assets. So, like any expense that is not cash, we add it back to net income when calculating cash flow from operations.

Interest

Interest expense is almost always paid in cash. There can be certain complex debt instruments that are exceptions, but if a company cannot pay its interest, then generally it is considered defaulting on its debt. So, for this reason, we almost always consider interest as cash. Therefore, we would not add it back to net income in the cash flow statement.

Taxes

Taxes can be deferred in some situations, which will be discussed later. The portion of taxes that we expensed but did not yet pay is referred to as "deferred taxes."

Table 2.1 summarizes the most common income statement line items and the related accounts if they can be deferred.

Keeping with the theme demonstrated previously, where we adjust the related revenue and expense items we did not pay or receive in cash from net income to get a measure of cash generated or spent, we can generalize this table toward cash flow from operating activities:

> Cash from Operating Activities
> = Net Income + Changes in Accounts Receivable + Changes in Inventory
> + Changes in Accounts Payable + Changes in Accrued Expenses
> + Changes in Prepaid Expenses + Depreciation + Deferred Taxes

Although we will discuss this later, there is a definition for Changes in Accounts Receivable + Changes in Inventory + Changes in Accounts Payable + Changes in Accrued Expenses + Changes in Prepaid Expenses called "changes in operating working capital," so we can rework the formula:

> Cash from Operating Activities
> = Net Income + Depreciation + Deferred Taxes
> + Changes in Operating Working Capital

Note the actual changes in each individual line item could be positive or negative. This will be explained in the section on Working Capital later in this chapter.

To be complete, cash from operating activities should include adjustments based on any and all income statement line items that are noncash. So, you may see "+ Other Noncash Items" toward the end of the formula to capture those adjustments.

TABLE 2.1 Most Common Income Statement Line Items

Net Income Line Item	Possible Deferrable Items?	Effect on Cash from Operations
Revenue	Yes	Changes in accounts receivable
Cost of Goods Sold	Yes	Changes in inventory; changes in accounts payable
Operating Expenses	Yes	Changes in accrued expenses; changes in prepaid expenses
Depreciation	Yes	Depreciation
Interest	No	None (some exceptions)
Taxes	Yes	Deferred taxes

Cash from Operating Activities
= Net Income + Depreciation + Deferred Taxes + Other Noncash Items
+ Changes in Operating Working Capital

The important lesson here is to gain the conceptual understanding of how cash from operating activities is derived from the income statement. As we get into more complex case studies and analyses, and for due diligence purposes, you will learn that it is important to understand cash flow as derived from individual income statement line items, rather than memorizing a standard formula. This is especially important in leveraged buyouts when analyzing smaller private companies that maybe do not have a complete set of financials. The ability to derive an operating working capital schedule and cash flow from operations from an income statement will be useful. This is just the fundamental beginning of such analyses.

CASH FLOW FROM INVESTING ACTIVITIES

Now that we have a measure of cash generated from our operations, there are two other areas from which cash can be generated or spent: investing activities and financing activities. Cash flow from investing activities is cash generated or spent from buying or selling assets, businesses, or other investments or securities. More specifically, the major categories are:

- Capital expenditures (investments in property, plant, and equipment)
- Buying or selling assets
- Buying, selling, spinning off, or splitting off businesses or portions of business entities
- Investing in or selling marketable and nonmarketable securities

CASH FLOW FROM FINANCING ACTIVITIES

Cash flow from financing activities is defined as cash generated or spent from equity or debt. More specifically:

- Raising or buying back equity or preferred securities
- Raising or paying back debt
- Distributions to equity holders (noncontrolling interests and dividends)

The sum of the cash flow from operating activities, cash flow from investing activities, and cash flow from financing activities gives us a total measure of how much cash is generated or has been spent over a given period.

THE BALANCE SHEET

The balance sheet is a measure of a company's financial position at a specific point in time. The balance sheet's performance is broken up into three major categories: assets, liabilities, and shareholders' equity; the company's total value of assets must always equal the sum of its liabilities and shareholders' equity:

Assets = Liabilities + Shareholders' Equity

ASSETS

An asset is a resource held to produce some economic benefit. Examples of assets are cash, inventory, accounts receivable, and property. Assets are separated into two categories: current assets and noncurrent assets.

Current Assets

A current asset is an asset whose economic benefit is expected to come within one year. Examples of common current assets follow.

Cash and Cash Equivalents Cash is currency on hand. Cash equivalents are assets that are readily convertible into cash, such as money market holdings, short-term government bonds or Treasury bills, marketable securities, and commercial paper. Cash equivalents are often considered as cash because they can be easily liquidated when necessary.

Accounts Receivable Accounts receivable (AR) are sales made on credit. The revenue for the sale has been recognized, but the customer did not pay for the sale in cash. An asset is recorded for the amount of the sale and remains until the customer has paid. If AR increases by $100, for example, then we must have booked a sale. So, revenue increases by $100.

Income Statement	
Revenue	100.0
Taxes (@ 40%)	(40.0)
Net Income	**60.0**

The resulting net income increase of $60 flows to the cash flow statement. We then need to remove the $100 in AR, as an increase in AR of $100 results in an operating working capital cash outflow of $100. Combined with the net income increase of $60, we have a total cash change of –$40.

Cash Flow			Balance Sheet	
Net Income	60.0		Cash	(40.0)
Changes in Accounts Receivable	(100.0)		Accounts Receivable	100.0
Total Changes in Cash	**(40.0)**		Retained Earnings (Net Income)	60.0

In the balance sheet, cash is reduced by $40, AR increases by $100, and retained earnings increases by $60. Note the relationship between the changes in accounts receivable on the cash flow statement and accounts receivable on the balance sheet: cash down, asset up. The balance sheet balances: Total assets (–$40 + $100 = $60) less liabilities ($0) equals retained earnings ($60).

When the customer finally pays, cash is received and the AR on the balance sheet is removed.

Cash Flow			Balance Sheet	
Net Income	**0.0**		Cash	100.0
Changes in Accounts Receivable	100.0		Accounts Receivable	(100.0)
Total Changes in Cash	**100.0**		Retained Earnings (Net Income)	0.0

Inventory Inventory is the raw materials and the goods that are ready for sale. When raw materials are acquired, inventory is increased by the amount of material purchased. Once goods are sold and recorded as revenue, the value of the inventory is reduced and a cost of goods sold (COGS) expense is recorded. Let's say, for example, we are selling chairs.

If inventory increases by $50, then we have most likely purchased inventory, resulting in a cash outflow. Cash is reduced by $50 and an inventory asset is created. Note the relationship between the changes in inventory on the cash flow statement and inventory on the balance sheet: cash down, asset up.

Cash Flow			Balance Sheet	
Net Income	0.0		Cash	(50.0)
Changes in Inventory	(50.0)		Inventory	50.0
Total Changes in Cash	**(50.0)**		Retained Earnings (Net Income)	0.0

If inventory decreases by $50, it is most likely related to a sale of that inventory, which is expensed as COGS. Note that the additional expense affects taxes and the resulting net income is –$30. An asset sold results in a cash increase; when added to the –$30 of net income, it gives us a total $20 change in cash.

Income Statement	
COGS	(50.0)
Taxes (@ 40%)	20.0
Net Income	**(30.0)**

Cash Flow			Balance Sheet	
Net Income	(30.0)		Cash	20.0
Changes in Inventory	50.0		Inventory	(50.0)
Total Changes in Cash	**20.0**		Retained Earnings (Net Income)	(30.0)

Inventory is reduced by 50. Net income affects retained earnings. The balance sheet balances: Total assets ($20 – $50 = –$30) less liabilities ($0) equals retained earnings (–$30).

Prepaid Expense Prepaid expense is an asset created when a company pays for an expense in advance of when it is billed or incurred. Let's say we decide to prepay rent expense by $100. Cash goes into a prepaid expense account. Note the relationship between the changes in prepaid expense on the cash flow statement and prepaid expense on the balance sheet: cash down, asset up.

Cash Flow			Balance Sheet	
Net Income	0.0		Cash	(100.0)
Changes in prepaid expense	(100.0)		Prepaid expense	100.0
Total Changes in Cash	**(100.0)**		Retained Earnings (Net Income)	0.0

When the expense is actually incurred, it is then expensed in the selling, general, and administrative (SG&A) account; after tax we get −$60 in net income.

Income Statement	
SG&A	(100.0)
Taxes (@ 40%)	40.0
Net Income	**(60.0)**

The −$60 in net income flows into retained earnings on the balance sheet. The prepaid expense asset is reduced, causing a change in prepaid expense inflow.

Cash Flow			Balance Sheet	
Net Income	(60.0)		Cash	40.0
Changes in prepaid expense	100.0		Prepaid expense	(100.0)
Total Changes in Cash	**40.0**		Retained Earnings (Net Income)	(60.0)

The balance sheet balances: Total assets ($40 − $100 = −$60) less liabilities ($0) equals shareholders' equity (−$60).

Noncurrent Assets

Noncurrent assets are not expected to be converted into cash within one year. Some examples of noncurrent assets follow.

Property, Plant, and Equipment (PP&E) Property, plant, and equipment are assets purchased in order to further the company's operations. Also known as fixed assets, examples of PP&E are buildings, factories, and machinery.

Intangible Assets An intangible asset is an asset that cannot be physically touched. Intellectual property, such as patents, trademarks, and copyrights, along with goodwill and brand recognition are all examples of intangible assets.

LIABILITIES

A liability is any debt or financial obligation of a company. There are current liabilities and noncurrent liabilities.

Current Liabilities

Current liabilities are company debts or obligations that are owed within one year. Some examples of current liabilities follow.

Accounts Payable Accounts payable are obligations owed to a company's suppliers. If a company, for example, purchases $500 in raw materials from its supplier on credit, the company incurs a $500 account payable. The company increases the accounts payable by $500 until it pays the supplier.

Cash Flow		Balance Sheet	
Net Income	0.0	Cash	500.0
Changes in Accounts Payable	500.0	Accounts Payable	500.0
Total Changes in Cash	**500.0**	Retained Earnings (Net Income)	0.0

Once the supplier is paid, the account payable is reduced by $500, and cash on the balance sheet goes down by $500. Note the relationship between the changes in accounts payable on the cash flow statement and accounts payable on the balance sheet: cash up, liability up.

Accrued Liabilities Accrued liabilities are expenses that have been incurred but have not yet been paid. If a company receives a utility bill of $1,000, for example, which is expensed under SG&A, an accrued liabilities account is also recorded for $1,000 in the balance sheet.

Income Statement	
SG&A	(1,000.0)
Taxes (@ 40%)	400.0
Net Income	(600.0)

After taxes, the net income effect is –$600, which flows to cash flow. Note the relationship between the changes in accrued liabilities on the cash flow statement and accrued liabilities on the balance sheet: cash up, liability up.

Cash Flow		Balance Sheet	
Net Income	(600.0)	Cash	400.0
Changes in accrued liabilities	1,000.0	Accrued liabilities	1,000.0
Total Changes in Cash	**400.0**	Retained Earnings (Net Income)	(600.0)

Once the bill has been paid, the accrued liabilities is reduced, and cash in the balance sheet goes down by $1,000.

Cash Flow		Balance Sheet	
Net Income	0.0	Cash	(1,000.0)
Changes in accrued liabilities	(1,000.0)	Accrued liabilities	(1,000.0)
Total Changes in Cash	**(1,000.0)**	Retained Earnings (Net Income)	0.0

Short-Term Debts Short-term debts are debts that come due within one year.

Noncurrent Liabilities

Noncurrent liabilities are company debts or obligations due beyond one year. Some examples of noncurrent liabilities follow.

Long-Term Debts Long-term debts are debts due beyond one year.

Deferred Taxes Deferred taxes result from timing differences between net income recorded for generally accepted accounting principles (GAAP) purposes and net income recorded for tax purposes. Deferred taxes can act as a liability or an asset. We will discuss deferred taxes in more detail in the next section.

DEPRECIATION

Depreciation is accounting for the aging of assets.

> *Depreciation is an income tax deduction that allows a taxpayer to recover the cost or other basis of certain property. It is an annual allowance for the wear and tear, deterioration, or obsolescence of the property.*
>
> *Most types of tangible property (except land), such as buildings, machinery, vehicles, furniture, and equipment are depreciable. Likewise, certain intangible property, such as patents, copyrights, and computer software is depreciable.*
>
> *(from www.irs.gov)*

In other words, as a company owns and utilizes an asset, its value will most likely decrease. As discussed in the balance sheet chapter, if an asset value decreases, there must be another change to one of the other line items in the balance sheet to offset the asset reduction. Accounting rules state that the reduction in asset value can be expensed, with the idea being that the asset's aging or wear and tear is partly due to utilization of the asset to produce or generate revenue. If the item is expensed, net income is reduced, which in turn will reduce the retained earnings in the shareholders' equity section of the balance sheet.

Let's take an example of an asset that has a depreciation expense of $5,000. Depreciation expense reduces net income after taxes, as shown. Net income drives the cash flow statement, but since depreciation is a noncash expense it is added back to cash.

Income Statement			Cash Flow	
Depreciation	(5,000.0)		**Net Income**	**(3,000.0)**
Taxes (@ 40%)	2,000.0		Depreciation	5,000.0
Net Income	**(3,000.0)**		**Total Changes in Cash**	**2,000.0**

In the balance sheet, net income drives retained earnings. Depreciation will lower the value of the asset being depreciated (the plant, property, and equipment [PP&E]).

Cash Flow			Balance Sheet Adjustments	
Net Income	**(3,000.0)**		Cash	2,000.0
Depreciation	5,000.0		PP&E	(5,000.0)
Total Changes in Cash	**2,000.0**		Retained Earnings (Net Income)	(3,000.0)

There are several methods allowed to depreciate assets. Each has its benefits under certain conditions. In this chapter we will learn about the most popular methods and how they are utilized. The two major categories are:

1. Straight-line depreciation
2. Accelerated depreciation

STRAIGHT-LINE DEPRECIATION

The straight-line method of depreciation evenly ages the asset by the number of years that asset is expected to last—it's useful life. For example, if we purchase a car for $50,000 and that car has a useful life of 10 years, the depreciation would be $5,000 per year. So next year the asset will have depreciated by $5,000 and its value would be reduced to $45,000. In the following year, the asset will be depreciated by another $5,000 and be worth $40,000. By year 10, the asset will be worth $0 and have been fully depreciated.

One can also assign a residual value (also known as scrap value) to an asset, which is some minimal value an asset can be worth after the end of its useful life. So, for example, if the car after year 10 can be sold for $1,000 for spare parts, then $1,000 is the residual value. In this case, by year 10, the value of the car should be $1,000, not $0. In order to account for residual value in the depreciation formula, we need to depreciate the value of the car less this residual value, or $50,000 minus $1,000, which is $49,000. The depreciation will now be $4,900 per year, which means the next year the value of the car will be $44,100. And by year 10, the final value of the car will be $1,000. So the definition for straight-line depreciation is:

$$\text{Depreciation} = (\text{Fair Value of Asset} - \text{Residual Value})/\text{Useful Life}$$

ACCELERATED DEPRECIATION

Accelerating depreciation allows a greater depreciation expense earlier in the life of the asset, and a lower depreciation in the later years. The most common reason for accelerating depreciation is that a higher depreciation expense will produce a lower taxable net income, and therefore lower taxes. There are several methods of accelerating depreciation, the most common of which are:

- Declining balance
- Sum of the year's digits
- Modified Accelerated Cost Recovery System (MACRS)

Declining Balance

The declining balance method takes a percentage of the net property balance each year. The net property balance is reduced each year by the depreciation expensed in that particular year.

The percentage applied is calculated by dividing 1 by the life of the asset times an accelerating multiplier:

$$1/\text{Useful Life} \times \text{Accelerating Multiplier}$$

The multiplier is most commonly 2.0 or 1.5.

In the car example, the asset has a life of 10 years. If we assume 2.0 as the accelerating multiplier, then the declining balance percentage is:

$$1/10 \times 2 = 20\%$$

TABLE 2.2 Declining Balance Example

Period Ending December 31	2016E	2017E	2018E	2019E	2020E
Net property, plant & equipment	50,000.0	40,000.0	32,000.0	25,600.0	20,480.0
Accelerated depreciation (%)	20%	20%	20%	20%	20%
Depreciation expense	10,000.0	8,000.0	6,400.0	5,120.0	4,096.0

We will apply 20 percent to the net property balance each year to calculate the accelerated depreciation of the car. So, 20 percent of $50,000 is $10,000. The net balance is $40,000 ($50,000 – $10,000). In year 2 we will apply 20 percent to the $40,000, which gives us $8,000. The new net balance is $32,000 ($40,000 – $8,000). And in year 3, we will apply 20 percent to the $32,000 to get $6,400. (See Table 2.2.)

Sum of the Year's Digits

To use the sum of the year's digits method, we first take the sum of the digits from 1 to the life of the asset. For example, an asset with a useful life of 10 years will have a sum of 55: $1 + 2 + 3 + 4 + 5 + 6 + 7 + 8 + 9 + 10$. For year 1, the percentage will be 10/55 or 18.18 percent (rounded to the hundredth place). For year 2, the percentage will be 9/55 or 16.36 percent. For year 3 it is 8/55 or 14.55 percent, and so on. This percentage is applied to the base value of the asset and is not reduced by the depreciation each year like in the declining balance method.

$$\text{Year 1 depreciation} = \$50,000 \times 18.18\% \text{ or } \$9,090$$

$$\text{Year 2 depreciation} = \$50,000 \times 16.36\% \text{ or } \$8,180$$

$$\text{Year 3 depreciation} = \$50,000 \times 14.55\% \text{ or } \$7,275$$

$$\text{Year 4 depreciation} = \$50,000 \times 12.73\% \text{ or } \$6,365$$

$$\text{Year 5 depreciation} = \$50,000 \times 10.91\% \text{ or } \$5,455$$

Notice in Table 2.3 that we are basing the future depreciation on the original balance each year. This differs from the declining balance method, where we calculate depreciation on the net property balance each year (property net of depreciation).

Modified Accelerated Cost Recovery System (MACRS)

The Modified Accelerated Cost Recovery System (MACRS) is the U.S. tax method of depreciation.

TABLE 2.3 Sum of the Year's Digits Example

Period Ending December 31	2016E	2017E	2018E	2019E	2020E
Net property, plant & equipment	50,000.0				
Accelerated depreciation (%)	18.18%	16.36%	14.55%	12.73%	10.91%
Depreciation expense	9,090.0	8,180.0	7,275.0	6,365.0	5,455.0

The MACRS method is a predefined set of percentages based on the asset's useful life. These percentages are applied to the base value of the asset each year. (You can look up these percentages at www.irs.gov.) There are several conventions used, each with a different set of calculated percentages, including the half-year convention and the mid-quarter convention. The differences in conventions are dependent on when exactly the asset is placed in service and starts depreciating. The half-year convention, shown in Table 2.4, assumes that the asset is not placed in service and does not begin depreciating until midyear.

When looking at the "3-year" percentages, notice that the first percentage is actually lower (33.33 percent) than the next year's percentage (44.45 percent), which is not really accelerating. The half-year convention assumes the asset is not placed in service, and so does not start depreciating until midyear, so an adjustment had been made to that first percentage.

The mid-quarter convention, shown in Table 2.5, assumes that the asset starts depreciating in the middle of the first quarter. So here the starting percentage of 58.33 percent is higher than that of the half-year convention. Because the asset is placed in service in the first quarter rather than at midyear, the asset will begin depreciating earlier, and will therefore have a greater depreciation expense by the end of the first year.

There are also mid-quarter convention tables where the asset is placed in service in the second, third, and fourth quarters.

Determining which table to use really depends on when the assets are placed in service, which is often unobtainable information. So, by default, we typically use the mid-quarter convention where the asset is placed in service in the first quarter, as it results

TABLE 2.4 3-, 5-, 7-, 10-, 15-, and 20-Year Property Half-Year Convention

Year	Depreciation Rate for Recovery Period					
	3-Year	5-Year	7-Year	10-Year	15-Year	20-Year
1	33.33%	20.00%	14.29%	10.00%	5.00%	3.750%
2	44.45	32.00	24.49	18.00	9.50	7.219
3	14.81	19.20	17.49	14.40	8.55	6.677
4	7.41	11.52	12.49	11.52	7.70	6.177
5		11.52	8.93	9.22	6.93	5.713
6		5.76	8.92	7.37	6.23	5.285
7			8.93	6.55	5.90	4.888
8			4.46	6.55	5.90	4.522
9				6.56	5.91	4.462
10				6.55	5.90	4.461
11				3.28	5.91	4.462
12					5.90	4.461
13					5.91	4.462
14					5.90	4.461
15					5.91	4.462
16					2.95	4.461
17						4.462
18						4.461
19						4.462
20						4.461
21						2.231

TABLE 2.5   3-, 5-, 7-, 10-, 15-, and 20-Year Property Mid-Quarter Convention Placed in Service in First Quarter

Year	Depreciation Rate for Recovery Period					
	3-Year	5-Year	7-Year	10-Year	15-Year	20-Year
1	58.33%	35.00%	25.00%	17.50%	8.75%	6.563%
2	27.78	26.00	21.43	16.50	9.13	7.000
3	12.35	15.60	15.31	13.20	8.21	6.482
4	1.54	11.01	10.93	10.56	7.39	5.996
5		11.01	8.75	8.45	6.65	5.546
6		1.38	8.74	6.76	5.99	5.130
7			8.75	6.55	5.90	4.746
8			1.09	6.55	5.91	4.459
9				6.56	5.90	4.459
10				6.55	5.91	4.459
11				0.82	5.90	4.459
12					5.91	4.460
13					5.90	4.459
14					5.91	4.460
15					5.90	4.459
16					0.74	4.460
17						4.459
18						4.460
19						4.459
20						4.460
21						0.565

in the greatest depreciation expense in the first year. It is always recommended that you consult an asset appraiser and a tax professional to be sure you are using the correct methods of depreciation.

For an asset with a 10-year useful life, using Table 2.5, we would apply 17.50 percent to the value of the asset to get year 1 depreciation expense. For year 2, the percentage will be 16.50 percent. See Table 2.6 for the first five years' depreciation calculations for an asset originally worth $50,000.

Note that quite often there are differences between the income statement reported for generally accepted U.S. accounting (GAAP) purposes and the income statement for tax purposes. One of the major differences can be the method of depreciation. Common depreciation methods under U.S. GAAP include straight-line, declining balance, and sum of the year's digits. Tax accounting uses the Modified Accelerated Cost Recovery System (MACRS). The differences in the net income caused by using a different depreciation

TABLE 2.6   Modified Accelerated Cost Recovery System

Period Ending December 31	2016E	2017E	2018E	2019E	2020E
Net property, plant & equipment	50,000.0				
Accelerated depreciation (%)	17.50%	16.50%	13.20%	10.56%	8.45%
Depreciation expense	8,750.0	8,250.0	6,600.0	5,280.0	4,225.0

method when filing GAAP reports versus tax statements can cause a deferred tax liability. We discuss this in more detail next.

DEFERRED TAXES

A deferred tax asset is defined as an asset on a company's balance sheet that may be used to reduce income tax expense. A deferred tax asset is most commonly created after receiving a net operating loss (NOL), which occurs when a company's expenses exceed its sales. The IRS allows a company to offset the loss against taxable income in another year. The NOL can be carried back two to five years or carried forward up to 20 years. Note that the amount of years a company can carry back or carry forward a loss depends on several business factors that need to be considered by the IRS on a case-by-case basis. More information on the specific criteria can be found at www.irs.gov. It is always strongly recommended to verify treatment of NOLs with a certified accountant or tax professional.

NOL Carryback Example

Income Statement	2013	2014	2015
EBT	750.0	1,500.0	(1,000.0)
Taxes (@ 40%)	(300.0)	(600.0)	0.0
Net Income	450.0	900.0	(1,000.0)

The company in this example has suffered a net loss in 2015. So, it files for a two-year carryback, which allows the company to offset the 2015 loss by receiving a refund on taxes paid in the prior two years. So that $1,000 loss becomes a balance from which taxes can be deducted in other years.

NOL Applied to 2013	
Beginning Balance	$1,000.0
Taxable Income	750.0
Tax Refund (@ 40%)	300.0
NOL Balance	250.0

We first apply the $1,000 loss to the $750 of taxable income in 2013, which results in a $300 refund. This leaves us with $250 ($1,000 – $750) of NOLs left to apply to 2014.

NOL Applied to 2014	
Beginning Balance	$250.0
Taxable Income	1,500.0
Tax Refund (@ 40%)	100.0
NOL Balance	0.0

In 2014, we have $1,500 of taxable income. However, with only $250 in NOLs left, we can receive a refund on only $250 of the $1,500. So that's a $100 refund ($250 × 40%). Combined with the $300 refund, we have a total of $400 refunded.

If the company had little or no taxable income in the prior years, it can elect to carry forward the net operating losses for up to 20 years depending on various considerations. Let's take another example, where, after the two-year carryback credits have been applied, an NOL balance still exists.

Income Statement	2013	2014	2015
EBT	100.0	200.0	(1,000.0)
Taxes (@ 40%)	(40.0)	(80.0)	0.0
Net Income	60.0	120.0	(1,000.0)

The company in this example has also suffered a net loss in 2015. The company files for a two-year carryback, which allows it to offset the 2015 loss by receiving a refund on taxes paid in the prior two years.

NOL Applied to 2013	
Beginning Balance	$1,000.0
Taxable Income	100.0
Tax Refund (@ 40%)	40.0
NOL Balance	900.0

We first apply the $1,000 loss to the $100 taxable income in 2013, which results in a $40 refund. This leaves us with $900 ($1,000 − $100) of NOLs left to apply to 2014.

NOL Applied to 2014	
Beginning Balance	$900.0
Taxable Income	200.0
Tax Refund (@ 40%)	80.0
NOL Balance	700.0

In 2014, we have $200 of taxable income. Applying the NOL will result in an $80 refund, or $120 in total refunds when combined with the 2013 tax refund. But notice we still have $700 in NOLs left. These can be used to offset future taxes. This $700 balance becomes a deferred tax asset until it is used or is no longer usable.

Deferred Tax Liability

A deferred tax liability is caused by temporary accounting differences between the income statement filed for GAAP purposes and the income statement for tax purposes. One common cause of a deferred tax liability is having differing methods of depreciation in a

GAAP income statement versus that in a tax income statement. A company can produce a GAAP set of financials using straight-line depreciation, for example, yet have a tax set of financials using the MACRS method of depreciation. This causes a deferred tax liability, reducing taxes in the short term.

Let's take a simple example of a company with $100,000 in earnings before interest, taxes, depreciation, and amortization (EBITDA). For GAAP purposes let's assume we will use the straight-line depreciation of $5,000 ($50,000/10). Let's also say we have decided to accelerate the depreciation for tax purposes using the MACRS method of depreciation. For an asset with a 10-year useful life, the depreciation is $8,750 (17.5% × $50,000). This will create the income statements shown in Table 2.7 for GAAP purposes and for tax purposes.

The GAAP income statement in the left column shows a lower depreciation expense and shows $95,000 in earnings before taxes (EBT). The right column, however, the tax income statement, shows a higher depreciation expense because it has been accelerated. This creates a lower EBT of $91,250, and results in $1,500 ($38,000 – $36,500) of lower taxes. Now, the GAAP-reported taxes of $38,000, which is the larger amount, is the tax number we see in a company's annual report or 10-K. The lower amount of taxes filed for tax purposes is the amount of taxes filed to the IRS that the company actually has to pay this year. So, the difference between the taxes reported and the taxes paid ($1,500) becomes a noncash item. Just like any expense that the company did not yet pay in cash, this noncash portion of taxes is added back to net income in the cash flow statement. This is a deferred tax liability.

Note that this is a great method to use in order to free up cash in the short term. The deferred tax amount of $1,500 calculated previously can also be calculated by subtracting the accelerated depreciation expense from the straight-line depreciation and multiplying by the tax rate:

$$\text{Deferred Tax Liability} = (\text{Accelerated Depreciation} - \text{Straight-Line Depreciation}) \times \text{Tax Rate}$$

or

$$(\$8,750 - \$5,000) \times 40\% = \$1,500$$

In modeling, we build a projected straight-line depreciation schedule and, if needed, an accelerated depreciation schedule. We then subtract the projected straight-line

TABLE 2.7 Income Statements for GAAP and Tax Purposes

Income Statement	GAAP (Straight-Line Depreciation)	Tax (MACRS Depreciation)
EBITDA	$100,000.0	$100,000.0
Depreciation	(5,000.0)	(8,750.0)
EBIT	95,000.0	91,250.0
Interest	0.0	0.0
EBT	95,000.0	91,250.0
Taxes (@ 40%)	(38,000.0)	(36,500.0)
Net Income	$57,000.0	$54,750.0

depreciation from the accelerated depreciation and multiply by the tax rate to estimate deferred tax.

WORKING CAPITAL

Working capital is a measure of a company's current assets less its current liabilities. However, for modeling purposes, we focus on a narrower definition of working capital called operating working capital (OWC). Operating working capital is also defined as current assets less current liabilities. However, OWC does not include cash and cash equivalents as part of current assets, and does not include debts as part of current liabilities.

"Cash equivalents" are assets that are readily convertible into cash, such as money market holdings, short-term government bonds and Treasury bills, marketable securities, and commercial paper. Cash equivalents are often considered as cash because they can be easily liquidated when necessary.

So, removing cash and cash equivalents, we are left with the following for current assets:

- Accounts receivable
- Inventory
- Prepaid expenses

And removing debts, we are left with the following for current liabilities:

- Accounts payable
- Accrued expenses

Note that there are other possible current assets or current liabilities; the aforementioned are just a few of the most common examples.

Each of these line items is most closely related to the company's operations. For example, accounts receivable is the portion of revenue we did not collect in cash, and accrued expenses is the portion of expenses we did not yet pay in cash. For this reason, operating working capital is a good measure of how much cash is coming in from the day-to-day operations. Another way to look at this is: Operating working capital helps track how well a company is managing its cash generating from day-to-day operations. In contrast, working capital, because it includes cash, cash equivalents, and debts, may not give the clearest measure of just the day-to-day operations.

How do we know if the individual operating working capital items are really performing well? If we see accounts receivable, for example, increasing year over year, this could mean we have an ever-growing collections problem. However, this could also mean that the receivables are growing because the revenue is growing, which would be a good indicator of strong business growth. So it is not enough to look at these operating working capital line items independently in order to determine their performance; we need to compare these line items to some related income statement line item. We use a measure called "days" to track how well we are collecting our receivables or paying our payables. Days are measured by dividing the receivable or payable by their related income statement item and multiplying by 360.

For example, let's say in 2015 the accounts receivable balance is $25,000 and the revenue is $100,000.

Income Statement		Operating Working Capital	
Revenue	100,000.0	Accounts Receivable	25,000.0
COGS	10,000.0	Inventory	7,500.0
Operating Expenses	85,000.0	Prepaid Expenses	1,000.0
EBITDA	**5,000.0**	Accounts Payable	12,500.0
		Accrued Expenses	15,000.0
		Net Working Capital	**6,000.0**

The accounts receivable divided by the revenue gives us 25 percent. So, 25 percent of our 2015 revenue has not yet been collected. We multiply this percentage by the number of days in one year to get an equivalent number representing how many days these receivables have been left outstanding; $25\% \times 360 = 90$, so of the 2015 revenue, 90 days are outstanding. As a rule of thumb, many companies require customer receipts to be paid within 30 days. However, depending on the business, 60, 90, or even more days could be acceptable. Ninety could be considered high or it could be okay, depending on the business model and the product sold. Notice that we have used 360 days instead of 365. Either way is acceptable; however, we more commonly use 360 because this is divisible by 12, which would make the modeling simpler if we ever wanted to break the year column down into 12 months:

$$Accounts\ Receivable\ Days = \frac{Accounts\ Receivable}{Revenue} \times 360$$

It is important to note that we have made a simplifying assumption in this formula for clarity. We took the last year's accounts receivable balance as the numerator in the calculation. In the actual analysis, it is important to take an average of the ending balances from the year being analyzed and the previous year. Because balance sheet items are balances at a specific point in time, averaging the current year's and previous year's performances gives a better indicator of measurement for the entire year. Income statement and cash flow items actually give us total performance over an entire period, so averaging does not apply. The complete formula for accounts receivable days in 2015 is:

$$2015\ Accounts\ Receivable\ Days = \frac{Average\ (2015\ Accounts\ Receivable, 2014\ Accounts\ Receivable)}{2015\ Revenue} \times 360$$

Let's take another example using a liability: accrued expenses. Let's say the accrued expenses balance in 2015 is \$15,000, and is made up of unpaid office rent. The 2015 income statement expense is \$85,000. The accrued expenses of \$15,000 divided by \$85,000 gives us 17.6 percent. So, 17.6 percent of our 2015 expenses have not yet been paid. We multiply this percentage by the number of days in one year to get an equivalent number representing how many days these payables have been left outstanding; $17.6\% \times 360 = 63.4$, so of the 2015 expense, 63.4 days are still outstanding, which could be considered too high in this case, especially considering that rent should typically be paid every 30 days.

$$Accrued\ Expenses\ Days = \frac{Accrued\ Expenses}{Operating\ Expenses} \times 360$$

We again simplified the example for purposes of instruction. When performing the actual analysis, we take the average of the accrued expenses balance in the year being analyzed and in the prior year:

$$2015\ Accrued\ Expenses\ Days = \frac{Average\ (2015\ Accrued\ Expenses, 2014\ Accrued\ Expenses)}{2015\ Operating\ Expenses} \times 360$$

In modeling, we use the calculated historical days to predict future working capital line items. You can get more information on the specific modeling in the book *Financial Modeling and Valuation: A Practical Guide to Investment Banking and Private Equity.*

DEBT SCHEDULE

The debt schedule is designed to track every major type of debt a company has, and the associated interest and payment schedules for each. It also helps track the cash available that could be used to pay down those debts and any interest income that could be generated from cash or cash equivalents available. Simply put, a debt schedule helps us better track the debt and interest. There is also a very important "circular reference" that is created once the debt schedule is complete and properly linked through the rest of the model. This circular reference is crucial in helping us determine various debt situations, such as the absolute maximum amount of debt a company can raise while making sure there is still enough cash to meet the interest payments. You can get more information on the specific modeling in the book *Financial Modeling and Valuation: A Practical Guide to Investment Banking and Private Equity.*

CHAPTER 3

Financial Statements Questions

1) Walk me through the three financial statements.

The income statement, the cash flow statement, and the balance sheet are the core financial statements. The income statement is a measure of profitability—revenue less expenses is taxed and creates net income. The cash flow statement tracks how much cash has been spent or generated from three major areas: operating activities, investing activities, and financing activities. The balance sheet is a snapshot of a company's resources (assets), its obligations (liabilities), and equity. The assets must always equal the sum of a company's equity and liabilities.

2) Walk me through an income statement (more detailed).

The income statement always starts with revenue, a company's sales, and builds down to net income. Cost of goods sold is the costs most directly associated to the revenue and is reduced from the revenue to produce gross profit (revenue – COGS = gross profit). Operating expenses are the next series of costs and consist of sales, general, and administrative expenses, and marketing and advertising expenses, to name the two most common. Gross profit less operating expenses make EBITDA. Depreciation and amortization are the costs related to the aging of tangible and intangible assets respectively. EBITDA less D&A makes EBIT. Interest expense is reduced from EBIT to get EBT. EBT is then tax affected to get net income.

You can also add: After net income there are two major sections reserved for equity distributions (noncontrolling interest expenses and dividends) and non-recurring or extraordinary events. Earnings per share is the net income divided by the shares outstanding.

3) What is EBITDA?

EBITDA stands for earnings before interest taxes depreciation and amortization.

4) EBITDA is $500MM. Which of the following has the greatest impact to EBITDA? Assume all is equal except for the below variables.
   a. Costs increase by $10MM.
   b. Pricing increases by 10%.
   c. Volume increases by 10%.

The answer is b. Since revenue is a product of pricing and volume, each of b and c would impact revenue. An increase in price of 10% would certainly increase revenue by 10% or $50MM. However, increasing volume, or units produced, would increase costs as well, assuming COGS is variable and based on units produced. Therefore, that potential increase in costs would offset the revenue benefits in some way.

So it's safe to say that b would have a larger impact than c. We would immediately eliminate a once we realized the impact of b is greater.

5) Walk me through a cash flow statement (more detailed).

The cash flow statement is a measure of how much cash is generated or spent over a given period. The statement is broken up into three major sections: cash flow from operating activities, cash flow from investing activities, and cash flow from financing activities. Cash flow from operating activities is the cash generated from net income, or the net income less all non-cash items from the income statement. This consists of net income plus depreciation and amortization, deferred taxes, other non-cash items, and changes in working capital. Cash flow from investing activities is cash generated or spent from investments. This includes capital expenditures, acquisitions and divestitures, and purchases and sales of securities to name the major few. Cash flow from financing activities is cash generated or spent from debt, equity, or distributions. This consists mainly of monies raised from or used to pay debts, monies received from equity and other securities, monies spent from share buybacks, and monies spent from dividend and other equity distributions. The sum of these three cash flow components completes the cash flow statement.

6) What is cash flow from operations?

Cash flow from operations is defined by net income + D&A + deferred taxes + other non-cash items + changes in working capital.

7) What is the difference between net income and cash flow?

Net income measures profitability whose components may or may not have impacted cash. Cash flow tracks just the cash impacts generated or received from operations, investing, and financing activities.

8) Why would an investor care about cash flow versus net income?

This question is quite similar to the previous, but it's important that one grasps these concepts because questions around them could be asked several different ways. An investor is more apt to base his investment using the cash flow statement as it tracks the "true" measure of how much cash has been generated or spent over a period. Net income may report profitability, but how much of that profitability had actually been converted into cash? If none, for example, the investor would be less likely to see his investment returned. "Cash is king" holds true in this context. And this is why we more commonly look at cash flow in a discounted cash flow analysis as opposed to net income.

9) How does maintenance CAPEX differ from growth CAPEX?

Maintenance CAPEX is the funds expended to extend the useful life of existing assets, whereas expansion CAPEX is the purchase of new assets to grow the business.

10) Walk me through a balance sheet (more detailed).

The balance sheet is a measure of a company's assets, liabilities, and shareholder's equity at a given point in time. The company's assets, a resource with economic value that is expected to provide some future benefit, is broken up into current and non-current. Current assets are resources whose economic benefit is expected to come due within one year. Examples of current assets are cash, accounts receivable, and inventories. Examples of long-term assets are property, plant and equipment (PP&E), goodwill, intangible assets, and investments in securities. A liability is a debt or obligation and is also broken up into current and non-current sections. Current liabilities are debts or obligations the come due within one year. Examples of current liabilities are accounts payable, accrued expenses, and short-term debts. Examples of long-term liabilities are long-term debts and deferred tax liabilities. Shareholder's equity consists of retained earnings and share capital less Treasury shares. The sum of the shareholder's equity and the total liabilities must equal the total value of assets:

$$\text{Total Assets} = \text{Total Liabilities} + \text{Shareholder's Equity}$$

11) How do the three statements link together?

Note there can be many ways to answer this question. Here is a suggested solution:
    Net income from the income statement flows into the top of the cash flow statement and into the shareholder's equity section of the balance sheet. Each and every line item in the cash flow statement impacts a line item in the balance sheet: an asset, liability, or shareholder's equity. Total cash and cash equivalents at the bottom of the cash flow statement impacts the cash line item at the top of the balance sheet. Depreciation created on its own schedule flows into the income statement, into the cash flow statement, and impacts PP&E on the balance sheet. Changes in each working capital line item from the working capital schedule flow into the working capital section of the cash flow statement, and subsequently impact each respective balance sheet line item. Interest expense and interest income, derived from the debt schedule, flows into the income statement. Finally, any debt issuances or paydowns depicted in the debt schedule flow into the financing activities in the cash flow statements and further into the respective debt balances on the balance sheet.

12) Walk me through the circular reference in a model.

A circular reference can begin in the debt schedule with some issuance or paydown of debt. When debt is paid down, for example, the interest expense is reduced. This reduction in interest expense flows into the income statement and increases net income. The increase in net income flows into the cash flow statement and increases the cash flow before debt paydown balance. Cash flow before debt paydown flows back into the debt schedule, increasing the amount of funds that can be used to pay down debt. If we have more funds, we can pay down more debt, interest expense will reduce further, impact the income statement, increase net income, increase the cash balance further, and the cycle will continue.

13) What is working capital used for?

Working capital is a measure of a company's current assets less its current liabilities. Working capital is often looked at as a measure of a company's near-term liquidity or operating efficiency as current assets (resources that will be converted into cash within a year) less liabilities (debt or obligations due within one year) can help determine if there will be enough cash in the short term to cover a company's upcoming liabilities or obligations.

14) How does operating working capital differ from working capital?

Operating working capital is a company's current assets excluding cash and current liabilities excluding debts. Bankers often look at operating working capital as by eliminating cash and debts, you are left with line items most closely related to a company's core operations (e.g., accounts receivable, inventories, accounts payable).

15) What is a deferred tax liability? How is such a liability created?

A deferred tax liability is a tax balance due that has not yet been paid in cash. Deferred tax liabilities are created from timing differences between book accounting (GAAP) and tax accounting.

16) How is a deferred tax asset created?

A deferred tax asset can be created if a business has a net operating loss (NOL). An asset can also be created by receiving government tax credits (investing in certain energy, for example).

17) If you had to choose only one of the three core statements to determine the financial viability of a company, which statement would you choose?

The cash flow statement provides a true measure of cash produced by the business as opposed to an income statement, which may or may not include non-cash items. To an investor, cash is the true measure of performance. This is partially why the discounted cash flow is a valuable valuation method.

18) If I had to choose only two statements to assess a company's performance, which two would I use?

The income statement and the balance sheet. A cash flow statement can be created from an income statement and two years of a balance sheet.

PRACTICE QUESTIONS

Use the space available to answer the following examples. The answers are at the end of the chapter.

19) If accounts receivable increases by $10, please explain the effects on the income statement, cash flow statement, and balance sheet (assume 40% tax rate).

Income Statement	Cash Flow	Balance Sheet

20) If accounts receivable now decreases by $10, please explain the effects on the income statement, cash flow statement, and balance sheet.

Income Statement	Cash Flow	Balance Sheet

21) If accrued expenses increase by $30, please explain the effects on the income statement, cash flow statement, and balance sheet. Assume accrued expenses are related to SG&A. Assume a 40% tax rate.

Income Statement	Cash Flow	Balance Sheet

22) If accrued expenses now decrease by $30, please explain the effects on the income statement, cash flow statement, and balance sheet.

Income Statement	Cash Flow	Balance Sheet

23) If depreciation expense increased by $20, please explain the effects on the income statement, cash flow statement, and balance sheet. Assume a 40% tax rate.

Income Statement	Cash Flow	Balance Sheet

24) We are in the business of buying and selling widgets, and we have just started the company. We can purchase these widgets for $100 each if we are buying in bulk of 50 and the purchase can be deferred as an account payable. We have not yet made any sales. Please explain the effects on the income statement, cash flow statement, and balance sheet.

Income Statement	Cash Flow	Balance Sheet

25A) In the first period we have sold 15 widgets for $500 each in cash. Please explain the effects on the income statement, cash flow statement, and balance sheet. Assume a 40% tax rate.

Income Statement	Cash Flow	Balance Sheet

25B) What does the final balance sheet look like after the results from Question 24 and Question 25A?

Final Balance Sheet

26A) Let's now assume we have sold 15 widgets *on credit*. Please explain the effects on the income statement, cash flow statement, and balance sheet. Assume a 40% tax rate.

Income Statement	**Cash Flow**	**Balance Sheet**

26B) What does the final balance sheet look like after the results from Questions 24–26A?

Final Balance Sheet

27A) Let's now assume we have sold the remaining 20 widgets, 10 in cash and 10 on credit. Please explain the effects on the income statement, cash flow statement, and balance sheet. Assume a 40% tax rate.

Income Statement	**Cash Flow**	**Balance Sheet**

27B) What does the final balance sheet look like after the results from Questions 24–27A?

Final Balance Sheet

28A) Let's now assume we have collected on all receivables and paid all payables. Please explain the effects on the income statement, cash flow statement, and balance sheet.

| Income Statement | Cash Flow | Balance Sheet |

28B) What does the final balance sheet look like after the results from Questions 24–28A?

Final Balance Sheet

29A) Let's now assume we have incurred overhead costs of $1,500 that have been paid in cash. Please explain the effects on the income statement, cash flow statement, and balance sheet. Assume a 40% tax rate.

Income Statement   **Cash Flow**   **Balance Sheet**

29B) What does the final balance sheet look like after the results from Questions 24–29A?

Final Balance Sheet

30A) Let's assume we have received a rent bill of $5,000 which we have decided to defer as an accrued expense. Please explain the effects on the income statement, cash flow statement, and balance sheet. Assume a 40% tax rate.

Income Statement   **Cash Flow**   **Balance Sheet**

30B) What does the final balance sheet look like after the results from Questions 24–30A?

Final Balance Sheet

---

*Advanced—Questions 31–35 are a bit more advanced. We will cover and practice these in more detail in the M&A chapter:

31A) Now let's say we want to purchase property for $15,000. Since we don't have 15,000 in cash on our balance sheet, we will first raise debt to fund the difference. Let's say we raise $3,000, allowing some cushion for interest payments. The debt has an interest rate of 10%. Please explain the effects on the income statement, cash flow statement, and balance sheet of the debt raise. Focus on just the debt raise; we will handle the interest impact later.

Income Statement	**Cash Flow**	**Balance Sheet**

31B) What does the final balance sheet look like after the results from Questions 24–31A?

Final Balance Sheet

32A) Now let's say the debt has an interest rate of 10%. Please explain the effects on the income statement, cash flow statement, and balance sheet of the interest expense on the debt raised. Assume a 40% interest rate.

Income Statement	**Cash Flow**	**Balance Sheet**

32B) What does the final balance sheet look like after the results from Questions 24–32A?

Final Balance Sheet

33A) Now what is the income statement, cash flow, and balance sheet impact on the property purchase? Ignore impacts on depreciation for the time being.

Income Statement	Cash Flow	Balance Sheet

33B) What does the final balance sheet look like after the results from Questions 24–33A?

Final Balance Sheet

34A) Now what is the income statement, cash flow, and balance sheet impact on the depreciation expense associated with this new property? Assume a 10-year useful life and no residual value. Tax rate is 40%.

Income Statement   **Cash Flow**   **Balance Sheet**

34B) What does the final balance sheet look like after the results from Questions 24–34A?

Final Balance Sheet

35A) Now let's see that the company also accelerates depreciation on the new property for deferred tax purposes. What is the income statement, cash flow, and balance sheet impact? Assume the double declining balance method. Tax rate is 40%.

Income Statement	Cash Flow	Balance Sheet

35B) What does the final balance sheet look like after the results from Questions 24–35A?

Final Balance Sheet

---

36) If accounts receivable increases by $15, please explain the effects on the income statement, cash flow statement, and balance sheet (assume 40% tax rate).

Income Statement   **Cash Flow**   **Balance Sheet**
---

37) If accounts receivable now decreases by $15, please explain the effects on the income statement, cash flow statement, and balance sheet.

Income Statement	Cash Flow	Balance Sheet

38) If accounts receivable increases by $300, please explain the effects on the income statement, cash flow statement, and balance sheet (assume a 40% tax rate).

Income Statement	Cash Flow	Balance Sheet

39) If accounts receivable now decreases by $300, please explain the effects on the income statement, cash flow statement, and balance sheet.

Income Statement	Cash Flow		Balance Sheet

40) If accounts receivable increases by $1,250, please explain the effects on the income statement, cash flow statement, and balance sheet (assume a 40% tax rate).

Income Statement	Cash Flow		Balance Sheet

41) If accounts receivable now decreases by $1,250, please explain the effects on the income statement, cash flow statement, and balance sheet.

Income Statement	Cash Flow	Balance Sheet

42) If inventory *increases* by $20, please explain the effects on the income statement, cash flow statement, and balance sheet.

Income Statement	Cash Flow	Balance Sheet

43) If inventory *decreases* by $20, please explain the effects on the income statement, cash flow statement, and balance sheet (assume a 40% tax rate).

Income Statement	Cash Flow	Balance Sheet

44) If inventory *increases* by $500, please explain the effects on the income statement, cash flow statement, and balance sheet.

Income Statement	Cash Flow	Balance Sheet

45) If inventory *decreases* by $500, please explain the effects on the income statement, cash flow statement, and balance sheet (assume a 40% tax rate).

Income Statement	Cash Flow	Balance Sheet

46) If inventory *increases* by $2,250, please explain the effects on the income statement, cash flow statement, and balance sheet (assume a 40% tax rate).

Income Statement	Cash Flow	Balance Sheet

47) If inventory *decreases* by $1,750, please explain the effects on the income statement, cash flow statement, and balance sheet (assume a 40% tax rate).

Income Statement	Cash Flow	Balance Sheet

48) If accrued expenses increase by $50, please explain the effects on the income statement, cash flow statement, and balance sheet. Assume accrued expenses are related to operating expenses. Assume a 40% tax rate.

Income Statement	Cash Flow	Balance Sheet

49) If accrued expenses now decrease by $50, please explain the effects on the income statement, cash flow statement, and balance sheet.

Income Statement	Cash Flow	Balance Sheet

50) If accrued expenses increase by $250, please explain the effects on the income statement, cash flow statement, and balance sheet. Assume accrued expenses are related to SG&A. Assume a 40% tax rate.

Income Statement	Cash Flow	Balance Sheet

51) If accrued expenses now decrease by $250, please explain the effects on the income statement, cash flow statement, and balance sheet.

Income Statement	Cash Flow	Balance Sheet

52) If depreciation expense increases by $75, please explain the effects on the income statement, cash flow statement, and balance sheet. Assume a 40% tax rate.

Income Statement	Cash Flow	Balance Sheet

53) If depreciation expense increases by $250, please explain the effects on the income statement, cash flow statement and balance sheet. Assume a 40% tax rate.

Income Statement	Cash Flow	Balance Sheet

54A) Let's say we have property valued at $25,000. What is the income statement, cash flow, and balance sheet impact on the depreciation expense associated with this property? Assume a 10-year useful life and no residual value. Tax rate is 40%.

Income Statement	Cash Flow	Balance Sheet

54B) Now let's see that the company also accelerates depreciation on the new property for deferred tax purposes. What is the income statement, cash flow, and balance sheet impact? Assume the double declining balance method. Tax rate is 40%.

Income Statement	Cash Flow	Balance Sheet

55A) Let's say we have property valued at $750,000. What is the income statement, cash flow, and balance sheet impact on the depreciation expense associated with this property? Assume a 15-year useful life and no residual value. Tax rate is 40%.

Income Statement	Cash Flow	Balance Sheet

55B) Now let's see the company also accelerates depreciation on the new property for deferred tax purposes. What is the income statement, cash flow, and balance sheet impact? Let's use the MACRS method, assuming 25% in the first year. Tax rate is 40%.

Income Statement	Cash Flow	Balance Sheet

56) We are in the business of buying and selling watches, and we have just started the company. We can purchase these watches for $50 each if we are buying in bulk of 30 and the purchase can be deferred as an account payable. We have not yet made any sales. Please explain the effects on the income statement, cash flow statement, and balance sheet.

Income Statement	Cash Flow	Balance Sheet

57A) In the first period we have sold 10 watches for $200 each in cash. Please explain the effects on the income statement, cash flow statement, and balance sheet. Assume a 40% tax rate.

Income Statement	Cash Flow	Balance Sheet

57B) What does the final balance sheet look like after the results from Question 56 and Question 57A?

Final Balance Sheet

58A) Let's now assume we have sold 10 watches *on credit*. Please explain the effects on the income statement, cash flow statement, and balance sheet. Assume a 40% tax rate.

Income Statement	Cash Flow	Balance Sheet

58B) What does the final balance sheet look like after the results from Questions 56–58A?

Final Balance Sheet

59A) Let's now assume we have sold the remaining 10 watches, 5 in cash and 5 on credit. Please explain the effects on the income statement, cash flow statement and balance sheet. Assume a 40% tax rate.

Income Statement	Cash Flow	Balance Sheet

59B) What does the final balance sheet look like after the results from Questions 56–59A?

Final Balance Sheet

60A) Let's now assume we have collected on all receivables and paid all payables. Please explain the effects on the income statement, cash flow statement, and balance sheet.

Income Statement   **Cash Flow**   **Balance Sheet**

60B) What does the final balance sheet look like after the results from Questions 56–60A?

Final Balance Sheet

61) We are in the business of buying and selling hats. We can purchase the raw material for these hats for $3 each if we are buying in bulk of 45 and the purchase can be deferred as an account payable. We have not yet made any sales. Please explain the effects on the income statement, cash flow statement, and balance sheet.

Income Statement	Cash Flow	Balance Sheet

62A) In the first period we have sold 15 hats for $10 each in cash. Please explain the effects on the income statement, cash flow statement, and balance sheet. Assume a 40% tax rate.

Income Statement	Cash Flow	Balance Sheet

62B) What does the final balance sheet look like after the results from Question 61 and Question 62A?

Final Balance Sheet

63A) Let's now assume we have sold 15 hats *on credit*. Please explain the effects on the income statement, cash flow statement, and balance sheet. Assume a 40% tax rate.

Income Statement   **Cash Flow**   **Balance Sheet**

63B) What does the final balance sheet look like after the results from Questions 61–63A?

Final Balance Sheet

64A) Let's now assume we have sold the remaining 15 hats, 10 in cash and 5 on credit. Please explain the effects on the income statement, cash flow statement, and balance sheet. Assume a 40% tax rate.

Income Statement   **Cash Flow**   **Balance Sheet**

64B) What does the final balance sheet look like after the results from Questions 61–64A?

Final Balance Sheet

65A) Let's now assume we have collected on all receivables and paid all payables. Please explain the effects on the income statement, cash flow statement, and balance sheet.

Income Statement   Cash Flow   Balance Sheet

65B) What does the final balance sheet look like after the results from Questions 61–65A?

Final Balance Sheet

---

66) We are in the business of buying and selling appliances, and we have just started the company. We can purchase items in bulk for $300 each if we are buying in bulk of 60 and the purchase can be deferred as an account payable. We have not yet made any sales. Please explain the effects on the income statement, cash flow statement, and balance sheet.

Income Statement	**Cash Flow**	**Balance Sheet**

67A) In the first period we have sold 20 appliances for $500 each in cash. Please explain the effects on the income statement, cash flow statement, and balance sheet. Assume a 40% tax rate.

Income Statement	Cash Flow	Balance Sheet

67B) What does the final balance sheet look like after the results from Question 66 and Question 67A?

Final Balance Sheet

68A) Let's now assume we have sold 15 *on credit*. Please explain the effects on the income statement, cash flow statement, and balance sheet. Assume a 40% tax rate.

Income Statement	Cash Flow	Balance Sheet

68B) What does the final balance sheet look like after the results from Questions 66–68A?

Final Balance Sheet

69A) Let's now assume we have sold the remaining 25 appliances, 10 in cash and 15 on credit. Please explain the effects on the income statement, cash flow statement, and balance sheet. Assume a 40% tax rate.

Income Statement	Cash Flow	Balance Sheet

69B) What does the final balance sheet look like after the results from Questions 66–69A?

Final Balance Sheet

70A) Let's now assume we have collected on all receivables and paid all payables. Please explain the effects on the income statement, cash flow statement, and balance sheet.

Income Statement	Cash Flow	Balance Sheet

70B) What does the final balance sheet look like after the results from Questions 66–70A?

Final Balance Sheet

71) We have a business that has incurred $1,500 in various operating expenses. What is the impact on the income statement, cash flow statement, and balance sheet. Assume a 40% tax rate.

Income Statement	Cash Flow	Balance Sheet

72) Those expenses must be paid immediately, but we have no cash. So we will raise a $1,200 revolving line of credit to supplement the cash need. What is the impact on the income statement, cash flow statement, and balance sheet of the debt raise? Ignore the effects of interest expense.

Income Statement	Cash Flow	Balance Sheet

73) The revolving line of credit incurs a 10% interest. What is the impact on the income statement, cash flow statement, and balance sheet? Assume a 40% interest rate.

Income Statement	Cash Flow	Balance Sheet

74) We have a company that's incurred $10,000 in unexpected expenses. $10,000 of debt is raised to fund the expense payment at 5% interest. What is the impact on the income statement, cash flow statement, and balance sheet? Assume a 40% interest rate.

Income Statement	Cash Flow	Balance Sheet

ANSWERS

19) If accounts receivable increases by $10, please explain the effects on the income statement, cash flow statement, and balance sheet (assume 40% tax rate).

Income Statement	Cash Flow	Balance Sheet
Revenue +$10	Net Income +$6	Cash −$4
Taxes −$4	Accounts Receivable −$10	Accounts Receivable +$10
Net Income +$6	Change in Cash −$4	Retained Earnings +$6

20) If accounts receivable now decreases by $10, please explain the effects on the income statement, cash flow statement, and balance sheet.

Income Statement	Cash Flow	Balance Sheet
No Change	Accounts Receivable +$10	Cash +$10
	Change in Cash +$10	Accounts Receivable −$10

21) If accrued expenses increase by $30, please explain the effects on the income state-ment, cash flow statement, and balance sheet. Assume accrued expenses are related to SG&A. Assume a 40% tax rate.

Income Statement	Cash Flow	Balance Sheet
SG&A −$30	Net Income −$18	Cash +$12
Taxes +$12	Accrued Expenses +$30	Accrued Expenses +$30
Net Income −$18	Change in Cash +$12	Retained Earnings −$18

22) If accrued expenses now decrease by $30, please explain the effects on the income statement, cash flow statement, and balance sheet.

Income Statement	Cash Flow	Balance Sheet
No Change	Accrued Expenses −$30	Cash −$30
	Change in Cash −$30	Accrued Expenses −$30

23) If depreciation expense increased by $20, please explain the effects on the income statement, cash flow statement, and balance sheet. Assume a 40% tax rate.

Income Statement	Cash Flow	Balance Sheet
Depreciation −$20	Net Income −$12	Cash +$8
Taxes +$8	Depreciation +$20	PP&E −$20
New Income −$12	Change in Cash +$8	Retained Earnings −$12

24) We are in the business of buying and selling widgets, and we have just started the company. We can purchase these widgets for $100 each if we are buying in bulk of 50 and the purchase can be deferred as an account payable. We have not yet made any sales. Please explain the effects on the income statement, cash flow statement, and balance sheet.

Income Statement	Cash Flow	Balance Sheet
No Change	Inventory −$5,000	Inventory +$5,000
	Accounts Payable +$5,000	Accounts Payable +$5,000

25A) In the first period we have sold 15 widgets for $500 each in cash. Please explain the effects on the income statement, cash flow statement, and balance sheet. Assume a 40% tax rate.

Income Statement	Cash Flow	Balance Sheet
Revenue +$7,500	Net Income +$3,600	Cash +$5,100
COGS −$1,500	Inventory +$1,500	Inventory −$1,500
EBIT +$6,000	Cash +$5,100	Retained Earnings +$3,600
Tax −$2,400		
Net Income +$3,600		

25B) What does the final balance sheet look like after the results from Question 24 and Question 25A?

Final Balance Sheet

Cash +$5,100
Inventory $3,500
Accounts Payable +$5,000
Retained Earnings +$3,600

26A) Let's now assume we have sold 15 widgets *on credit*. Please explain the effects on the income statement, cash flow statement, and balance sheet. Assume a 40% tax rate.

Income Statement	Cash Flow	Balance Sheet
Revenue +$7,500	Net Income +$3,600	Cash −$2,400
Cogs −$1,500	Accounts Receivable −$7,500	Accounts Receivable +$7,500
EBIT +$6,000	Inventory +$1,500	Inventory −$1,500
Tax −$2,400	Cash −$2,400	Retained Earnings +$3,600
Net Income +$3,600		

26B) What does the final balance sheet look like after the results from Questions 24–26A?

Final Balance Sheet

Cash +$2,700
Accounts Receivable +$7,500
Inventory +$2,000
Accounts Payable +$5,000
Retained Earnings +$7,200

27A) Let's now assume we have sold the remaining 20 widgets, 10 in cash and 10 on credit. Please explain the effects on the income statement, cash flow statement, and balance sheet. Assume a 40% tax rate.

Income Statement	Cash Flow	Balance Sheet
Revenue +$10,000	Net Income +$4,800	Cash +$1,800
Cogs −$2,000	Accounts Receivable	Accounts Receivable +$5,000
EBIT +$8,000	−$5,000	Inventory −2,000
Tax −$3,200	Inventory +$2,000	Retained Earnings +$4,800
Net Income +$4,800	Cash +$1,800	

27B) What does the final balance sheet look like after the results from Questions 24–27A?

Final Balance Sheet

Cash +$4,500
Accounts Receivable +$12,500
Inventory $0
Accounts Payable +$5,000
Retained Earnings +$12,000

28A) Let's now assume we have collected on all receivables and paid all payables. Please explain the effects on the income statement, cash flow statement, and balance sheet.

Income Statement	Cash Flow	Balance Sheet
No Changes	Accounts Receivable	Cash +$7,500
	+$12,500	Accounts Receivable
	Accounts Payable −$5,000	−$12,500
	Cash +$7,500	Accounts Payable −$5,000

28B) What does the final balance sheet look like after the results from Questions 24–28A?

Final Balance Sheet

Cash +$12,000
Accounts Receivable $0
Inventory $0
Accounts Payable $0
Retained Earnings +$12,000

29A) Let's now assume we have incurred overhead costs of $1,500 that have been paid in cash. Please explain the effects on the income statement, cash flow statement, and balance sheet. Assume a 40% tax rate.

Income Statement	Cash Flow	Balance Sheet
SG&A −$1,500	Net Income −$900	Cash −$900
Tax +600	Cash −$900	Retained Earnings −$900
Net Income −$900		

29B) What does the final balance sheet look like after the results from Questions 24–29A?

Final Balance Sheet

Cash +$11,100
Accounts Receivable $0
Inventory $0
Accounts Payable $0
Retained Earnings +$11,100

30A) Let's assume we have received a rent bill of $5,000, which we have decided to defer as an accrued expense. Please explain the effects on the income statement, cash flow statement, and balance sheet. Assume a 40% tax rate.

Income Statement	Cash Flow	Balance Sheet
SG&A −$5,000	Net Income −$3,000	Cash +$2,000
Tax +2,000	Accrued Expenses +$5,000	Accrued Expenses +$5,000
Net Income −$3,000	Cash +$2,000	Retained Earnings −$3,000

30B) What does the final balance sheet look like after the results from Questions 24–30A?

Final Balance Sheet

Cash +$13,100
Accounts Receivable $0
Inventory $0
Accounts Payable $0
Accrued Expenses +$5,000
Retained Earnings +$8,100

31A) Now let's say we want to purchase property for $15,000. Since we don't have 15,000 in cash on our balance sheet, we will first raise debt to fund the difference. Let's say we raise $3,000, allowing some cushion for interest payments. The debt has an interest rate of 10%. Please explain the effects on the income statement, cash flow statement, and balance sheet of the debt raise. Focus on just the debt raise; we will handle the interest impact later.

Income Statement	Cash Flow	Balance Sheet
No Change	Debt Raise +$3,000 Cash +$3,000	Cash +$3,000 Debt +$3,000

31B) What does the final balance sheet look like after the results from Questions 24–31A?

Final Balance Sheet

Cash +$16,100
Accounts Receivable $0
Inventory $0
Accounts Payable $0
Accrued Expenses +$5,000
Debt +3,000
Retained Earnings +$8,100

32A) Now let's say the debt has an interest rate of 10%. Please explain the effects on the income statement, cash flow statement, and balance sheet of the interest expense on the debt raised. Assume a 40% interest rate.

Income Statement	Cash Flow	Balance Sheet
Interest −$300 Tax +120 Net Income −180	Net Income −$180 Cash −$180	Cash −$180 Retained Earnings −$180

32B) What does the final balance sheet look like after the results from Questions 24–32A?

Final Balance Sheet

Cash +$15,920
Accounts Receivable $0
Inventory $0
Accounts Payable $0
Accrued Expenses +$5,000
Debt +3,000
Retained Earnings +$7,920

33A) Now what is the income statement, cash flow, and balance sheet impact on the property purchase? Ignore impacts on depreciation for the time being.

Income Statement	Cash Flow	Balance Sheet
No Change	Property Purchase −$15,000 Cash −$15,000	Cash −15,000 PP&E +15,000

33B) What does the final balance sheet look like after the results from Questions 24–33A?

Final Balance Sheet

Cash +$920
PP&E +$15,000
Accrued Expenses +$5,000
Debt +3,000
Retained Earnings +$7,920

34A) Now what is the income statement, cash flow, and balance sheet impact on the depreciation expense associated with this new property? Assume a 10-year useful life and no residual value. Tax rate is 40%.

Income Statement	Cash Flow	Balance Sheet
Depreciation −$1,500 Tax +$600 Net Income −$900	Net Income −$900 Depreciation +$1,500 Cash +$600	Cash +$600 PP&E −1,500 Retained Earnings −$900

34B) What does the final balance sheet look like after the results from Questions 24–34A?

Final Balance Sheet

Cash +$1,520
PP&E +$13,500
Accrued Expenses +$5,000
Debt +3,000
Retained Earnings +$7,020

35A) Now let's see that the company also accelerates depreciation on the new property for deferred tax purposes. What is the income statement, cash flow, and balance sheet impact? Assume the double declining balance method. Tax rate is 40%.

   So to apply the double declining balance method, you need to take the reciprocal of the useful life and multiply by 2. So $1/10 \times 2 = 20\%$. The accelerated depreciation in the first period is 20% of the original property value, or $3,000 (20% × $15,000). A deferred tax liability is calculated by taking the accelerated depreciation minus the straight line depreciation and multiplying by the tax rate. So ($3,000 − $1,500) × 40% is $600. The deferred taxes do not impact the income statement.

Income Statement	Cash Flow	Balance Sheet
No Change	Deferred Tax +$600 Cash +$600	Cash +$600 Deferred Tax +$600

35B) What does the final balance sheet look like after the results from Questions 24–35A?

Final Balance Sheet

Cash +$2,120
PP&E +$13,500
Accrued Expenses +$5,000
Debt +3,000
Deferred Tax +600
Retained Earnings +$7,020

36) If accounts receivable increases by $15, please explain the effects on the income statement, cash flow statement, and balance sheet (assume 40% tax rate).

Income Statement	Cash Flow	Balance Sheet
Revenue +$15 Taxes −$6 Net Income +$9	Net Income +$9 Accounts Receivable −$15 Change in Cash −$6	Cash −$6 Accounts Receivable +$15 Retained Earnings +$9

37) If accounts receivable now decreases by $15, please explain the effects on the income statement, cash flow statement, and balance sheet.

Income Statement	Cash Flow	Balance Sheet
No Change	Accounts Receivable +$15 Change in Cash +$15	Cash +$15 Accounts Receivable −$15

38) If accounts receivable increases by $300, please explain the effects on the income statement, cash flow statement, and balance sheet (assume a 40% tax rate).

Income Statement	Cash Flow	Balance Sheet
Revenue +$300	Net Income +$180	Cash −$120
Taxes −$120	Accounts Receivable −$300	Accounts Receivable +$300
Net Income +$180	Change in Cash −$120	Retained Earnings +$180

39) If accounts receivable now decreases by $300, please explain the effects on the income statement, cash flow statement, and balance sheet.

Income Statement	Cash Flow	Balance Sheet
No Change	Accounts Receivable +$300	Cash +$300
	Change in Cash +$300	Accounts Receivable −$300

40) If accounts receivable increases by $1,250, please explain the effects on the income statement, cash flow statement, and balance sheet (assume a 40% tax rate).

Income Statement	Cash Flow	Balance Sheet
Revenue +$1,250	Net Income +$750	Cash −$500
Taxes −$500	Accounts Receivable	Accounts Receivable +$1,250
Net Income +$750	−$1,250	Retained Earnings +$750
	Change in Cash −$500	

41) If accounts receivable now decreases by $1,250, please explain the effects on the income statement, cash flow statement, and balance sheet.

Income Statement	Cash Flow	Balance Sheet
No Change	Accounts Receivable	Cash +$1,250
	+$1,250	Accounts Receivable
	Change in Cash +$1,250	−$1,250

42) If inventory *increases* by $20, please explain the effects on the income statement, cash flow statement, and balance sheet.

Income Statement	Cash Flow	Balance Sheet
No change	Inventory −$20	Cash −$20
	Change in Cash −$20	Inventory +$20

43) If inventory *decreases* by $20, please explain the effects on the income statement, cash flow statement, and balance sheet (assume a 40% tax rate).

Income Statement	Cash Flow	Balance Sheet
COGS −$20	Net Income −$12	Cash +$8
Taxes +$8	Inventory +$20	Inventory −$20
Net Income −$12	Change in Cash +$8	Retained Earnings −$12

44) If inventory *increases* by $500, please explain the effects on the income statement, cash flow statement, and balance sheet.

Income Statement	Cash Flow	Balance Sheet
No change	Inventory −$500	Cash −$500
	Change in Cash −$500	Inventory +$500

45) If inventory *decreases* by $500, please explain the effects on the income statement, cash flow statement, and balance sheet (assume a 40% tax rate).

Income Statement	Cash Flow	Balance Sheet
COGS −$500	Net Income −$300	Cash +$200
Taxes +$200	Inventory +$500	Inventory −$500
Net Income −$300	Change in Cash +$200	Retained Earnings −$300

46) If inventory *increases* by $2,250, please explain the effects on the income statement, cash flow statement, and balance sheet (assume a 40% tax rate).

Income Statement	Cash Flow	Balance Sheet
No change	Inventory −$2,250	Cash −$2,250
	Change in Cash −$2,250	Inventory +$2,250

47) If inventory *decreases* by $1,750, please explain the effects on the income statement, cash flow statement, and balance sheet (assume a 40% tax rate).

Income Statement	Cash Flow	Balance Sheet
COGS −$1,750	Net Income −$1,050	Cash +$700
Taxes +$700	Inventory +$1,750	Inventory +$1,750
Net Income −$1,050	Change in Cash +$700	Retained Earnings −$1,050

48) If accrued expenses increase by $50, please explain the effects on the income statement, cash flow statement, and balance sheet. Assume accrued expenses are related to operating expenses. Assume a 40% tax rate.

Income Statement	Cash Flow	Balance Sheet
OpEx −$50	Net Income −$30	Cash +$20
Taxes +$20	Accrued Expenses +$50	Accrued Expenses +$50
Net Income −$30	Change in Cash +$20	Retained Earnings −$30

49) If accrued expenses now decrease by $50, please explain the effects on the income statement, cash flow statement, and balance sheet.

Income Statement	Cash Flow	Balance Sheet
No Change	Accrued Expenses −$50	Cash −$50
	Change in Cash −$50	Accrued Expenses −$50

50) If accrued expenses increase by $250, please explain the effects on the income statement, cash flow statement, and balance sheet. Assume accrued expenses are related to SG&A. Assume a 40% tax rate.

Income Statement	Cash Flow	Balance Sheet
OpEx −$250	Net Income −$150	Cash +$100
Taxes +$100	Accrued Expenses +$250	Accrued Expenses +$250
Net Income −$150	Change in Cash +$100	Retained Earnings −$150

51) If accrued expenses now decrease by $250, please explain the effects on the income statement, cash flow statement, and balance sheet.

Income Statement	Cash Flow	Balance Sheet
No Change	Accrued Expenses −$250	Cash −$250
	Change in Cash −$250	Accrued Expenses −$250

52) If depreciation expense increases by $75, please explain the effects on the income statement, cash flow statement, and balance sheet. Assume a 40% tax rate.

Income Statement	Cash Flow	Balance Sheet
Depreciation −$75	Net Income −$45	Cash +$30
Taxes +$30	Depreciation +$75	PP&E −$75
New Income −$45	Change in Cash +$30	Retained Earnings −$45

53) If depreciation expense increases by $250, please explain the effects on the income statement, cash flow statement and balance sheet. Assume a 40% tax rate.

Income Statement	Cash Flow	Balance Sheet
Depreciation −$250	Net Income −$150	Cash +$100
Taxes +$100	Depreciation +$250	PP&E −$250
New Income −$150	Change in Cash +$100	Retained Earnings −$150

54A) Let's say we have property valued at $25,000. What is the income statement, cash flow, and balance sheet impact on the depreciation expense associated with this property? Assume a 10-year useful life and no residual value. Tax rate is 40%.

Income Statement	Cash Flow	Balance Sheet
Depreciation −$2,500	Net Income −$1,500	Cash +$1,000
Tax +$1,000	Depreciation +$2,500	PP&E −$2,500
Net Income −$1,500	Cash +$1,000	Retained Earnings −$1,500

54B) Now let's see that the company also accelerates depreciation on the new property for deferred tax purposes. What is the income statement, cash flow, and balance sheet impact? Assume the double declining balance method. Tax rate is 40%.

So to apply the double declining balance method, you need to take the reciprocal of the useful life and multiply by 2. So $1/10 \times 2 = 20\%$. The accelerated depreciation in the first period is 20% of the original property value, or $5,000 (20% × $25,000). A deferred tax liability is calculated by taking the accelerated depreciation minus the straight line depreciation and multiplying by the tax rate. So ($5,000 − $2,500) × 40% is $1,000. The deferred taxes do not impact the income statement.

Income Statement	Cash Flow	Balance Sheet
No Change	Deferred Tax +$1,000	Cash +$1,000
	Cash +$1,000	Deferred Tax +$1,000

55A) Let's say we have property valued at $750,000. What is the income statement, cash flow, and balance sheet impact on the depreciation expense associated with this property? Assume a 15-year useful life and no residual value. Tax rate is 40%.

Income Statement	Cash Flow	Balance Sheet
Depreciation −$50,000	Net Income −$30,000	Cash +$20,000
Tax +$20,000	Depreciation +$50,000	PP&E −$50,000
Net Income −$30,000	Cash +$20,000	Retained Earnings −$30,000

55B) Now let's see the company also accelerates depreciation on the new property for deferred tax purposes. What is the income statement, cash flow, and balance sheet impact? Let's use the MACRS method, assuming 25% in the first year. Tax rate is 40%.

    The accelerated depreciation in the first period is 25% of the net property value, or $187,500 (25% × $750,000). A deferred tax liability is calculated by taking the accelerated depreciation minus the straight line depreciation and multiplying by the tax rate. So ($187,500 − $50,000) × 40% is $55,000. The deferred taxes do not impact the income statement.

Income Statement	Cash Flow	Balance Sheet
No Change	Deferred Tax +$55,000 Cash +$55,000	Cash +$55,000 Deferred Tax +$55,000

56) We are in the business of buying and selling watches, and we have just started the company. We can purchase these watches for $50 each if we are buying in bulk of 30 and the purchase can be deferred as an account payable. We have not yet made any sales. Please explain the effects on the income statement, cash flow statement, and balance sheet.

Income Statement	Cash Flow	Balance Sheet
No Change	Inventory −$1,500 Accounts Payable +$1,500	Inventory +$1,500 Accounts Payable +$1,500

57A) In the first period we have sold 10 watches for $200 each in cash. Please explain the effects on the income statement, cash flow statement, and balance sheet. Assume a 40% tax rate.

Income Statement	Cash Flow	Balance Sheet
Revenue +$2,000 Cogs −$500 EBIT +$1,500 Tax −$600 Net Income +$900	Net Income +900 Inventory +$500 Cash +$1,400	Cash +$1,400 Inventory −$500 Retained Earnings +$900

57B) What does the final balance sheet look like after the results from Question 56 and Question 57A?

Final Balance Sheet

Cash +$1,400
Inventory +$1,000
Accounts Payable +$1,500
Retained Earnings +$900

58A) Let's now assume we have sold 10 watches *on credit*. Please explain the effects on the income statement, cash flow statement, and balance sheet. Assume a 40% tax rate.

Income Statement	Cash Flow	Balance Sheet
Revenue +$2,000	Net Income +900	Cash −$600
Cogs −$500	Inventory +$500	Inventory −$500
EBIT +$1,500	Accounts Receivable	Accounts Receivable +$2,000
Tax −$600	−$2,000	Retained Earnings +$900
Net Income +$900	Cash −$600	

58B) What does the final balance sheet look like after the results from Questions 56–58A?

Final Balance Sheet

Cash +$800
Inventory +$500
Accounts Receivable +$2,000
Accounts Payable +$1,500
Retained Earnings +$1,800

59A) Let's now assume we have sold the remaining 10 watches, 5 in cash and 5 on credit. Please explain the effects on the income statement, cash flow statement and balance sheet. Assume a 40% tax rate.

Income Statement	Cash Flow	Balance Sheet
Revenue +$2,000	Net Income +$900	Cash +$400
Cogs −$500	Inventory +$500	Accounts Receivable +$1,000
EBIT +$1,500	Accounts Receivable	Inventory −$500
Tax −$600	−$1,000	Retained Earnings +$900
Net Income +$900	Cash +$400	

59B) What does the final balance sheet look like after the results from Questions 56–59A?

Final Balance Sheet

Cash +$1,200
Inventory $0
Accounts Receivable +$3,000
Accounts Payable +$1,500
Retained Earnings +$2,700

60A) Let's now assume we have collected on all receivables and paid all payables. Please explain the effects on the income statement, cash flow statement, and balance sheet.

Income Statement	Cash Flow	Balance Sheet
No Changes	Accounts Receivable +$3,000	Cash +$1,500
	Accounts Payable −$1,500	Accounts Receivable −$3,000
	Cash +$1,500	Accounts Payable −$1,500

60B) What does the final balance sheet look like after the results from Questions 56–60A?

Final Balance Sheet

Cash +$2,700
Inventory $0
Accounts Receivable +$0
Accounts Payable +$0
Retained Earnings +$2,700

---

61) We are in the business of buying and selling hats. We can purchase the raw material for these hats for $3 each if we are buying in bulk of 45 and the purchase can be deferred as an account payable. We have not yet made any sales. Please explain the effects on the income statement, cash flow statement, and balance sheet.

Income Statement	Cash Flow	Balance Sheet
No Change	Inventory −$135	Inventory +$135
	Accounts Payable +$135	Accounts Payable +$135

62A) In the first period we have sold 15 hats for $10 each in cash. Please explain the effects on the income statement, cash flow statement, and balance sheet. Assume a 40% tax rate.

Income Statement	Cash Flow	Balance Sheet
Revenue +$150	Net Income +$63	Cash +$108
Cogs −$45	Inventory +$45	Inventory −$45
EBIT +$105	Cash +$108	Retained Earnings +$63
Tax −$42		
Net Income +$63		

62B) What does the final balance sheet look like after the results from Question 61 and Question 62A?

Final Balance Sheet

Cash +$108
Inventory +$90
Accounts Payable +$135
Retained Earnings +$63

63A) Let's now assume we have sold 15 hats *on credit*. Please explain the effects on the income statement, cash flow statement, and balance sheet. Assume a 40% tax rate.

Income Statement	Cash Flow	Balance Sheet
Revenue +$150	Net Income +$63	Cash −$42
Cogs −$45	Inventory +$45	Inventory −$45
EBIT +$105	Accounts Receivable −$150	Accounts Receivable +$150
Tax −$42	Cash −$42	Retained Earnings +$63
Net Income +$63		

63B) What does the final balance sheet look like after the results from Questions 61–63A?

Final Balance Sheet

Cash +$66
Inventory +$45
Accounts Receivable +$150
Accounts Payable +$135
Retained Earnings +$126

64A) Let's now assume we have sold the remaining 15 hats, 10 in cash and 5 on credit. Please explain the effects on the income statement, cash flow statement, and balance sheet. Assume a 40% tax rate.

Income Statement	Cash Flow	Balance Sheet
Revenue +$150	Net Income +$63	Cash +$58
Cogs −$45	Inventory +$45	Inventory −$45
EBIT +$105	Accounts Receivable −$50	Accounts Receivable +$50
Tax −$42	Cash +$58	Retained Earnings +$63
Net Income +$63		

64B) What does the final balance sheet look like after the results from Questions 61–64A?

Final Balance Sheet

Cash +$124
Inventory +$0
Accounts Receivable +$200
Accounts Payable +$135
Retained Earnings +$189

65A) Let's now assume we have collected on all receivables and paid all payables. Please explain the effects on the income statement, cash flow statement, and balance sheet.

Income Statement	Cash Flow	Balance Sheet
No Changes	Accounts Receivable +$200	Cash +$65
	Accounts Payable −$135	Accounts Receivable −$200
	Cash +$65	Accounts Payable −$135

65B) What does the final balance sheet look like after the results from Questions 61–65A?

Final Balance Sheet

Cash +$189
Inventory +$0
Accounts Receivable +$0
Accounts Payable +$0
Retained Earnings +$189

66) We are in the business of buying and selling appliances, and we have just started the company. We can purchase items in bulk for $300 each if we are buying in bulk of 60 and the purchase can be deferred as an account payable. We have not yet made any sales. Please explain the effects on the income statement, cash flow statement, and balance sheet.

Income Statement	Cash Flow	Balance Sheet
No Change	Inventory −$18,000 Accounts Payable +$18,000	Inventory +$18,000 Accounts Payable +$18,000

67A) In the first period we have sold 20 appliances for $500 each in cash. Please explain the effects on the income statement, cash flow statement, and balance sheet. Assume a 40% tax rate.

Income Statement	Cash Flow	Balance Sheet
Revenue +$10,000 Cogs −$6,000 EBIT +$4,000 Tax −$1,600 Net Income +$2,400	Net Income +2,400 Inventory +$6,000 Cash +$8,400	Cash +$8,400 Inventory −$6,000 Retained Earnings +$2,400

67B) What does the final balance sheet look like after the results from Question 66 and Question 67A?

Final Balance Sheet

Cash +$8,400
Inventory +$12,000
Accounts Payable +$18,000
Retained Earnings +$2,400

68A) Let's now assume we have sold 15 *on credit*. Please explain the effects on the income statement, cash flow statement, and balance sheet. Assume a 40% tax rate.

Income Statement	Cash Flow	Balance Sheet
Revenue +$7,500 Cogs −$4,500 EBIT +$3,000 Tax −$1,200 Net Income +$1,800	Net Income +$1,800 Inventory +$4,500 Accounts Receivable −$7,500 Cash −$1,200	Cash −$1,200 Inventory −$4,500 Accounts Receivable +$7,500 Retained Earnings +$1,800

68B) What does the final balance sheet look like after the results from Questions 66–68A?

Final Balance Sheet

Cash +$7,200
Inventory +$7,500
Accounts Receivable +$7,500
Accounts Payable +$18,000
Retained Earnings +$4,200

69A) Let's now assume we have sold the remaining 25 appliances, 10 in cash and 15 on credit. Please explain the effects on the income statement, cash flow statement, and balance sheet. Assume a 40% tax rate.

Income Statement	Cash Flow	Balance Sheet
Revenue +$12,500	Net Income +$3,000	Cash +$3,000
Cogs −$7,500	Inventory +$7,500	Accounts Receivable +$7,500
EBIT +$5,000	Accounts Receivable	Inventory −$7,500
Tax −$2,000	−$7,500	Retained Earnings +$3,000
Net Income +$3,000	Cash +$3,000	

69B) What does the final balance sheet look like after the results from Questions 66–69A?

Final Balance Sheet

Cash +$10,200
Inventory +$0
Accounts Receivable +$15,000
Accounts Payable +$18,000
Retained Earnings +$7,200

70A) Let's now assume we have collected on all receivables and paid all payables. Please explain the effects on the income statement, cash flow statement, and balance sheet.

Income Statement	Cash Flow	Balance Sheet
No Changes	Accounts Receivable	Cash −$3,000
	+$15,000	Accounts Receivable
	Accounts Payable	−$15,000
	−$18,000	Accounts Payable
	Cash −$3,000	−$18,000

70B) What does the final balance sheet look like after the results from Questions 66–70A?

Final Balance Sheet

Cash +$7,200
Inventory +$0
Accounts Receivable +$0
Accounts Payable +$0
Retained Earnings +$7,200

---

71) We have a business that has incurred $1,500 in various operating expenses. What is the impact on the income statement, cash flow statement, and balance sheet? Assume a 40% tax rate.

Income Statement	Cash Flow	Balance Sheet
SG&A −$1,500	Net Income −$900	Cash −$900
Tax +600	Cash −$900	Retained Earnings −$900
Net Income −$900		

72) Those expenses must be paid immediately, but we have no cash. So we will raise a revolving line of credit of $1,200 to supplement the cash need. What is the impact on the income statement, cash flow statement, and balance sheet of the debt raise? Ignore the effects of interest expense.

Income Statement	Cash Flow	Balance Sheet
No Change	Revolver +$1,200	Cash +$1,200
	Cash +$1,200	Revolver +$1,200

73) The revolving line of credit incurs a 10% interest. What is the impact on the income statement, cash flow statement, and balance sheet? Assume a 40% interest rate.

Income Statement	Cash Flow	Balance Sheet
Interest −$120	Net Income −$72	Cash −$72
Tax +$48	Cash −$72	Retained Earnings −$72
Net Income −$72		

74) We have a company that's incurred $10,000 in unexpected expenses. $10,000 of debt is raised to fund the expense payment at 5% interest. What is the impact on the income statement, cash flow statement, and balance sheet? Assume a 40% interest rate.

Answer:
On paper I would recommend to do this in steps to ensure no mistakes are made. First the movement of the expense:

Income Statement	Cash Flow	Balance Sheet
Expenses −$10,000	Net Income −$6,000	Cash −$6,000
Tax +$4,000	Cash −$6,000	Retained Earnings −$6,000
Net Income −$6,000		

Then the debt:

Income Statement	Cash Flow	Balance Sheet
No Change	Debt +$10,000	Cash +$10,000
	Cash +$10,000	Debt +$10,000

Then the interest:

Income Statement	Cash Flow	Balance Sheet
Interest −$500	Net Income −$300	Cash −$300
Tax +$200	Cash −$300	Retained Earnings −$300
Net Income −$300		

And finally add all three together:

Income Statement	Cash Flow	Balance Sheet
Expenses −$10,000	Net Income −$6,300	Cash +$3,700
Interest −$500	Debt +$10,000	Debt +$10,000
Tax +$4,200	Cash +$3,700	Retained Earnings −$6,300
Net Income −$6,300		

Valuation

Valuation is a crucial topic for investment banking interview preparation. If a technical question is asked in a first-round interview, it is very likely that the technical question will center on valuation. You may simply be asked to explain various valuation concepts. Or you may be given an actual case study to perform on paper or in Excel. So it's important not only to understand valuation concepts but to be able to interpret concepts for various technical analyses. We will cover all variations after the following overview. If you need additional detail or valuation understanding, I recommend reading Section Two of the book *Financial Modeling and Valuation*.

CHAPTER 4

Valuation Overview

The most important question before even getting into valuation mechanics is "What is value?" To help answer this question, we note there are two major categories of value:

1. *Book value*. Book value is the value of an asset or entire business entity as determined by its books, or the financials.
2. *Market value*. Market value is the value of an asset or entire business entity as determined by the market.

BOOK VALUE

The book value can be determined by the balance sheet. The total book value of a company's property, for example, can be found under the net property, plant, and equipment (PP&E) in the assets section of the balance sheet. The book value of the shareholders' interest in the company (not including the noncontrolling interest holders) can be found under shareholders' equity.

MARKET VALUE

The market value of a company can be defined by its market capitalization, or shares outstanding times share price.

Both the book value and market value represent the equity value of a business. The equity value of a business is the value of the business attributable to just equity holders—that is, the value of the business excluding debt lenders, noncontrolling interest holders, and other obligations.

Shareholders' equity, for example, is the value of the company's assets less the value of the company's liabilities. So this shareholders' equity value (making sure noncontrolling interest is not included in shareholders' equity) is the value of the business excluding lenders and other obligations—an equity value. The market value, or market capitalization, is based on the stock price, which is inherently an equity value since equity investors value a company's stock after payments to debt lenders and other obligations.

ENTERPRISE VALUE

Enterprise value (also known as firm value) is defined as the value of the entire business, including debt lenders and other obligations. We will see why the importance of enterprise value is that it approaches an approximate value of the operating assets of an entity. To be more specific, "debt lenders and other obligations" can include short-term debts, long-term debts, current portion of long-term debts, capital lease obligations, preferred securities, noncontrolling interests, and other nonoperating liabilities (e.g., unallocated pension funds). So, for complete reference, enterprise value can be calculated as:

Enterprise value
= Equity value
+ Short-term debts
+ Long-term debts
+ Current portion of long-term debts
+ Capital lease obligations
+ Preferred securities
+ Noncontrolling interests
+ Other nonoperating liabilities (e.g., unallocated pension funds)
– Cash and cash equivalents

We will explain why subtracting "cash and cash equivalents" is significant. So, to arrive at enterprise value on a book value basis, we take the shareholders' equity (book value) and add back any potential debts and obligations less cash and cash equivalents. Similarly, if we add to market capitalization (market value) any potential debts and obligations less cash and cash equivalents, we approach the enterprise value of a company on a market value basis.

Here is a quick recap:

Valuation Category	Book Value	Market Value
Equity Value	Shareholders' Equity	Market Capitalization
Enterprise Value	Shareholders' Equity plus potential debts and obligations less cash and cash equivalents	Market Capitalization plus potential debts and obligations less cash and cash equivalents

Let's take the example of a company that has shareholders' equity of $10 million according to its balance sheet. Let's also say it has $5 million in total liabilities. We will assume no noncontrolling interest holders in these examples to better illustrate the main idea. As per the balance sheet formula (where Assets = Liabilities + Shareholders' Equity), the total value of the company's assets is $15 million. So $10 million is the book equity value of the company.

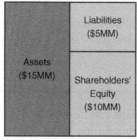

Book Value

Let's now say the company trades in the market at a premium to its book equity value; the market capitalization of the company is $12 million. The market capitalization of a company is an important value, because it is current; it is the value of a business as determined by the market (Share Price × Shares Outstanding). When we take the market capitalization and add the total liabilities of $5 million, we get a value that represents the value of the company's total assets as determined by the market.

Market Value

However, in valuation we typically take market capitalization or book value and add back not the total liabilities, but just debts and obligations as noted earlier to get to enterprise value. The balance sheet formula can help us explain why:

$$\text{Shareholder's Equity} + \text{Liabilities} = \text{Assets}$$

Using this equation, let's list out the actual balance sheet items:

Shareholders' Equity [or Market Capitalization] + Accounts Payable
+ Accrued Expenses + Short-Term Debt + Long-Term Debt = Cash
+ Accounts Receivable + Inventory + Property, Plant, and Equipment

To better illustrate the theory, in this example we assume the company has no non-controlling interests, no preferred securities, and no other nonoperating liabilities such as unallocated pension funds; it has just short-term debt, long-term debt, and cash.

We will abbreviate some line items so the formula is easier to read:

$$\text{SE [or Mkt. Cap.]} + \text{AP} + \text{AE} + \text{STD} + \text{LTD} = \text{Cash} + \text{AR} + \text{Inv.} + \text{PP\&E}$$

Now we need to move everything that's not related to debt—the accounts payable (AP) and accrued expenses (AE)—to the other side of the equation. We can simply subtract AP and AE from both sides of the equation to get:

$$\text{SE [or Mkt. Cap.]} + \text{STD} + \text{LTD} = \text{Cash} + \text{AR} + \text{Inv.} + \text{PP\&E} - (\text{AP} + \text{AE})$$

And we can regroup the terms on the right to get:

$$\text{SE [or Mkt. Cap.]} + \text{STD} + \text{LTD} = \text{Cash} + \text{PP\&E} + \text{AR} + \text{Inv.} - \text{AP} - \text{AE}$$

Notice that AR + Inv. − AP − AE, or current assets less current liabilities, is working capital, so:

$$\text{SE [or Mkt. Cap.]} + \text{STD} + \text{LTD} = \text{Cash} + \text{PP\&E} + \text{WC}$$

Now remember that enterprise value is shareholders' equity (or market capitalization) plus debt *less cash,* so we need to subtract cash from both sides of the equation:

$$\text{SE [or Mkt. Cap.]} + \text{STD} + \text{LTD} - \text{Cash} = \text{PP\&E} + \text{WC}$$

Short-term debt plus long-term debt less cash and cash equivalents is also known as net debt. So, this gives us:

$$\text{SE [or Mkt. Cap.]} + \text{Net Debt} = \text{PP\&E} + \text{WC}$$

This is a very important formula. So, when adding net debt to shareholders' equity or market capitalization, we are backing into the value of the company's PP&E and working capital in the previous example, or more generally the core operating assets of the business. So, enterprise value is a way of determining the implied value of a company's core operating assets. Further, enterprise value based on market capitalization, or

$$\text{Enterprise Value} = \text{Market Capitalization} + \text{Net Debt}$$

is a way to approach the value of the operating assets as determined by the market.

Book Value	Market Value

Note that we had simplified the example for illustration. If the company had noncontrolling interests, preferred securities, or other nonoperating liabilities such as unallocated pension funds in addition to debts, the formula would read:

Enterprise Value = Market Capitalization + Net Debt + Noncontrolling Interests
+ Preferred Securities + Capital Lease Obligations + Other Nonoperating Liabilities

Quite often people wonder why cash needs to be removed from net debt in this equation. This is also a very common investment banking interview question. And, as illustrated here, cash is not considered an operating asset; it is not an asset that will be generating future income for the business (arguably). And so, true value of a company to an investor is the value of just those assets that will continue to produce profit and growth in the future. This is one of the reasons why, in a discounted cash flow (DCF) analysis, we are concerned only about the cash being produced from the operating assets of the business. It is also crucial to understand this core valuation concept, because the definition of an operating asset, or the interpretation of which portions of the company will provide future value, can differ from company to market to industry. Rather than depending on simple formulas, it is important to understand the reason behind them in this rapidly changing environment so you can be equipped with the proper tools to create your own formulas. For example, do Internet businesses rely on PP&E as the core operating assets? If not, would the current enterprise value formula have meaning? How about in emerging markets?

MULTIPLES

Multiples are metrics that compare the value of a business relative to its operations. A company could have a market capitalization value of $100 million, but what does that mean in relation to its operating performance? If that company is producing $10 million in net income, then its value is 10 times the net income it produces; "10 × net income" is a market value multiple. These multiples are used to compare the performance of one company to another. So let's say I wanted to compare this business to another business that also has $100 million in market cap. How would I know which business is the better investment? The market capitalization value itself is arbitrary in this case unless it is compared to the actual performance of the business. So if the other company is producing $5 million in net income, its multiple is 20×; its market capitalization is 20 times the net income it produces. As an investor, I would prefer to invest in the lower multiple, as it is the cheaper investment; it is more net income for a lower market price. So, multiples help us compare relative values to a business's operations.

Other multiples exist, depending on what underlying operating metric one would like to use as the basis of comparison: Earnings before interest and taxes (EBIT); earnings before interest, taxes, depreciation, and amortization (EBITDA); and revenue can be used instead of net income. But how do we determine which are better metrics to compare? Let's take an example of two companies with similar operations. (See Table 4.1.)

Let's say we want to consider investing in either Company A or Company B. Company A is a small distribution business, a package delivery business that has generated $10,000 in revenue in a given period. This is a startup company run and operated by one person. It has a cost structure that has netted $5,000 in EBITDA. Company B is also a small delivery business operating in a different region. Company B is producing the same revenue and has the same operating cost structure, so it is also producing $5,000 in EBITDA. The current owner of Company A operates his business out of his home. He parks the delivery truck in his garage, so he has minimal depreciation costs and no interest expense. The owner of Company B, however, operates

TABLE 4.1 Business Comparison

Metric	Company A	Company B
Revenue	$10,000.0	$10,000.0
Cost of Goods Sold (COGS)	3,500.0	3,500.0
Operating Expenses	1,500.0	1,500.0
EBITDA	5,000.0	5,000.0
Depreciation	500.0	3,000.0
EBIT	4,500.0	2,000.0
Interest	0.0	2,000.0
EBT	4,500.0	0.0
Taxes (@ 35%)	1,575.0	0.0
Net Income	2,925.0	0.0

his business differently. He has built a warehouse for storage and to park the truck. This has increased the depreciation expense and has created additional interest expense, bringing net income to $0. If we were to compare the two businesses based on net income, Company A is clearly performing better than Company B. But, what if we are only concerned about the core operations? What if we are only concerned about the volume of packages being delivered, the number of customers, and the direct costs associated to the deliveries? What if we were looking to acquire Company A or B, for example? In that case, let's say we don't care about Company B's debt and its warehouse, as we would sell the warehouse and pay down the debt. Here, EBITDA would be a better underlying comparable measure. From an operations perspective, looking at EBITDA, both companies are performing well, and we could have been misled in that case by looking only at net income.

So, although market capitalization/net income is a common multiple, there are other multiples using metrics such as EBIT or EBITDA. However, since EBIT and EBITDA are values before interest is taken into account, we cannot compare them to market capitalization. Remember that market capitalization, based on the share price, is the value of a business after lenders are paid; EBITDA (before interest) is the value before lenders have been paid. So, adding net debt (plus potentially other items as discussed previously in the enterprise value section) back to market capitalization gives us a numerator (enterprise value) that we can use with EBIT or EBITDA as a multiple:

$$\text{Enterprise Value/EBIT}$$

or

$$\text{Enterprise Value/EBITDA}$$

So, in short, if a financial metric you want to use as the comparable metric is after debt or interest, it must be related to market capitalization—this is a market value multiple. If the financial metric is before debt or interest, it is related to enterprise value—an enterprise value multiple.

Market Value Multiples	Enterprise Value Multiples
Market Capitalization/Net Income	Enterprise Value/Sales
Price per Share/EPS	Enterprise Value/EBITDA
Market Capitalization/Book Value	Enterprise Value/EBIT

THREE CORE METHODS OF VALUATION

The value definitions and multiples from earlier in the chapter are applied in several ways to best approach how much an entity could be worth. There are three major methods utilized to approach this value:

1. Comparable company analysis
2. Precedent transactions analysis
3. Discounted cash flow analysis

Each of these three methods is based on wide-ranging variables and could be considered quite subjective. Also, the methods approach value from very different perspectives. So we can have relatively strong support of value from a financial perspective if all three methods fall within similar valuation ranges.

Note that a leveraged buyout can also be considered a fourth method of valuation. The required exit in order to achieve a desired return on investment is the value of the business to the investor. This is a valuation method sometimes used by funds.

Comparable Company Analysis

The comparable company analysis compares one company with companies that are similar in size, product, and geography. The comparable company analysis utilizes multiples as a measure of comparison. If the peers' multiples are consistently higher than the multiples of the company we are valuing, it could mean that our company is undervalued. Conversely, if the peers' multiples are consistently lower than the multiples of the company we are valuing, it could mean that our company is overvalued. The comparable company analysis has one major advantage over the other valuation methods:

- *It is the most current of all three analyses.* It gives a market perspective. The comparable company analysis is based on the most recent stock prices and financials of the company.

However, the comparable company analysis has the following drawbacks:

- *It may be difficult to find companies to compare.* If the company has a unique business model, is in a niche industry, or is not the size of a public company, it may be difficult to find the right peer group.
- *The markets as a whole may be undervalued or overvalued.* We could be in a market environment where the entire industry is overvalued or undervalued. If so, our analysis will be flawed.

Precedent Transactions Analysis

The precedent transactions analysis assesses relative value by looking at multiples of historical transactions. The perspective is that the value of the company we are valuing is relative to the price others have paid for similar companies. So, if we look for other companies similar to ours that have been acquired, we can compare their purchase multiples to assess the approximate value of our business.

Purchase Multiples Purchase multiples are similar to market multiples (described previously), except the numerator in a purchase multiple is based on the price paid for an entity as opposed to the current market value.

Enterprise value/net income, for example, is based on (market capitalization + net debt)/net income in a market multiple. But in a purchase multiple, enterprise value/net income is based on (purchase price + net debt)/net income. Net debt is plus potentially noncontrolling interests, preferred securities, unallocated pension funds (and arguably other nonoperating liabilities), as discussed previously in the enterprise value section.

A precedent transactions analysis has this major advantage over the other valuation methods:

■ *The purchase price includes a premium.* This could be advantageous if we were look-ing to acquire a company. It would help us determine how much of a premium we would need to consider in order to convince the owner or shareholders to hand over the company to us.

And there are several major drawbacks to the analysis:

■ *Historical analysis.* Precedent transactions by definition are historical transactions. The analysis may be irrelevant if we are in a completely different economic environment.
■ *Difficult-to-find relevant transactions.* Especially in an environment where there are not many acquisitions, it may not be possible to find acquisitions similar to the one we are analyzing.
■ *Difficult-to-get data.* Even if we do find relevant transactions, it is not always easy to find the data to create the multiples (Table 4.2).

Discounted Cash Flow Analysis

The discounted cash flow (DCF) analysis is known as the most technical of the three major methods, as it is based on the company's cash flows. The discounted cash flow method takes the company's projected unlevered free cash flow (UFCF) and discounts it back to present value. We typically project the company's cash flows over a fixed time horizon (five to seven years, for example). We then create a terminal value, which is the value of the business from the last projected year into perpetuity. The enterprise value of

TABLE 4.2 Multiples

	Market Value	Enterprise Value (EV)
Market Multiples	Market Cap/Net Income Price per Share/EPS (P/E)	EV/EBIT EV/EBITDA EV/Sales (where EV is Market Cap + Net Debt*)
Purchase Multiples	Purchase Price/Net Income	EV/EBIT EV/EBITDA EV/Sales (where EV is Purchase Price + Net Debt*)

Note: "Potential debts and obligations" can include short-term debts, long-term debts, current portion of long-term debts, capital lease obligations, preferred securities, noncontrolling interests, and other nonoperating liabilities (e.g., unallocated pension funds).
*Plus potentially noncontrolling interests, preferred securities, and unallocated pension funds (and arguably other nonoperating liabilities), as discussed in the enterprise value section.

the business is the sum of the present value of all the projected cash flows and the present value of the terminal value.

$$DCF\ Enterprise\ Value = Present\ Value\ (PV)\ of\ UFCF\ Year\ 1 + \cdots$$
$$+ PV\ of\ UFCF\ Year\ n + PV\ of\ Terminal\ Value$$

The discounted cash flow analysis has this major advantage over the other valuation methods:

- *It is the most technical.* It is based on the company's cash flows from the model projections, as opposed to the comparable company analysis, which is mainly driven by market data.

The analysis also has several disadvantages:

- *Terminal value.* Although the first projected years are based on modeled cash flows, the terminal value accounts for a very significant portion of the overall valuation. That terminal value is based on a multiple or a perpetuity.
- *Model projections.* The model projections could be inaccurate; they could be overstated or understated, depending on what is driving the projections.
- *Discount rate.* The discount rate may be difficult to estimate.

Again, while all three major valuation methodologies have significant drawbacks, they do have strengths. It is important to play the strengths of each off of the others to come up with an approximate value of the entire business. If you are interested in seeing how that is technically done, I recommend reading my book, *Financial Modeling and Valuation: A Practical Guide to Investment Banking and Private Equity* (John Wiley & Sons, 2013), which steps through a complete valuation analysis of Walmart.

CHAPTER 5

Valuation Questions

1) What is the difference between book value and market value of a public company?

Book value is the shareholders' equity as listed on a company's balance sheet; market value is the market capitalization (# of shares × $/share) of a business.

2) How is the market value of a business calculated?

Market value is calculated by multiplying the number of shares outstanding by the current share price.

3) How is the enterprise value of a business calculated?

Enterprise value is calculated by adding net debt to a company's market value. Net debt is the company's total debts (plus capital leases, certain convertible securities, and non-controlling interests if any) less cash.

4) Why is it important to remove cash from net debt to arrive at an enterprise value of a business?

Removing cash leaves us with a value that represents the core operating assets of a business.

5) What is the difference between a market multiple and a purchase multiple?

A market multiple is a multiple based on the current valuation of a company; a purchase multiple is based on the price paid for a company.

6) Why is Market Value/EBITDA not a good comparable multiple?

Market value is the value of a business after lenders have been paid; EBITDA (before interest) is a metric before lenders have been paid.

7) What are the three major methods of valuation?

   a. Comparable company analysis
   b. Precedent transactions analysis
   c. Discounted cash flow analysis

8) What is the purpose of the discounted cash flow analysis?

The discounted cash flow analysis values a company based on its projected unlevered free cash flows and an estimated terminal value.

9) Why do we typically discount cash flows as opposed to net income?

Investors prefer cash flow as it is seen as a "truer" measure of output. Net income may show profitability, but net income profitability does not necessarily mean cash generation. An investor would prefer to know cash output to best predict cash return. This is why we more commonly refer to a discounted cash flow analysis as opposed to a discounted net income analysis.

10) What is one major advantage of the discounted cash flow analysis?

It is the most technical analysis of the three. It is based on the company's cash flows from the model projections, as opposed to the comparable company analysis, which is mainly driven by market data.

11) What are a few major disadvantages of the discounted cash flow analysis?

a. *Terminal value.* Although the first projected years are based on modeled cash flows, the terminal value accounts for a very significant portion of the overall valuation. That terminal value is based on a multiple or a perpetuity.
b. *Model projections.* The model projections could be inaccurate; they could be overstated or understated depending on what is driving the projections.
c. *Discount rate.* The discount rate may be difficult to estimate. We will go through standard techniques, but these standards do not apply in all situations.

12) What is the purpose of the comparable company analysis?

The comparable company analysis ("comps") compares companies that are similar in product size, product, and geography to the company we are valuing.

13) What is one major advantage of the comparable company analysis?

It is the most current of all three analyses—it gives a market perspective. The comparable company analysis is based on the most recent stock prices and financials of the company.

14) What are the major disadvantages of the comparable company analysis?

a. It may be difficult to find companies to compare. If the company has a unique business model, is in a very "niche" industry, or is not the size of a public company, it may be difficult to find the right comparables.
b. The markets may be under- or overvalued. We could be in a market environment where the entire industry in overvalued or undervalued. If so, our analysis will be flawed.

15) What is the purpose of the precedent transactions analysis?

The precedent transactions analysis assesses relative value by looking at multiples of historical transactions.

16) What is one major advantage of the precedent transactions analysis?

Purchase price includes a premium. This could be advantageous if we were looking to acquire a company. It would help us determine how much of a premium we would need to consider in order to convince the owner or shareholders to hand over the company.

17) What are the major disadvantages of the precedent transactions analysis?

    a. *Historical analysis.* Precedent transactions by definition are historical transactions. The analysis may be irrelevant if we are in a completely different economic environment.

    b. *Difficult to find relevant transactions.* Especially in an environment where there are not many acquisitions, it may not be possible to find acquisitions similar to the one we are analyzing.

    c. *Difficult to get data.* Even if we do find relevant transactions, it is not always easy to find the data to create the multiples.

18) What is the formula for calculating unlevered free cash flows?

    EBIT + D&A + Deferred Tax + other non-cash items + Working Capital – Capital Expenditures – Taxes

19) What is the formula to properly discount a cash flow?

$$UFCF * (1 + Discount\ Rate)^{period}$$

20) What is the weighted average cost of capital formula?

$$\frac{Debt}{Debt + Equity} * COD * (1 - tax\%) + \frac{Equity}{Debt + Equity} * COE$$

21) What is a typical WACC of a standard business?

    A standard WACC can range from 9% to 12%.

22) What is the cost of equity? Please include the formula.

    The cost of equity is the expected return to equity investors relative to the investment risk.

$$COE = Rf + Beta * (Rm - Rf)$$

23) What is the market risk premium for the United States?

    6% (It can range from approximately 5% to 6% depending on the source.)

24) Is market risk premium the average return of the market?

    No. The market risk premium (MRP) is Rm – Rf. Rm is the average return of the "market."

25) Please explain the terminal value and the two methods. The terminal value of a company estimates the value of the business after the last projected year. There are two major methods for calculating the terminal value of a company.

    ▪ Multiple method
    ▪ Perpetuity method

26) What is the formula for the perpetuity method?

$$\frac{UFCF * (1 + g)}{(r - g)}$$

27) Walk me through a DCF.

"A DCF, or discounted cash flow analysis, aims to value a business by projecting a company's cash flows and estimating a terminal value. First the company's unlevered free cash flows are projected out a certain number of years, let's say five, for example. Unlevered free cash flows can be defined by a company's EBIT plus depreciation amortization, deferred taxes, and other non-cash items and adjusted further by changes in working capital, capital expenditures, and taxes. These cash flows are discounted back to present value using some discount rate, typically the weighted average cost of capital. Then a terminal value is calculated to establish an expected value of the business after the final projected year (Year 5 in this example). A terminal value can be calculated in two ways: (1) taking a multiple of the final year's EBITDA or (2) using the perpetuity formula on the final year's unlevered free cash flow. This terminal value is then discounted back to present value and added to the sum of the present value of the first five years' cash flow to get a total value of the business."

28) Of the three major valuation methods, which method typically results in the highest valuation?

The precedent transactions analysis would result in the highest valuation because these statistics include a purchase premium.

29) Of the three major valuation methods, which method typically results in the lowest valuation?

This answer can depend on several items. Remember it's not only about giving the correct answer; it's how that answer is supported. *How* you answer the question is important. The comparable company analysis is based on market multiples, so if the market is highly valued, this analysis could produce results higher than the DCF. However, the DCF is based on a financial model. If the model has been constructed based on aggressive metrics, the DCF analysis could produce higher results than the comparable company analysis. I typically build conservative models that, coupled with the fact that cash flows are discounted back to present value, usually result in the DCF being lower than the comparable company analysis. As long as you are comfortable with the drivers of each, you can properly defend your answer.

30) In a comparable company analysis why would one possibly use EV/EBITDA multiples as opposed to P/E multiples?

Because EBITDA is before interest, and enterprise value (EV) is before debt, the EV/EBITDA metric is a better measure of a company's core operations. This could result in more comparable metrics as opposed to a P/E multiple, which includes the impacts of debts, depreciation, and other income or expense items.

PRACTICE CASES

These next few examples are designed to be 45-minute cases and answered on paper. I have provided blank pages to work out answers on your own. The solutions are provided at the end of the chapter.

31) You are a new analyst at a large investment bank. You are assigned to value an entity for potential investment using the discounted cash flow analysis. What is the

value of the business (assuming five-year projections)? The following assumptions are given:

EBITDA is $100 at Year 0 and grows 5% each year.

The company has $150MM of long-term debt on its balance sheet (7% interest rate).

The company has $100MM of equity on its balance sheet.

Assume ongoing CAPEX to be 5% EBITDA.

Assume the CAPEX has a useful life of 10 years with no residual value. Depreciation can be accelerated (for deferred tax purposes) using the following simplified MACRS schedule:

Year 1	Year 2	Year 3	Year 4	Year 5
25%	20%	15%	12%	10%

The company has an effective tax rate of 35%.

Assume 30 days working capital for accounts receivable, 15 for inventory, 25 for accounts payable, and 10 for accrued expenses. For simplification, assume all working capital line items are projected off of EBITDA.

You have already done some research and found the risk-free rate of return is 2%, and the market has returned 11% over the past 10 years.

Use a 7.0× EBITDA for the EBITDA terminal value multiple. Assume a 1% perpetuity growth rate.

Assume the company has a beta of 1.5.

32) You are working on an M&A transaction and need to value the potential target company. What is the value of the business (assuming five-year projections)? The following assumptions are given:

EBITDA is $75 at Year 0 and grows 10% each year.

The company has $50MM of long-term debt on its balance sheet (10% interest rate).

The company has $50MM of equity on its balance sheet.

Assume ongoing CAPEX to be 4% EBITDA.

Assume the CAPEX has a useful life of 10 years with no residual value. Depreciation can be accelerated (for deferred tax purposes) using the following simplified MACRS schedule:

Year 1	Year 2	Year 3	Year 4	Year 5
25%	20%	15%	12%	10%

The company has an effective tax rate of 40%.

Assume 20 days working capital for accounts receivable, 10 for inventory, 5 for accounts payable, and 30 for accrued expenses. For simplification, assume all working capital line items are projected off of EBITDA.

You have already done some research and found the risk-free rate of return is 3% and the market has returned 13% over the past 10 years.

Use a 5.0× EBITDA for the EBITDA terminal value multiple.

Assume a 1% perpetuity growth rate.

Assume the company has a beta of 1.5.

This analysis is meant to be done on paper so feel free to use the space provided.

33) You are an analyst in a fund analyzing a potential investment. What is the value of the business (assuming five-year projections)? The following assumptions are given:

EBITDA is $30 at Year 0 and grows 2% each year.

The company has $75MM of long-term debt on its balance sheet (7% interest rate).

The company has $100MM of equity on its balance sheet.

Assume ongoing CAPEX to be 10% EBITDA.

Assume the CAPEX has a useful life of 10 years with no residual value. Depreciation can be accelerated (for deferred tax purposes) using the following simplified MACRS schedule:

Year 1	Year 2	Year 3	Year 4	Year 5
25%	20%	15%	12%	10%

The company has an effective tax rate of 35%.

Assume 25 days working capital for accounts receivable, 5 for inventory, 10 for accounts payable, and 30 for accrued expenses. For simplification, assume all working capital line items are projected off of EBITDA.

You have already done some research and found the risk-free rate of return is 3%, and the market has returned 12% over the past 10 years.

Use a 15.0× EBITDA for the EBITDA terminal value multiple.

Assume a 2% perpetuity growth rate.

Assume the company has a beta of 0.5.

This analysis is meant to be done on paper, so feel free to use the space provided.

The next two questions are *slightly* more detailed. These are designed to be done in Excel rather than on paper. Again, in all such cases time management becomes key.

34) You are at a final-round investment banking interview. You have 45 minutes to complete this valuation. The following assumptions are given:

> Five-year time frame.
> Revenue is $1,000MM at Year 0 and grows 7% each year.
> COGS is 35% of revenue.
> Operating expenses are projected at 15% of revenue.
> The company has $2,500MM of long-term debt on its balance sheet (10% interest rate).
> The company has $1,250MM of equity on its balance sheet.
> Assume ongoing CAPEX to be 3% revenue.
> Assume the CAPEX has a useful life of 10 years with no residual value.
> Depreciation can be accelerated (for deferred tax purposes) using the following simplified MACRS schedule:

Year 1	Year 2	Year 3	Year 4	Year 5
25%	20%	15%	12%	10%

> The company has an effective tax rate of 35%.
> Assume 30 days working capital for accounts receivable, 10 for inventory, 10 for accounts payable, and 25 for accrued expenses.
> You have already done some research and found the risk-free rate of return is 2%, and the market has returned 10% over the past 10 years.
> Use a 7.5× EBITDA for the EBITDA terminal value multiple.
> Assume a 1% perpetuity growth rate.
> Assume the company has a beta of 1.75.
> As time management is key, try to keep the analysis concise, yet still tasking all assumptions into consideration. In 45 minutes, a full-scale model will be unlikely. It is recommended to keep this to one page.

35) For extra practice, here is a second case of the same style:

> You are at a final-round investment banking interview. You have 45 minutes to complete this valuation. The following assumptions are given:
> Five-year time frame.
> Revenue is $2,750MM at Year 0 and grows 15% each year.
> COGS is 27% of revenue.
> Operating expenses are projected at 12% of revenue.
> The company has $3,450MM of long-term debt on its balance sheet (10% interest rate).
> The company has $1,340MM of equity on its balance sheet.
> Assume ongoing CAPEX to be 5% revenue.
> Assume the CAPEX has a useful life of 25 years with no residual value. Depreciation can be accelerated (for deferred tax purposes) using the following simplified MACRS schedule:

Year 1	Year 2	Year 3	Year 4	Year 5
25%	20%	15%	12%	10%

The company has an effective tax rate of 35%.

Assume 25 days working capital for accounts receivable, 5 for inventory, 15 for accounts payable, and 30 for accrued expenses.

You have already done some research and found the risk-free rate of return is 3.5%, and the market has returned 12% over the past 10 years.

Use a 6.0× EBITDA for the EBITDA terminal value multiple.

Assume a 0.5% perpetuity growth rate.

Assume the company has a beta of 2.5.

ANSWERS

31) I will explain the answer to this first example and paste the solution. This is an analysis designed to be done on paper with a calculator as opposed to in Excel. You'll be surprised how much more difficult it is to do this on paper when already used to Excel, so this is where practice helps.

The first thing I would recommend doing is lay out the overall DCF structure. This will not only be a proper guide for your analysis but also help with time management, which is key in case studies.

Note if you are getting slight differences in calculations, it may be due to rounding. Although I'm presenting these numbers in three decimal places, I did not round when calculating the results.

Unlevered Free Cash Flow	Year 1	Year 2	Year 3	Year 4	Year 5
EBIT					
D&A					
Deferred Tax					
WC					
CAPEX					
Taxes					
Total UFCF					

Next we can slowly fill this out, beginning with EBIT. In order to get EBIT, we need to project EBITDA and calculate D&A. EBITDA begins at $100MM (Year 0) and grows at 5%, so,

	Year 0	Year 1	Year 2	Year 3	Year 4	Year 5
EBITDA	100.000	105.000	110.250	115.763	121.551	127.628
% Growth	5%	5%	5%	5%	5%	5%

We don't really need to see Year 0 as we just want the five-year projections.

Next we can calculate D&A to get to EBIT. D&A is dependent on CAPEX, which is 5% of EBITDA as per the assumptions, or:

	Year 1	Year 2	Year 3	Year 4	Year 5
CAPEX	(5.250)	(5.513)	(5.788)	(6.078)	(6.381)
% of EBITDA	5%	5%	5%	5%	5%

With these CAPEX projections, we can calculate straight-line depreciation:

	Year 1	Year 2	Year 3	Year 4	Year 5
CAPEX	5.250	5.513	5.788	6.078	6.381
Useful Life	10	10	10	10	10
Depreciation					
Year 1	0.525	0.525	0.525	0.525	0.525
Year 2		0.551	0.551	0.551	0.551
Year 3			0.579	0.579	0.579
Year 4				0.608	0.608
Year 5					0.638
Total	0.525	1.076	1.655	2.263	2.901

EBITDA less D&A will give us EBIT:

	Year 1	Year 2	Year 3	Year 4	Year 5
EBITDA	105.000	110.250	115.763	121.551	127.628
D&A	0.525	1.076	1.655	2.263	2.901
EBIT	104.475	109.174	114.107	119.288	124.727

So now we have EBIT, D&A, and CAPEX so far. We calculate taxes as 35% of EBIT:

Unlevered Free Cash Flow	Year 1	Year 2	Year 3	Year 4	Year 5
EBIT	104.475	109.174	114.107	119.288	124.727
D&A	0.525	1.076	1.655	2.263	2.901
Deferred Tax					
WC					
CAPEX	(5.250)	(5.513)	(5.788)	(6.078)	(6.381)
Taxes	(36.566)	(38.211)	(39.938)	(41.751)	(43.655)
Total UFCF					

We need to figure out deferred taxes and working capital. We can use the MACRS schedule to calculate accelerated depreciation for deferred tax purposes:

	Year 1	Year 2	Year 3	Year 4	Year 5
CAPEX	5.250	5.513	5.788	6.078	6.381
MACRS (%)	25%	20%	15%	12%	10%
Depreciation					
Year 1	1.313	1.050	0.788	0.630	0.525
Year 2		1.378	1.103	0.827	0.662
Year 3			1.447	1.158	0.868
Year 4				1.519	1.216
Year 5					1.595
Total	1.313	2.428	3.337	4.134	4.866

Deferred Taxes = (Accelerated Depreciation − Straight Line) × Tax%:

	Year 1	Year 2	Year 3	Year 4	Year 5
Accelerated Depreciation	1.313	2.428	3.337	4.134	4.866
Straight-Line Depreciation	0.525	1.076	1.655	2.263	2.901
Tax (%)	*35%*	*35%*	*35%*	*35%*	*35%*
Deferred Taxes	**0.276**	**0.473**	**0.589**	**0.655**	**0.688**

The assumptions suggested 30 days over EBITDA for accounts receivable. So we could apply $30/360 \times$ EBITDA in each year to get:

Working Capital	Year 0	Year 1	Year 2	Year 3	Year 4	Year 5
Accounts Receivable	8.333	8.750	9.188	9.647	10.129	10.636
Days	*30*	*30*	*30*	*30*	*30*	*30*

Note we also need Year 0 information so we can later calculate the changes from Year 0 to Year 1. We can now do the same for inventory, but using 15 days as per the example. $15/360 \times$ EBITDA gives us:

Working Capital	Year 0	Year 1	Year 2	Year 3	Year 4	Year 5
Accounts Receivable	8.333	8.750	9.188	9.647	10.129	10.636
Days	*30*	*30*	*30*	*30*	*30*	*30*
Inventory	4.167	4.375	4.594	4.823	5.065	5.318
Days	*15*	*15*	*15*	*15*	*15*	*15*
Total Assets	**12.500**	**13.125**	**13.781**	**14.470**	**15.194**	**15.954**

And we have also totaled the assets. For the liabilities, the assumption was 25 days for accounts payable and 10 for accrued expenses:

Working Capital	Year 0	Year 1	Year 2	Year 3	Year 4	Year 5
Accounts Receivable	8.333	8.750	9.188	9.647	10.129	10.636
Days	*30*	*30*	*30*	*30*	*30*	*30*
Inventory	4.167	4.375	4.594	4.823	5.065	5.318
Days	*15*	*15*	*15*	*15*	*15*	*15*
Total Assets	**12.500**	**13.125**	**13.781**	**14.470**	**15.194**	**15.954**
Accounts Payable	6.944	7.292	7.656	8.039	8.441	8.863
Days	*25*	*25*	*25*	*25*	*25*	*25*
Accrued Liabilities	2.778	2.917	3.063	3.216	3.376	3.545
Days	*10*	*10*	*10*	*10*	*10*	*10*
Total Liabilities	**9.722**	**10.208**	**10.719**	**11.255**	**11.817**	**12.408**

We then subtract the total liabilities from the total assets and calculate the year-over-year change:

Working Capital	Year 0	Year 1	Year 2	Year 3	Year 4	Year 5
Accounts Receivable	8.333	8.750	9.188	9.647	10.129	10.636
Days	*30*	*30*	*30*	*30*	*30*	*30*
Inventory	4.167	4.375	4.594	4.823	5.065	5.318
Days	*15*	*15*	*15*	*15*	*15*	*15*
Total Assets	**12.500**	**13.125**	**13.781**	**14.470**	**15.194**	**15.954**
Accounts Payable	6.944	7.292	7.656	8.039	8.441	8.863
Days	*25*	*25*	*25*	*25*	*25*	*25*
Accrued Liabilities	2.778	2.917	3.063	3.216	3.376	3.545
Days	*10*	*10*	*10*	*10*	*10*	*10*
Total Liabilities	**9.722**	**10.208**	**10.719**	**11.255**	**11.817**	**12.408**
Working Capital	**2.778**	**2.917**	**3.063**	**3.216**	**3.376**	**3.545**
Changes in Working Capital		(0.139)	(0.146)	(0.153)	(0.161)	(0.169)

We can now complete our UFCF, adding in the deferred taxes, working capital, and totaling:

Unlevered Free Cash Flow	Year 1	Year 2	Year 3	Year 4	Year 5
EBIT	104.475	109.174	114.107	119.288	124.727
D&A	0.525	1.076	1.655	2.263	2.901
Deferred Tax	0.276	0.473	0.589	0.655	0.688
WC	(0.139)	(0.146)	(0.153)	(0.161)	(0.169)
CAPEX	(5.250)	(5.513)	(5.788)	(6.078)	(6.381)
Taxes	(36.566)	(38.211)	(39.938)	(41.751)	(43.655)
Total UFCF	**63.320**	**66.854**	**70.472**	**74.216**	**78.111**

Now that we have UFCF, we need to discount each to present value. First we need to figure out a discount rate, using the standard WACC formula:

$$\frac{Debt}{Debt + Equity} * COD * (1 - tax\%) + \frac{Equity}{Debt + Equity} * COE$$

The COD is the given interest rate of 7%. The COE is calculated using the following formula:

$$COE = Rf + Beta * (Rm - Rf)$$

So we first get the COE and plug this into the WACC formula. COE = 2% + 1.5 × (11% − 2%) = 15.5%. The Beta, Rm, and Rf were all given in the example. The debt and equity was also given in the example question so we can plug all data into the WACC formula:

$$\frac{150}{150 + 100} * 7\% * (1 - 35\%) + \frac{100}{150 + 100} * 15.5\%$$

This gives us a WACC of 8.93%. With this percentage we can discount each cash flow using the formula:

$$UFCF * (1 + Discount\ Rate)^{period}$$

where *period* is the cash flow year. The PV of each year's UFCF is totaled.

	Year 1	Year 2	Year 3	Year 4	Year 5
Total UFCF	63.320	66.854	70.472	74.216	78.111
Period	1	2	3	4	5
PV of UFCF	58.130	56.342	54.523	52.712	50.930
Sum of UFCF	272.636				

This represents the implied value of the business from Year 1 through Year 5. We now need to calculate the terminal value (TV), which will represent the implied value of the business after Year 5. It is the sum of the TV and the UFCF that gives us the total enterprise value of the business. We will use both methods to calculate the TV and compare.

Starting with the EBITDA method, we multiply the given EBITDA multiple by the Year 5 EBITDA:

$$7 \times 127.628 = 893.396$$

This is the implied value of the business after Year 5. We must discount this value back to PV. So the PV of the TV is:

$$582.514$$

We add this to the PV of the UFCF to get 855.150.

For the perpetuity method we use the following formula:

$$\frac{UFCF * (1 + g)}{(r - g)}$$

where r is the WACC and g is the given rate of growth. So we can plug in using the Year 5 UFCF:

$$\frac{78.111 * (1 + 1\%)}{(8.93\% - 1\%)} = 994.856$$

We then discount this to PV to get 648.669. We add this to the PV of the UFCF to get 921.305.

So the enterprise value of the business is 855.150 based on the EBITDA method and 921.305 based on the perpetuity method. If asked for an equity value, you would simply subtract the Net Debt (in this case $150) from each.

Note if you need more help with these topics and analysis, please read the book *Financial Modeling and Valuation*.

32) Here is the solution:

Enterprise Value

EBITDA method	545.086
Perpetuity Method	562.793

The UFCFC buildup: The WACC was calculated at 12%.

Unlevered Free Cash Flow

EBIT	82.170	90.057	98.733	108.276	118.774
D&A	0.330	0.693	1.092	1.532	2.015
Deferred Tax	0.198	0.350	0.451	0.522	0.574
WC	0.104	0.115	0.126	0.139	0.153
CAPEX	(3.300)	(3.630)	(3.993)	(4.392)	4.832)
Taxes	(32.868)	(36.023)	(39.493)	(43.310)	(47.509)
Total UFCF	46.634	51.562	56.916	62.766	69.174
Period	1	2	3	4	5
Discounted CF	41.638	41.105	40.512	39.889	39.251
NPV of UFCF	202.394				

And the TV calculations:

Terminal Value

EBITDA Method	120.788
Multiple	5.0x
EBITDA TV	603.941
Net PV	342.692
Perpetuity	69.174
Growth Rate	1%
Perpetuity TV	635.146
Net PV	360.399

Supporting the UFCF buildup is the EBIT and EBITDA calculations:

Income Statement	Year 1	Year 2	Year 3	Year 4	Year 5
EBITDA	82.500	90.750	99.825	109.808	120.788
% Growth	*10%*	*10%*	*10%*	*10%*	*10%*
D&A	0.330	0.693	1.092	1.532	2.015
EBIT	82.170	90.057	98.733	108.276	118.774

Depreciation and deferred taxes:

Depreciation
St Line

	Year 1	Year 2	Year 3	Year 4	Year 5
CAPEX	$3	$4	$4	$4	$5
% of EBITDA	*4%*	*4%*	*4%*	*4%*	*4%*
Years	10	10	10	10	10
2010	0.330	0.330	0.330	0.330	0.330
2011		0.363	0.363	0.363	0.363
2012			0.399	0.399	0.399
2013				0.439	0.439
2014					0.483
Total	0.330	0.693	1.092	1.532	2.015

Accelerated

	Year 1	Year 2	Year 3	Year 4	Year 5
MACRS	25%	20%	15%	12%	10%
2010	0.825	0.660	0.495	0.396	0.330
2011		0.908	0.726	0.545	0.436
2012			0.998	0.799	0.599
2013				1.098	0.878
2014					1.208
Total	0.825	1.568	2.219	2.837	3.451
Difference	0.495	0.875	1.127	1.306	1.436
Tax Rate	40%	40%	40%	40%	40%
Deferred Taxes	0.198	0.350	0.451	0.522	0.574

Working capital:

Working Capital	Year 0	Year 1	Year 2	Year 3	Year 4	Year 5
AR	4.167	4.583	5.042	5.546	6.100	6.710
Days	*20*	*20*	*20*	*20*	*20*	*20*
Inventory	2.083	2.292	2.521	2.773	3.050	3.355
Days	*10*	*10*	*10*	*10*	*10*	*10*
Accounts Payable	1.042	1.146	1.260	1.386	1.525	1.678
Days	*5*	*5*	*5*	*5*	*5*	*5*
Accrued Exp.	6.250	6.875	7.563	8.319	9.151	10.066
Days	*30*	*30*	*30*	*30*	*30*	*30*
Total	(1.042)	(1.146)	(1.260)	(1.386)	(1.525)	(1.678)
		0.104	0.115	0.126	0.139	0.153

33) Here is the solution:

Enterprise Value	
EBITDA method	442.920
Perpetuity Method	416.687

The UFCFC buildup: The WACC was calculated at 6.24%.

Unlevered Free Cash Flow					
EBIT	30.294	30.594	30.900	31.212	31.530
D&A	0.306	0.618	0.936	1.261	1.592
Deferred Tax	0.161	0.271	0.330	0.358	0.365
WC	0.017	0.017	0.017	0.018	0.018
CAPEX	(3.060)	(3.121)	(3.184)	(3.247)	(3.312)
Taxes	(10.603)	(10.708)	(10.815)	(10.924)	(11.035)
Total UFCF	17.114	17.671	18.185	18.677	19.158
Period	1	2	3	4	5
Discounted CF	16.110	15.657	15.167	14.663	14.158
NPV of UFCF	75.755				

And the TV calculations:

Terminal Value	
EBITDA Method	33.122
Multiple	15.0x
EBITDA TV	496.836
Net PV	367.164
Perpetuity	19.158
Growth Rate	2%
Perpetuity TV	461.339
Net PV	340.932

Supporting the UFCF buildup is the EBIT and EBITDA calculations:

Income Statement	Year 1	Year 2	Year 3	Year 4	Year 5
EBITDA	30.600	31.212	31.836	32.473	33.122
% Growth	2%	2%	2%	2%	2%
D&A	0.306	0.618	0.936	1.261	1.592
EBIT	30.294	30.594	30.900	31.212	31.530

Depreciation and deferred taxes:

Depreciation St Line	Year 1	Year 2	Year 3	Year 4	Year 5
CAPEX	$3	$3	$3	$3	$3
% of EBITDA	*10%*	*10%*	*10%*	*10%*	*10%*
Years	10	10	10	10	10
2010	0.306	0.306	0.306	0.306	0.306
2011		0.312	0.312	0.312	0.312
2012			0.318	0.318	0.318
2013				0.325	0.325
2014					0.331
Total	0.306	0.618	0.936	1.261	1.592

Accelerated

	Year 1	Year 2	Year 3	Year 4	Year 5
MACRS	25%	20%	15%	12%	10%
2010	0.765	0.612	0.459	0.367	0.306
2011		0.780	0.624	0.468	0.375
2012			0.796	0.637	0.478
2013				0.812	0.649
2014					0.828
Total	0.765	1.392	1.879	2.284	2.636
Difference	0.459	0.774	0.943	1.023	1.043
Tax Rate	35%	35%	35%	35%	35%
Deferred Taxes	0.161	0.271	0.330	0.358	0.365

Working capital:

Working Capital	Year 0	Year 1	Year 2	Year 3	Year 4	Year 5
AR	2.083	2.125	2.168	2.211	2.255	2.300
Days	*25*	*25*	*25*	*25*	*25*	*25*
Inventory	0.417	0.425	0.434	0.442	0.451	0.460
Days	*5*	*5*	*5*	*5*	*5*	*5*
Accounts Payable	0.833	0.850	0.867	0.884	0.902	0.920
Days	*10*	*10*	*10*	*10*	*10*	*10*
Accrued Exp.	2.500	2.550	2.601	2.653	2.706	2.760
Days	*30*	*30*	*30*	*30*	*30*	*30*
Total	(0.833)	(0.850)	(0.867)	(0.884)	(0.902)	(0.920)
		0.017	0.017	0.017	0.018	0.018

34) You can find a sample solution on the Wiley website.

35) You can find a sample solution on the Wiley website.

Four

Mergers and Acquisitions

Mergers and acquisitions (M&A) is the general term for the process behind acquiring or divesting an asset or entity. An understanding of this topic is necessary for those interested in the Mergers and Acquisitions group in an investment bank or maybe in a fund that will be acquiring business entities. For the review section of this part, we will overview only the accretion/dilution analysis. This is the most covered M&A technical analysis in interviews. If you find an interest or need to review asset acquisitions, asset divestitures, or full-scale merger models, please read my book, *Mergers, Acquisitions, Divestitures, and Other Restructurings*.

CHAPTER 6

Mergers and Acquisitions Overview

The distinction between a merger, an acquisition, a divestiture, and other types of restructurings warrants some clarification. Transactions can come in a multitude of forms, can be a hybrid of several classifications, or in new markets can create a brand-new classification altogether. Often some of the definitions are used interchangeably or are categorized differently. There has really been no set standard on these definitions, but I will attempt to simplify and clarify. It is important to understand these core structures to better classify any individual transaction explored. Note that there are many excellent books that go through the subjective, regulatory, and legal aspects of mergers and acquisitions. This book is designed to give a technical and procedural approach, so I will only be brief on the major keywords.

Merger: A merger is fundamentally the combination of two or more business entities in which only one entity remains. The firms are typically similar in size. (Company A + Company B = Company A.)

Consolidation: A consolidation is a combination of more than one business entity; however, an entirely new entity is created. (Company A + Company B = Company C.)

Acquisition: An acquisition is the purchase of a business entity, entities, or an asset or assets. Although often used interchangeably an acquisition differs from a merger in that the acquiring company (the acquirer) is typically significantly larger than the asset or entity being purchased (the target).

Acquisitions can take several forms, including:

- **Acquisition of assets:** An acquisition of assets is the purchase of an asset, group of assets, and the direct liabilities associated with those assets.
- **Acquisition of equity:** An acquisition of equity is the purchase of equity interest in a business entity. The differences between an acquisition of assets and an acquisition of equity are important from a legal, regulatory, accounting, and modeling perspective and will be detailed further later in the book.
- **Leveraged buyout:** A leveraged buyout (LBO) is an acquisition using a significant amount of debt to meet the cost of acquisition. Please see my book, *Leveraged Buyouts: A Practical Guide to Investment Banking and Private Equity*, for a thorough analysis on leveraged buyouts.
- **Management buyout**—A management buyout (MBO) is a form of acquisition where a company's existing managers acquire a large part or all of the business entity.

Acquisitions can be considered *hostile* or *friendly* depending on the assertive nature of the process:

- **Friendly acquisition:** An acquisition accomplished in agreement with the target company's management and board of directors; a public offer of stock or cash is made by the acquiring firm, and the board of the target firm will publicly approve the terms.

- **Hostile acquisition:** An acquisition that is accomplished not by coming to an agreement with the target company's management or board of directors, but by going through other means to get acquisition approval such as directly to the company's shareholders; a tender offer and proxy fight are ways to solicit support from shareholders.

Mergers, consolidations, and acquisitions can be categorized further:

- **Horizontal:** A horizontal transaction is between business entities in the same industry. Such a combination would potentially increase market share of a business in that particular industry.
- **Vertical:** A vertical transaction is between business entities operating at different levels within an industry's supply chain. Synergies created by merging firms would benefit both. A good example is within the oil and gas industry. In the oil and gas industry you have exploration and production (E&P) companies that drill for oil. Once oil is found and the wells are producing and the energy is refined, distribution companies or pipeline companies transport the product to retail for access to the customer, such as a gas station. So, in this example, an E&P company purchasing a pipeline company or a gas station would represent vertical integration—a vertical merger. In contrast, an E&P company purchasing another E&P company is a horizontal merger.
- **Conglomerate**—A transaction between two or more unrelated business entities: entities that basically have no business activity in common. There are two major types of conglomerate transactions: pure and mixed. Pure conglomerate transactions involve business entities that are completely unrelated while mixed conglomerate transactions involve firms that are looking for product extensions or market extensions.

Divestiture: A divestiture is the sale of an interest of a business entity or an asset or group of assets.

- **Asset divestiture:** An asset divestiture is the sale of an asset or group of assets. In Part Four of this book we will discuss a simple asset divestiture.
- **Spin-off:** A spin-off occurs when a parent company creates a separate entity and distributes shares in that entity to its shareholders as a dividend.
- **Equity carveout:** An equity carveout occurs when a parent company sells a percentage of the equity of a subsidiary to the public. This is also known as a partial IPO.

Other restructurings: Merger, consolidations, acquisitions, and divestitures can all be considered types of business restructurings as they all involve some level of reorganization aimed to increase business profitability. Although the aforementioned are just major categories, other types of business restructurings can be considered to help fuel growth. A share buyback, for example, is when a company buys back shares in the open market. This creates an anti-dilutive effect, hopefully fueling an increase in company stock price. A workforce reduction is another example of a way to reduce costs and improve earnings performance. Each of these strategies aims in some way to improve business value. The purpose of this book is to attempt to quantify the benefits of any of these situations from a financial perspective.

THE M&A PROCESS

Although there are many facets to M&A and the industry is constantly evolving, it is important to understand the possible steps an acquirer would take in order to pursue a target business. This will further help one understand the M&A process. The early stages of the process are considered "friendly"; the latter "hostile."

Casual pass: A casual pass is an informal inquiry made to business management. This can literally be done via email, a letter, or a phone call. A solicitation to management to discuss a "strategic alternative" can be a suggestion for acquisition. Management can either respond or reject. A rejection would lead the acquirer to one of the next steps, and this can now be considered "hostile."

Bear hug: A bear hug is a letter to company management regarding an acquisition and demanding a rapid response. The letter is not a proposal but rather a demand and arrives without warning. Often the bear-hug action is made public and is utilized to encourage management to negotiate in a friendly manner.

Open market purchase: In an open market purchase the acquirer purchases shares in the open market. Although an interesting tactic, this can often end up unsuccessful if not all shareholders are willing to sell their shares. However, if successful, this could lower the overall cost of the transaction as one blanketed control premium is no longer negotiated, among other reasons. We will discuss the control premium later in the book.

Proxy contest: In a proxy contest the acquirer seeks to gain shareholders' support to change a decision of the board of directors or management in some way that allows the acquisition to proceed. A proxy letter can be mailed out to every shareholder in an attempt to garner support in the form of "votes." Although the proxy strategy comes in several forms, it can prove to be unsuccessful if the target company stock is held by a large number of individuals.

Tender offer: A tender offer is a direct solicitation to purchase shareholders' shares. Because a significant purchase premium is involved in order to try and ensure that enough shareholders would be willing to sell their shares and allow the acquisition to proceed, the tender offer is a costly method of acquiring a business.

It is *also* important to note, when acquiring assets, groups of assets, or business entities, there are three major methods of facilitating the acquisition:

1. Asset acquisition
2. Stock acquisition
3. 338(h)(10) election

Asset Acquisition

In an asset acquisition, the buyer purchases selected assets in the business and may take on the liabilities directly associated with the assets selected. Here, the net value of the assets purchased are *stepped up*, or written up, on the acquirer's tax balance sheet. In other words, if a buyer pays a higher value for an asset than what is stated on the seller's balance sheet, and that purchase price represents the fair market value of the asset, then that incremental value paid can be amortized over 15 years (under U.S. tax law) for tax purposes. This amortization is tax deductible. The value of the asset can also be *stepped down* or written down if the purchase price is less than what is stated on the seller's balance sheet.

Stock Acquisition

In a stock acquisition, the buyer purchases the target's stock from the selling shareholders. This would result in an acquisition of the entire business entity—all of the assets and liabilities of the seller (some exceptions will be later noted). In a stock acquisition, if the purchase price paid is higher than the value of the entity as per its balance sheet, the difference needs to be further scrutinized. Unlike in an acquisition of assets, where the difference can be amortized and tax deductible, here the difference cannot all be attributed to an asset step-up and may be attributed to other items such as intangible assets or goodwill. While intangible assets can still be amortized, goodwill cannot under GAAP rules. Because goodwill cannot be amortized, it will not receive the same tax benefits as amortizable assets.

338(h)(10) Elections

To a buyer, an acquisition of assets is generally preferred for several reasons: First, the buyer will not be subject to additional liabilities beyond those directly associated with the assets; and second, the buyer can receive the tax benefits of an asset step-up.

However, to a seller an acquisition of equity is generally preferred as the entire business, including most liabilities, are sold. This also avoids the double-taxation issue sellers face related to an asset purchase. (See Table 6.1.)

The 338(h)(10) election is a "best of both worlds" scenario that allows the buyer to record a stock purchase as an asset acquisition in that the buyer can still record the asset step-up. The section 338(h)(10) election historically has been available to buyers of subsidiaries only, but is now permitted in acquisitions of S corporations even though, by definition, S corporations do not fulfill the statute's requirement that the target be a subsidiary. Thus, an S corporation acquisition can be set up as a stock purchase, but it can be treated as an asset purchase followed by a liquidation of the S corporation for tax purposes.

See Table 6.1 from the popular website, "Breaking Into Wall Street" for a nice summary of all the major differences between an asset acquisition, a stock acquisition, and the 338(h)(10) election.

These major categories do have subcategories, and other methods of pursuing an acquisition do exist. But these major methods should help provide the most general perspective on acquisition procedure. Of course, *all* of the steps to an acquisition are vast and time consuming and consist of legal, regulation, research, and due diligence. But these are the major components designed to help you understand from a very high and investment banking–minded level where these acquisitions come from.

Next we will overview a key analysis utilized in merger and acquisitions—the accretion/dilution analysis. Understanding this method is not only important for an analyst, but key for potential M&A interview cases.

ACCRETION/DILUTION ANALYSIS

An accretion/dilution analysis is a common analysis in mergers and acquisitions. The analysis helps determine if an acquiring company's earnings per share (EPS) will increase (demonstrating accretion) or decrease (demonstrating dilution) after combining financials with a target company. To help understand the process, it is important to note that in a simple asset acquisition, funds are expended, and the PP&E is increased by the value of the asset purchased. But in an acquisition of an entire business entity, more than

TABLE 6.1 Types of Acquisitions

	Stock Purchase	Asset Purchase	338(h)(10) Election
Sellers	Shareholders	Corporate entity	Shareholders
Assets and Liabilities	Buyer gets everything	Buyer picks and chooses	Buyer gets everything
Valuation of Assets and Liabilities	Book values used, but modified for any step-ups or step-downs	Every single asset/liability must be valued separately	Book values used, but modified for any step-ups or step-downs
Seller Taxes	Single taxation—shareholders pay capital gains tax	Double taxation—taxes on purchase price minus fair market value as well as on shareholder proceeds	Double taxation—taxes on purchase price minus fair market value as well as on shareholder proceeds
Book Basis	Assets/liabilities stepped up or down for accounting purposes	Assets/liabilities stepped up or down for accounting purposes	Assets/liabilities stepped up or down for accounting purposes
Tax Basis	Buyer assumes seller's tax basis for assets/liabilities	Buyer receives tax step-up for assets/liabilities	Buyer receives tax step-up for assets/liabilities
Goodwill and Other Intangibles	Not amortized for tax purposes and not tax-deductible	Amortization is tax-deductible; amortized over 15 years for tax purposes	Amortization is tax-deductible; amortized over 15 years for tax purposes
Seller Net Operating Losses (NOLs)	Buyer can apply Section 382 after transaction to reduce taxes	Completely lost in transaction	Completely lost in transaction
Complexity	Inexpensive and quick to execute	Complex and time-consuming—need to value and transfer each asset	Inexpensive and quick to execute
Used For	Most public/large companies	Divestitures; distressed sales; some private companies	Private companies; compromise between buyer and seller
Preferred By	Sellers	Buyers	Both
Combined Balance Sheet	Add all seller's assets and liabilities (assume shareholders' equity is wiped out); adjust for write-ups, write-downs, and new items	Add only the seller's assets and liabilities that the buyer is acquiring; adjust for write-ups, write-downs, and new items created in acquisition	Add all seller's assets and liabilities (assume shareholders' equity is wiped out); adjust for write-ups, write-downs, and new items

(continued)

TABLE 6.1 (*Continued*)

	Stock Purchase	Asset Purchase	338(h)(10) Election
Goodwill Created	= Equity Purchase Price − Seller Book Value + Seller Existing Goodwill − PP&E Write-Up − Intangibles Write-Up − Seller Existing Deferred Tax Liability (DTL) + Write-Down of Seller Existing Deferred Tax Asset (DTA) + New DTL Created	= Equity Purchase Price − Seller Book Value + Seller Existing Goodwill − PP&E Write-Up − Intangibles Write-Up − Seller Existing DTL + Write-Down of Seller Existing DTA	= Equity Purchase Price − Seller Book Value + Seller Existing Goodwill − PP&E Write-Up − Intangibles Write-Up − Seller Existing DTL + Write-Down of Seller Existing DTA
Goodwill Treatment	Not amortized for accounting purposes; not amortized for tax purposes and not tax-deductible	Not amortized for accounting purposes; amortized over 15 years for taxes and tax-deductible	Not amortized for accounting purposes; amortized over 15 years for taxes and tax-deductible
Intangibles Treatment	Amortized for accounting purposes; not tax-deductible	Amortized for accounting purposes; tax-amortized over 15 years and tax-deductible	Amortized for accounting purposes; tax-amortized over 15 years and tax-deductible
Depreciation from PP&E Write-Up	Affects pretax income but not tax-deductible	Affects pretax income and tax-deductible	Affects pretax income and tax-deductible
New DTL Created	Total Asset Write-Up* Buyer Tax Rate	$0	$0
Annual NOL Usage Allowed	Seller's Equity Purchase Price* MAX (Previous Three Month's Adjusted Long-Term Rates)	$0	$0
DTA Write-Down	=MAX (0, NOL Balance − Allowed Annual Usage* Years until Expiration)	Subtract entire NOL balance from DTA	Subtract entire NOL balance from DTA

Source: "Breaking into Wall Street" (BIWS): samples.breakingintowallstreet.com.s3.amazonaws.com/22-BIWS-Acquisition-Types.pdf.

just the core PP&E is acquired. When purchasing a business entity, one is effectively taking into consideration the entire balance sheet, the value of which is indicated by the total assets less the total liabilities, or the shareholders' equity. So, where in a simple asset acquisition the price paid represents the net asset value (potentially at a premium), the price paid for a business entity represents the shareholders' equity (potentially at a premium). So, in a merger or acquisition of a business entity, we are effectively buying out shareholders' interest in the target business, represented by its shareholders' equity: We are using funds to buy out the target shareholders, and so those shareholders go away, and so does the shareholders' equity on the balance sheet. If you feel you need a stronger background on the fundamentals of acquiring assets, please see the book *Mergers, Acquisitions, Divestitures, and Other Restructurings*. To better illustrate this let's discuss the process.

There are three major steps to conducting a merger or acquisition analysis:

Step 1: Obtaining a purchase price

Step 2: Estimating sources and uses of funds

Step 3: Creating a pro-forma analysis

STEP 1: OBTAINING A PURCHASE PRICE

Before conducting the analysis, we first need to obtain a potential purchase price of the entity. Conducting a valuation analysis on the entity will help us arrive at an approximate current value of the entity. Although a valuation analysis is helpful in providing an indication of what the appropriate value of the entity is today, one will most likely have to consider a control premium. A control premium is the percentage above current market value one would consider paying to convince the business owner or shareholders to hand over the business or shares.

GROCERYCO EXAMPLE

Let's take an example involving two local grocery businesses. GroceryCo A is looking to acquire GroceryCo B in an attempt to increase market share in the region. GroceryCo A believes the combination of both companies' operations will lead to a more powerful entity and will help curb competition from other grocery stores. Let's say GroceryCo B has agreed to be acquired by GroceryCo A for a 20% premium above GroceryCo B's $10/share current stock price. So, GroceryCo A will pay $12/share for each GroceryCo B share ($10 × (1 + 20%)). Note that GroceryCo A needs to consider all shares including the possibility that target company stock options and warrants could be exercised upon acquisition; so we look at the total diluted shares outstanding. GroceryCo B has 250MM diluted shares outstanding, so the total acquisition price at the premium will be $3,000MM (250MM × $12).

STEP 2: ESTIMATING SOURCES AND USES OF FUNDS

Once a purchase price has been established, we have to determine the amount of funds we actually need raised to complete the acquisition (uses), and we need to know how we will obtain those funds (sources).

Uses of Funds

The uses of funds represent how much funding we need to complete the acquisition. These uses generally fall into three major categories:

1. Purchase price
2. Net debt
3. Transaction fees

Purchase Price As discussed previously in the purchase price section of this chapter, a target business is valued to establish an appropriate purchase price. A purchase price can be based on a premium above the company's market trading value, for example.

Net Debt Quite often, in addition to the purchase price, a buyer is responsible for raising additional funds to pay off the target company's outstanding debt obligations. Net debt can be loosely defined as the company's total debts less cash. This can also include other liabilities such as capital lease obligations and certain convertible securities. The need to pay down such obligations is dependent on several factors, including whether the company is public or private.

Public Company If the company is public, which means the buyer is buying all existing shares from the shareholders, the buyer must assume responsibility for obligations on the target company's balance sheet. Certainly the shareholders cannot be responsible for the corporate debt. So the buyer has to determine whether it can or should assume the debt that will carry over after purchase, or if it must raise additional funds to pay down those obligations. The buyer must conduct some due diligence on the company's debts. Most likely, when lenders lend to companies, those debts come with covenants and bylaws that state if there are any major company events, such as a change in control (an acquisition), those lenders would require to be paid back. If that is the case, then the buyer has no choice but to refinance or raise additional funds to pay those obligations. If there are no such requirements, then the buyer must make the decision whether it would prefer to pay back the obligations or take them on and just keep them outstanding on the balance sheet. That decision will most likely be based on the interest rates or other terms of the outstanding loans. If the buyer can get a loan with a better rate, the buyer will most likely prefer to pay back the old debt and raise new debt.

Private Company If the company is private, the buyer has most likely negotiated a purchase price based on some multiple. Remember that there are market value multiples and enterprise value multiples. The multiple becomes an important factor here because this multiple determines whether the purchase price is effectively a market value or an enterprise value. In other words, if the purchase price was derived based on a market value multiple, then of course the purchase price is an effective market value, whereas, if the purchase price was derived based on an enterprise value multiple, then the purchase price is an effective enterprise value. This is important to consider because if the purchase price negotiated is effectively an enterprise value, then that purchase price includes the value of debt. And that means we should not have to raise additional funds to pay down the target company's debt obligations. We are basically saying that the seller should be responsible for such obligations. Let's say, for example, that we negotiated to buy a company for 5× EBITDA. If the company's EBITDA is $100,000, then we will pay $500,000 for the company. However, since $500,000 is based on an enterprise value, which is the value of the business including obligations, then the $500,000 effectively includes the value of debt and obligations and the seller should assume responsibility for paying them down.

On the other hand, let's say we negotiated a purchase price based on a market value multiple of 10× net income. If the net income is $25,000, then the purchase price is $250,000. However, that purchase price is a market value (because it is based on net income—after debt and obligations), which means the value of debt is not included. Inherently, the buyer is now responsible for the obligations on the business. This should make sense because this is a lower purchase price than that obtained when we used the EBITDA multiple.

Let's say the total value of obligations is $250,000. If we have negotiated a purchase price based on EBITDA, then we pay $500,000 and are not responsible for the debt (the seller holds responsibility). However, if the negotiated purchase price is based on net income and the purchase price is $250,000, then we are responsible for raising additional funds to pay the obligations of $250,000, which totals $500,000.

	Public Company	Private Company
Valuation Methods Used	Percent premium above market price, multiples	Multiples
Net Debt Responsibility	Goes to the buyer; is either rolled over, refinanced, or paid down upon acquisition	Can go to the buyer or seller; depends on valuation method, negotiations, and debt contracts

So, depending on how the buyer has arrived at a purchase price, net debt may or may not need to be included in uses of funds. Note that we mention net debt as opposed to total debt, as net debt is the total debt less cash and cash equivalents. In other words, we assume if there is any outstanding cash on the target company balance sheet at acquisition, it will be used to pay target obligations. Note that for a private company, it is likely that a seller will pocket all outstanding cash before sale. In that situation, the cash will be $0 on the balance sheet.

Transaction Fees Transaction fees are expenses related to the pursuit and close of the transaction. Lawyers and investment bankers need to get paid for their services in helping the deal come together, for example. The buyer needs to allocate additional funds to pay such fees. The fees can run from a small retainer to a percentage of the transaction size. The amount depends on negotiations and firm-wide policy. Some of these fees can be capitalized. (See Table 6.2.) Examples of a few of the more common transaction fee categories follow.

Investment Banking Fees Investment banks will often be hired to help pursue the purchase or sale of a business on behalf of a client. The investment banking fees are often based on a percentage of the transaction value (1 percent to 3 percent, for example, or even less than 1 percent for some multibillion-dollar businesses). Investment banks also receive fees for conducting business valuations, seeking out other investing parties such as lenders, and conducting due diligence.

TABLE 6.2   Transaction Fee Table Example

Transaction Fees	Rate	Amount
Equity Investor	2.00%	$600,000
Senior Lender	0.50%	37,500
Mezzanine Lender	2.00%	120,000
Legal		150,000
Accounting		75,000
Environmental		10,000
Due Diligence		15,000
Human Resources		25,000
Miscellaneous		25,000
Total		$1,057,500

Legal Fees   Attorneys are needed for contract negotiation, regulatory review and approval, legal due diligence, preparation of documents for approval, and closing documents. There will also be attorney fees for negotiating, reviewing, and preparing the documents necessary for funding the transaction, which can include private placement memoranda for debt and/or equity. Investment banks also aid in authoring memoranda hand-in-hand with legal counsel.

Due Diligence Costs   Due diligence refers to examining and auditing a potential acquisition target. This process includes reviewing all financial records, appraising assets, and valuing the entity and anything deemed material to the sale.

Environmental Assessment   If land or property is involved in the acquisition, an environmental assessment may be required to assess the positive or negative impacts the asset may have on the environment.

Human Resources   Quite often if the strategy of a leveraged buyout is to improve the operational performance of the business, there will be a need to search for better talent. New management such as a CEO with a proven track record may be key to achieving such desired operational results. A human resources search may then need to be conducted.

Debt Fees   Lenders often charge a fee, either a flat rate or a certain percentage of the debt lent out. This percentage can be less than 1 percent for standard term loans or 1 percent to 3 percent for more aggressive types of debt. It can also vary significantly based on the size of debt lent. Sometimes fees charged associated with term loans can be capitalized and amortized on the balance sheet.

Equity Fees   The equity investor may also charge a fee upon transaction closing. Such fees are again dependent on the size of equity invested and are one of several ways a private equity fund can generate operating profit.

In summary, the purchase price, net debt, and transaction fees all represent the uses of cash. This is the amount of money a buyer needs to raise to meet the total cost of acquisition.

Sources of Funds

Now that we know how much we need to raise in total to fund the transaction, we need to source such funds. Funds are sourced either by raising equity or debt or by using cash on hand.

GROCERYCO EXAMPLE (CONT'D.)

In order to consider the total uses of funds, we need to look to GroceryCo B's balance sheet. Since we have negotiated a purchase price based on the public company's trading value, the purchase price is based on an equity value and does not include the value of the debt. Let's assume GroceryCo A would prefer to pay down the target company's debt as opposed to carrying it over to GroceryCo A's balance sheet. It is revealed that GroceryCo B has $150MM in long-term debt, $50MM in short-term debt, and $10MM in cash on its balance sheet. So, GroceryCo B has a total of $190MM in net debt. Let's also assume GroceryCo A will be responsible for $10MM in transaction fees. GroceryCo A will be funding 50% of the transaction by raising equity in the form of common stock, and 50% by raising long-term debt. So the total sources and uses will look like Figure 6.1.

Sources	$MM	Uses	$MM
Equity	1,600.0	Purchase Price	3,000.0
Debt	1,600.0	Net Debt	190.0
Cash	0.0	Transaction Fees	10.0
Total Sources	3,200.0	Total Uses	3,200.0

FIGURE 6.1   GroceryCo Sources and Uses of Funds

The total uses of cash must always match the total sources of cash.

STEP 3: CREATING A PRO-FORMA ANALYSIS

Once we have our sources and uses of funds, we can now proceed to determine the financial impact of the transaction. A pro-forma analysis ("pro-forma" is Latin for "as a matter of form" or "for the sake of form") is what we refer to as the process forecasting the results of a transaction. Once we have a financial summary of the two entities combined, we can analyze how the EPS has changed (accretion or dilution). An accretion/dilution analysis is a common way to assess the financial impact the combined entities have on EPS. If, after the combination, the EPS has increased, the transaction can be considered "accretive." If, however, the EPS has reduced, the transaction can be considered "dilutive."

So in order to proceed with determining the financial impact, we need to discuss how to combine two entities together. In short, you simply need to add the financials of Company B to the financials of Company A. The revenue of the combined entity, for example, is the revenue of Company A plus the revenue of Company B. From a general standpoint, it's that simple: To combine the income statements of two entities together, you would simply add each line item of entity A to entity B from revenue all the way down to net income.

However, adjustments need to be made based on transaction considerations. In order to understand these adjustments, it is important to reiterate and elaborate on the general

Income Statement	Company A	Company B	Pro Forma Income Statement	Comment
Revenue	Revenue A	Revenue B	Revenue (A + B)	
COGS	COGS A	COGS B	COGS (A + B)	
Operating Expenses	OpEx A	OpEx B	OpEx (A + B)	
EBITDA			**Revenue − COGS − Operating Expenses**	
Depreciation and Amortization	D&A A	D&A B	D&A (A + B)	
EBIT			**EBITDA − Depreciation and Amortization**	
Interest	Int. A	Int. B	Int. A	Company A Only (Assuming we are paying down Company B debt upon merger or acquisition)
EBT			**EBIT − Interest**	
Taxes			EBT × Tax%	
Net Income			**EBT − Taxes**	
Shares Outstanding	Shares A	Shares B	Shares A	Company A Only (Company B shareholders have been bought out)
EPS.			**Net Income/Shares Outstanding**	

FIGURE 6.2 Pro-Forma Analysis (Combining Two Entities Before Additional Transaction Adjustments)

concept discussed in the first paragraph of this chapter. In a merger or acquisition of a business entity, we are effectively buying out shareholders' interest in the target business. Note these funds can be in the form of cash on hand, equity or debt raised, or exchanging shares. However, to elaborate, as mentioned in the Uses of Funds section of this chapter, we often need to consider raising additional funds to pay down the target company's net debt. Although it may be unknown whether we truly need to do so (it depends on the debt contracts, which requires significant due diligence), it is conservative to assume we have to pay down those debts. Later, if we realize we do not need to pay down the company's debts, we can simply eliminate that assumption, which will only improve the outlook. So funds are needed not only to pay out target company shareholders, but to pay down the target company's net debt. Also, as per the Uses of Funds section, transaction fees need to be paid.

So when applying these concepts to an accretion/dilution analysis, where we are concerned with a combined (pro-forma) EPS, we simply add together everything from revenue down to net income, except for items relating to the target company's shareholders' equity and the target company's net debt. Again, this is because once merged or acquired, the target company's shareholders have been bought out and the debts have been paid down. And remember, we are working under the assumption that we are required to pay down the target company's net debts. So, on an income statement, the line items relating to the target company's net debt (net interest expense) and the line items relating to the target company's shareholders' equity (shares outstanding and dividends) will not be included in the analysis; they will be eliminated upon combination. Figure 6.2 is an example of two companies in the process of merging. Here I attempt to illustrate the core nature of a business combination from an income statement perspective and lay out the line items that typically need consolidation. Take a look at this example, then we will apply the consolidation process to GroceryCo.

GROCERYCO EXAMPLE

Let's look at the financials of the two GroceryCo companies and begin to analyze the pro-forma impact of the combination. GroceryCo A is producing $600MM in EBITDA, $334.8MM in net income, and has 750MM shares outstanding. This produces a $0.45 EPS. GroceryCo B is producing $250MM in EBITDA, $130.0MM in net income, and has 250MM shares outstanding. GroceryCo B is clearly smaller in terms of operation production (EBITDA) and so can be considered the "target." However, Company B's EPS is slightly greater at $0.52. So let's see what happens when the companies begin to merge. You can see in Figure 6.3, we have combined all of the GroceryCo A and GroceryCo B financials except for the interest expense and shares. So, first notice that the revenue in the "Pro-Forma GroceryCo" column is simply a sum of the two companies' revenue: $1,550MM. This holds true down through EBIT where $740MM is the sum of $525MM plus $215MM. However, the next line, interest expense, is taken solely from the acquiring company, GroceryCo A. GroceryCo B's interest is eliminated as we are assuming we have paid down their debt upon acquisition as depicted in the uses of funds. Now note that the EBT needs to be calculated by subtracting EBIT less the interest as you normally would in an income statement. We cannot calculate EBT by adding GroceryCo A's EBT plus GroceryCo B's EBT, as that would mistakenly take into account GroceryCo B's interest expense, which we want to eliminate. So, as soon as we start making

(continued)

adjustments to the pro-forma financials, we need to be careful with calculating the totals top-down so we can capture the effects of those adjustments. Keeping this in mind, we need to calculate taxes by multiplying the new EBT by the tax rate (in this case let's assume 35%), as opposed to adding GroceryCo A's taxes to GroceryCo B's. Again, we have an adjusted EBT, so we will have a new value of taxes. This gives us $474.5MM in pro-forma net income.

Income Statement ($MM)	GroceryCo A	GroceryCo B	Pro-Forma GroceryCo
Revenue	1,000.0	550.0	1,550.0
Expenses	400.0	300.0	700.0
EBITDA	600.0	250.0	850.0
D&A	75.0	35.0	110.0
EBIT	525.0	215.0	740.0
Interest Exp	10.0	15.0	10.0
EBT	515.0	200.0	730.0
Tax (35%)	180.3	70.0	255.5
Net Income	334.8	130.0	474.5
Shares	750.0	250.0	750.0
EPS	0.45	0.52	0.63

FIGURE 6.3   Pro-Forma GroceryCo

Next, assuming we have bought out GroceryCo B's shareholders, those shares have been eliminated. So we are left with just GroceryCo A's shares outstanding: the $750MM value.

So, in short, all core line items in GroceryCo B have been added to GroceryCo A except for those line items relating to GroceryCo B's net debt and equity; in this case that refers to GroceryCo B's interest expense and outstanding shares. This results in a $0.63 EPS: an increase from the original $0.45 in GroceryCo A's EPS, or a 40% EPS accretion to the acquiring company ($0.63/$0.45 − 1). Now, that's a very high accretion, but the analysis is not complete. Adjustments need to be made to this analysis. Let's read on.

Pro-Forma Transaction Adjustments   After the core combination is made, additional transaction adjustments need to be considered based on four major categories:

1. Post-merger cost savings
2. Amortization of newly allocated intangible assets
3. New interest expense
4. New shares raised

Adjustment 1: Post-Merger Cost Savings

Cost savings, also known as cost synergies, are cost reductions due to operating improvements implemented after the combination. Cost savings are very difficult to predict and even harder to realize. In smaller businesses they are scrutinized line item by line item. For example, if after an acquisition a CEO's salary will be reduced by half, you would naturally incorporate that adjustment into the model. But for larger businesses whose cost savings can span many different areas of operations, it may be more efficient to assume a small percentage of operating expenses or SG&A (0.5 percent to 3 percent, for example). This depends on not only how much cost savings you believe will be needed, but how much can actually be implemented.

Adjustment 2: Amortization of Newly Allocated Intangible Assets

Amortization is the accounting for the cost basis reduction of intangible assets (intellectual property such as patents, copyrights, and trademarks, for example) over their useful lives. When the purchase price for a business entity is greater than its book value, that difference can be allocated to several areas, including goodwill and intangible assets. The portion of that purchase price above book value that is allocated to intangible assets can be amortized, which results in an additional income statement expense. To fully understand this concept, let's clarify the concept of goodwill.

Goodwill Goodwill is an intangible asset that typically arises as a result of an acquisition. In U.S. GAAP accounting rules, the price paid for a business above the book value (shareholders' equity) is generally defined as goodwill. But several other adjustments are often made based on tangible and intangible assets and deferred taxes, which will affect our amount of purchase price over book value allocated to goodwill.

> *Goodwill arising from a transaction is calculated as the total purchase price minus the sum of the fair values of the acquired tangible and intangible assets, liabilities, contingent liabilities and deferred taxes.*
> (From "Intangible Assets and Goodwill in the Context of Business Combinations," *KPMG*, 2010, page 6, www.kpmg.com/PT/pt/IssuesAndInsights/ Documents/Intangible-assets-and-goodwill.pdf)

More specifically these adjustments are:

Step-Up of Existing Assets Notice the quote mentions the "fair values" of the acquired tangible and intangible assets. So, commonly pursuant to an acquisition, all of the assets are reevaluated and can be adjusted accordingly to their fair market values. This adjustment is called a "step-up" of assets. Note that a step-up of assets could result in additional deferred taxes.

New Intangible Assets Often in a merger or acquisition a portion of the purchase price above book value can be allocated to new intangible assets. The conceptual idea is that the reason an acquirer could pay more for the target company than what is stated on the book value is because they are paying for some intangible assets (branding, intellectual property, for example) that had not previously been identified and accounted for. It is beneficial to allocate as much of the purchase price over book value to intangible assets because, according to U.S. GAAP rules, intangible assets can be amortized. And of course, amortization is an income statement expense that reduces taxes.

Deferred Tax Adjustments In a purchase it is possible that a company's preexisting deferred tax assets and deferred tax liabilities will be adjusted or wiped out altogether. If that is the case, this will affect the amount of purchase price over book value allocated to goodwill. And again, a tangible asset step or new intangible assets could result in additional deferred taxes created.

In summary:

Purchase Price – Book Value
= Goodwill + Intangible Assets + Step-up of Existing Assets
+ Deferred Tax Adjustments

In modeling we often allocate 20 to 25 percent of the purchase price above book value toward intangible assets as a safe, conservative assumption. Let's take an example, conservatively assuming no additional asset step-ups or deferred tax adjustments:

An independent investor would like to buy a distribution business. The business has a book value of $20,000. The investor offers $30,000 for the company. This reflects a premium of $10,000 ($30,000 – $20,000 of shareholders' equity) of the purchase price over book value. The new balance sheet will have a shareholders' equity value of $30,000, reflecting the price paid. The investor estimates 25 percent of the $10,000 premium is attributable to intangible assets (e.g., the brand name "John's Trucks") and will be amortized for 15 years. The remainder is goodwill. The new balance sheet looks like Table 6.3.

Adjustment 3: New Interest Expense

If debt is being raised to fund the transaction, there will be new interest expense incurred. This is based on the funds raised times the interest rate.

Adjustment 4: New Shares Raised

If equity is being raised to fund the transaction, new shares are issued. The number of shares raised will be calculated by dividing the total funds needed by the stock price of the acquiring company or the company issuing the shares. Note that if the acquirer pays dividends to its shareholders, then raising additional shares in the open market would also result in an increase of total dividend payout.

These four transaction adjustments will increasingly affect the income statement post-combination. Let's revisit Figure 6.2, but with the added adjustments in place. (See Figure 6.4.)

So that's it! For a standard accretion/dilution analysis, these are the major adjustments that take place.

TABLE 6.3 Sample Balance Sheet Before and After LBO

John's Trucking Company (in $US 000s)	Before	After
Assets		
Cash	$0.0	$0.0
Intangible Assets	0.0	2.5
Goodwill	0.0	7.5
Truck	20.0	20.0
Total Assets	$20.0	$30.0
Liabilities		
Debt	$0.0	$0.0
Shareholders' Equity	$20.0	$30.0

Income Statement	Company A	Company B	Pro Forma Income Statement	Comment
Revenue	Revenue A	Revenue B	Revenue (A + B)	
COGS	COGS A	COGS B	COGS (A + B)	
Operating Expenses	OpEx A	OpEx B	OpEx (A + B)	
Adjustment: Post-merger cost savings			*Cost Savings*	New adjustment based on post merger cost savings
EBITDA			Revenue – COGS – Operating Expenses + Cost Savings	Cost savings would *increase* EBITDA
Depreciation and Amortization	D&A A	D&A B	D&A (A + B)	
Adjustment: New Amortization			*New Amortization*	New adjustment based on intangible asset allocation
EBIT			EBITDA – Depreciation and Amortization – New Amortization	
Interest	Int. A	Int. B	Int. A	Company A Only (Assuming we are paying down Company B debt upon merger or acquisition)
Adjustment: New Interest Expense			*New Interest*	New adjustment if debt is raised to fund transaction
EBT			EBIT – Interest – New Interest	EBIT – Interest
Taxes			EBT × Tax%	
Net Income			EBT – Taxes	
Shares Outstanding	Shares A	Shares B	Shares A	Company A Only (Company B shareholders have been bought out)
Adjustment: New Shares Raised			*New Shares*	New adjustment if equity is raised to fund transaction
Total Shares Outstanding			Shares A + New Shares	Shares Outstanding + New Shares Raised
EPS			Net Income/Shares Outstanding	

FIGURE 6.4 Accretion/Dilution Analysis Complete with Transaction Adjustments

GROCERYCO EXAMPLE

Let's now apply the four previous adjustments to the pro-forma analysis.

1. **Synergies.** Let's assume 1% of total combined expenses will be allocated to synergies. So, 1% of $700MM total Combined expenses, or $7MM, will be adjusted, and will reduce the expenses. (See Figure 6.5.)
2. **Amortization of newly allocated intangible assets.** Let's take the standard assumption that 25% of the purchase price above the target company's book value will be allocated to intangible assets and amortized over 15 years. GroceryCo B's book value is indicated by total shareholders' equity in the balance sheet. Let's say the total book value was $2,500MM. So the $3,000MM purchase price (from Figure 6.1) less the $2,500MM book value of GroceryCo B leaves us with $500MM that can be allocated across several items including goodwill and intangible assets. So assuming 25% of the $500MM will be allocated to intangible assets gives us $125MM. We amortize this over 15 years to get $8.3MM in intangible asset amortization per year. Simply put, the formula reads: ($3,000 − $2,500) × 25%/15. This $8.3MM will be an additional expense to the Depreciation and Amortization section. (See Figure 6.5.)

Income Statement ($MM)	GroceryCo A	GroceryCo B	Pro-Forma GroceryCo
Revenue	1000.0	550.0	1550.0
Expenses	400.0	300.0	700.0
Adj: Synergies (1% of Expenses)			*(7.0)*
EBITDA	600.0	250.0	857.0
D&A	75.0	35.0	110.0
Adj: Amortization of New Intangible Assets			8.3
EBIT	525.0	215.0	738.7
Interest Exp.	10.0	15.0	10.0
Adj: New Interest Expense			*160.0*
EBT	515.0	200.0	568.7
Tax (35%)	180.3	70.0	199.0
Net Income	334.8	130.0	369.6
Shares	750.0	250.0	750.0
Adj: New Shares			*106.7*
Total Shares			856.7
EPS	0.45	0.52	0.43

FIGURE 6.5   Pro-forma GroceryCo Accretion/Dilution Analysis with Transaction Adjustments

3. **New interest expense.** Since we are raising debt to fund the transaction, there will be additional interest expense in the combined entity. Let's assume the interest rate on new debt is 10%. Figure 6.1 illustrated our sources of funds, and more specifically the need to raise $1,600MM in debt to fund the acquisition. So 10% of the $1,600MM gives us an additional $160MM in interest expense per year. This will be added to our Interest section of the pro-forma income statement. (See Figure 6.5.)

4. **New shares.** Finally, since we are also raising equity to fund the acquisition, new shares will be issued. Issues will be raised by the acquirer and therefore at the acquirer share price. However, note often a large amount of shares can be raised at a small discount to the acquirer's current share price (~5%). In this example let's assume the shares are raised at the acquirer share price of $15 per share. So $1,600MM of equity raised at $15 per share gives us ($1,600/$15) 106.7MM new shares raised. This will be added to the total shares outstanding at the bottom of the pro-forma income statement. (See Figure 6.5.)

So we can see the resulting EPS of the new entity is $0.43. This represents a 4.4% EPS dilution to the original EPS of $0.45 (0.43 / 0.45 − 1).

$$\text{Accretion/Dilution} = \frac{\text{Pro-Forma EPS}}{\text{Acquiror EPS}} - 1$$

It is not uncommon to see a bit of dilution in such merger or acquisition transactions. We will lay out the overall drivers in an accretion/dilution analysis to better explain.

Let's first summarize the entire accretion/dilution analysis in a paragraph. This summary is not only a good recap, but a great way to position talking through an accretion dilution analysis in an investment banking interview:

SUMMARY

In order to assess the financial impact of the combination of two entities, you first need to obtain the purchase price. Once the purchase price is obtained, the sources and uses of funds need to be analyzed. The use of funds is comprised of the purchase price plus potentially paying down the target company's net debt and transaction fees. The sources of funds will be some combination of equity, debt, or cash on hand. Once we know the sources and uses of funds, we can begin combining the two entities by adding together Company A and Company B line items from revenue down to net income *except* for items relating to the target company's net debt (if we are assuming we are paying down the target company's net debt) and the target company's shareholder's equity (because we are paying off the shareholders). These items relate to the target company interest expense and target company shares and dividends on the income statement. In addition, we need to consider four major transaction adjustments: (1) post-merger cost savings, (2) the amortization of new intangible assets if we have been able to allocate a portion of the purchase price above book value toward new intangible assets, (3) new interest expense if we have raised debt to fund the transaction, and (4) new shares if we have raised equity to fund the transaction. We can then calculate a new EPS and compare with the original company's EPS in order to assess accretion dilution.

This is an accretion/dilution analysis in a nutshell. I would recommend reading this over and over again until it starts to make conceptual sense. The importance of this accretion/dilution analysis is twofold: First, for practical purposes, it gives a great initial understanding of the financial impact of a combination before going into the complete detail of building a full-scale model; and second, for instructional purposes it summarizes the major movements behind a merger or acquisition. It's a great way to capture all of the major mechanical transaction components without getting bogged down by all the detail found in a full-scale analysis. That being said, once you have a good conceptual understanding of the accretion/dilution mechanics, it should be fairly easy to see the major drivers for such an analysis.

DRIVERS

To strengthen your understanding of a merger and acquisition analysis, it is important to highlight some key variables affecting the pro-forma EPS. First, of course, in an acquisition the addition of the target company's EPS will be accretive to the acquiring company's EPS as long as the target company's EPS is positive. But the following transaction adjustments affect the combined EPS, resulting in total accretion or dilution:

- *Purchase price.* Of course the purchase price plays a major role in a transaction. The higher the purchase price, the more sources of funds needed to meet the cost. More equity or more debt raised will most likely reduce the pro-forma EPS further.
- *Sources of funds.* The amount of debt versus equity raised to meet the acquisition cost will affect EPS. Debt is most commonly less dilutive than equity, although this depends on the interest rate and the share price, respectively. If the company's share price is so high that it takes significantly fewer shares raised to meet the acquisition cost, the EPS dilution will be significantly reduced.
- *Post-merger cost savings.* The more cost savings incurred post transaction, the better off the net income will be. This will help improve the pro-forma EPS.
- *Amortization of newly identified intangible assets.* The more purchase price over book value allocated toward intangible assets, the greater the potential amortization will be. The amortization rate (useful life) will also affect the amortization value. This additional amortization will reduce the EPS; however, since this amortization is a non-cash expense, it is often a desirable expense to have. Amortization will help reduce taxes, yet since it is non-cash, it will just be added back in the cash flow statement.
- *New interest expense.* If debt is raised to fund the transaction, new interest expense will cause EPS dilution.
- *Interest rate.* The interest rate on the debt raised to fund the transaction would affect the EPS. Of course, a lower interest rate would result in less dilution.

- *New shares*. If equity is raised to fund the transaction, the additional outstanding shares will cause EPS dilution.
- *Share price*. If equity is raised to fund the transaction, the share price helps determine how many shares need to be raised. Total funds divided by the share price equals the number of shares raised. So, the higher the share price, the fewer shares needed to raise desired funds, and therefore less dilution.

Now that you have a basic understanding of the accretion/dilution analysis, let's go through some M&A interview questions and cases.

CHAPTER 7

Mergers and Acquisitions Questions

1) What is the difference between a merger and a consolidation?

   A merger is the combination of two or more business entities in which only one entity remains. A consolidation is a combination of more than one business entity; however, an entirely new entity is created.

2) What is the difference between a horizontal and vertical transaction?

   A horizontal transaction is between business entities in the same industry, where as a vertical transaction is between business entities operating at different levels within an industry's supply chain.

3) What are a few examples of acquisitions?

   1. Acquisition of assets
   2. Leveraged buyout
   3. Management buyout

4) What are three major ways to facilitate an acquisition?

   a. Acquisition of assets
   b. Acquisition of equity
   c. 338(h)10 election

5) What are examples of other restructurings?

   1. Share buyback
   2. Workforce reduction
   3. Debt reconsolidation

6) What are the key variables impacting EPS in a debt and equity raise, respectively?

   1. Interest rate on debt
   2. Price per share on equity

7) Is an equity raise or a debt raise typically more dilutive to EPS? What are the exceptions to the common rule?

Equity is typically more dilutive to EPS than debt. If the stock price is overvalued, raising equity can be less dilutive than raising debt. Or if the interest rate is higher than the cost of equity, raising debt can be more dilutive than raising equity.

8) Walk me through an accretion/dilution analysis.

An accretion/dilution analysis assesses the EPS impact of the combination of two entities. First, one needs to obtain the purchase price, and then the sources and uses of funds need to be analyzed. The uses of funds are comprised of the purchase price plus potentially paying down the target company's net debt and transaction fees. The sources of funds will be some combination of equity, debt, or cash on hand. Once we know the sources and uses of funds, we can begin combining the two entities by adding together each target and acquirer line item from revenue down to net income *except* for items relating to the target company's net debt (if we are assuming we are paying down the target company's net debt) and the target company's shareholders' equity (because we are paying off the shareholders). So, we do not include the target company interest expense and target company shares and dividends on the income statement. In addition, we need to consider four major transaction adjustments: (1) post-merger cost savings, (2) the amortization of new intangible assets if we have been able to allocate a portion of the purchase price above book value toward new intangible assets, (3) new interest expense if we have raised debt to fund the transaction, and (4) new shares if we have raised equity to fund the transaction. We can then calculate a new EPS and compare with the original company's EPS in order to assess accretion dilution.

9) Name the four major transaction adjustments in an accretion/dilution analysis.

1. Post-merger cost savings (synergies)
2. Amortization of identifiable intangible assets
3. New interest on raised debt
4. New shares and dividends on raised equity

10) Name four major components of purchase price over book value.

A. Goodwill
B. New intangible assets
C. Asset step-up
D. Deferred tax adjustments

PRACTICE QUESTIONS

Use the space available to answer the following examples. The answers are at the end of the chapter.

11) If $250MM of long-term debt is raised at 10% interest rate, what is the impact to the income statement, cash flow statement, and balance sheet? Assume a 40% tax rate. Ignore effects of interest income.

Income Statement	Cash Flow	Balance Sheet

12) If $250MM of common equity is raised at $10 per share, what is the impact to the income statement, cash flow statement, and balance sheet? Ignore effects of interest income.

Income Statement	Cash Flow	Balance Sheet

13) If $1,750MM of long-term debt is raised at a 7% interest rate, what is the impact to the income statement, cash flow statement, and balance sheet? Assume a 35% tax rate. Ignore effects of interest income.

Income Statement	Cash Flow	Balance Sheet

14) If $1,750MM of common equity is raised at $25 per share, what is the impact to the income statement, cash flow statement, and balance sheet? Ignore effects of interest income.

Income Statement	Cash Flow	Balance Sheet

15) If $325MM of long-term debt is raised at a 15% interest rate, what is the impact to the income statement, cash flow statement, and balance sheet? Assume a 40% tax rate. Ignore effects of interest income.

Income Statement	Cash Flow	Balance Sheet

16) If $325MM of common equity is raised at $25 per share, what is the impact to the income statement, cash flow statement, and balance sheet? Ignore effects of interest income.

Income Statement	Cash Flow	Balance Sheet

17) If an asset is purchased for $500MM, what is the impact to the income statement, cash flow statement, and balance sheet? Assume a 40% tax rate. Ignore effects of depreciation for the time being.

Income Statement	Cash Flow	Balance Sheet

18) What is the impact of straight-line depreciation on the $500MM asset to the income statement, cash flow statement, and balance sheet? Assume a 10-year useful life and a 40% tax rate.

Income Statement	Cash Flow	Balance Sheet

19) What is the impact of accelerated depreciation on the $500MM asset to the income statement, cash flow statement, and balance sheet? Assume a 25% accelerated rate, a 10-year useful life, and a 40% tax rate.

Income Statement	Cash Flow	Balance Sheet

20) If the $500MM asset is sold for $400, what would be the impact on the income statement, cash flow statement, and balance sheet? Assume a 40% tax rate on the asset gain (loss).

Income Statement	Cash Flow	Balance Sheet

21) If an asset was purchased for \$1,750MM, what is the impact to the income statement, cash flow statement, and balance sheet? Ignore effects of depreciation for the time being.

Income Statement	Cash Flow	Balance Sheet

22) What is the impact of straight-line depreciation on the \$1,750MM asset purchase to the income statement, cash flow statement, and balance sheet? Assume a 25-year useful life and a 35% tax rate.

Income Statement	Cash Flow	Balance Sheet

23) What is the impact of *accelerated* depreciation on the $1,750MM asset purchase to the income statement, cash flow statement, and balance sheet? Assume a 20% accelerated rate and a 35% tax rate.

Income Statement	Cash Flow	Balance Sheet

24) If the $1,750MM asset is sold for $2,000MM, what would be the impact on the income statement, cash flow statement, and balance sheet? Assume a 35% tax rate on the asset gain (loss).

Income Statement	Cash Flow	Balance Sheet

25) $175MM is raised to fund the purchase of an asset, $125MM is raised in equity, and $50MM is raised in debt. What is the impact of the *debt raise* to the income statement, cash flow statement, and balance sheet? Assume a 10% interest rate and a 40% tax rate. Ignore effects of interest income.

Income Statement	Cash Flow	Balance Sheet

26) If the $125 equity is raised at $10 per share, what is the impact to the income statement, cash flow statement, and balance sheet? Ignore effects of interest income.

Income Statement	Cash Flow	Balance Sheet

27) Now, what is the impact of the $175MM asset acquisition to the income statement, cash flow statement, and balance sheet? Assume a 40% tax rate. Ignore effects of depreciation for the time being.

Income Statement	Cash Flow	Balance Sheet

28) What is the impact of straight-line depreciation on the $175MM asset purchase to the income statement, cash flow statement, and balance sheet? Assume a 25-year useful life and a 40% tax rate.

Income Statement	Cash Flow	Balance Sheet

29) What is the impact of *accelerated* depreciation on the $175MM asset purchase to the income statement, cash flow statement, and balance sheet? Assume a 20% accelerated rate and a 40% tax rate.

Income Statement	Cash Flow	Balance Sheet

30) If the $175MM asset is sold for $150MM, what would be the impact on the income statement, cash flow statement, and balance sheet? Assume a 40% tax rate on the asset gain (loss).

Income Statement	Cash Flow	Balance Sheet

31) $425MM is raised to fund the purchase of an asset, $275MM is raised in equity, and $150MM is raised in debt. What is the impact of the *debt raise* to the income statement, cash flow statement, and balance sheet? Assume a 5% interest rate and a 40% tax rate. Ignore effects of interest income.

Income Statement	Cash Flow	Balance Sheet

32) If the $275 equity is raised at $25 per share, what is the impact to the income statement, cash flow statement, and balance sheet? Ignore effects of interest income.

Income Statement	Cash Flow	Balance Sheet

33) Now, what is the impact of the $425MM asset acquisition to the income statement, cash flow statement, and balance sheet? Assume a 40% tax rate. Ignore effects of depreciation for the time being.

Income Statement	Cash Flow	Balance Sheet

34) What is the impact of straight-line depreciation on the $425MM asset purchase to the income statement, cash flow statement, and balance sheet? Assume a 25-year useful life and a 40% tax rate.

Income Statement	Cash Flow	Balance Sheet

35) What is the impact of *accelerated* depreciation on the $425MM asset purchase to the income statement, cash flow statement, and balance sheet? Assume a 20% accelerated rate and a 40% tax rate.

Income Statement	Cash Flow	Balance Sheet

36) If the $425MM asset is sold for $475MM, what would be the impact on the income statement, cash flow statement, and balance sheet? Assume a 40% tax rate on the asset gain (loss).

Income Statement	Cash Flow	Balance Sheet

37) We have evaluated and would like to acquire a public company. The company is trading at $15 per share and has a total of 200MM diluted shares outstanding. We have negotiated a 25% purchase premium. The company has an LTM EBITDA of $500MM, $125MM of net debt outstanding. We will also assume $5MM of transaction fees. The net debt cannot carry over to the acquirer so it must be paid down. What are the total uses of funds?

38) We have evaluated and would like to acquire a private business, so we look to public comparable companies (if they exist) to assess a proper value. We assume the comparable company analysis results in a range of 7.0× to 9.0× EBITDA. The company has an LTM EBITDA of $100MM and $75MM of net debt outstanding. If we assume $2MM of transaction fees and an 8.0× EBITDA purchase price, what are the total uses of funds?

39) Company A is looking to acquire Company B through a combination of cash and shares. Specifically, Company B is being acquired for $1 per share and in addition each Company B share will be exchangeable for 0.5× Company A shares. Company A trades at $10 per share. Company B trades at $5 per share and has 100MM diluted shares outstanding. What is the purchase price of the transaction?

40) Company A is looking to acquire Company B through a combination of cash and shares. Specifically, Company B is being acquired for 0.75× Company A shares. Company A trades at $16 per share. Company B trades at $10 per share and has 250MM diluted shares outstanding. The acquirer will also pay down Company B net debt. Company B has $150MM in long-term debt, $50MM in short-term debt, and $10MM in cash. If we assume 2% of the purchase price will go to transaction fees, what are the total uses of cash?

41) Company A is looking to acquire Company B through a combination of cash and shares. Specifically, Company B is being acquired for $2 per share and in addition each Company B share will be exchangeable for 1.5× Company A shares. Company A trades at $10 per share. Company B trades at $20 per share and has 100MM basic shares outstanding. Company B also has 10MM stock options exercisable at a strike price of $15. What is the total purchase price of the transaction?

PRACTICE CASES

These next few examples are designed to be 45-minute cases and answered on paper. I have provided blank pages to work out answers on your own. The solutions are provided at the end of the chapter.

42) Company A is looking to acquire Company B through a combination of cash and shares. You have been assigned to determine the accretion or dilution to Company A's earnings. Company B is being acquired for $1 per share, and in addition each Company B share will be exchangeable for 0.5× Company A shares. In addition, Company A has no cash on hand; it will raise additional funds in debt to pay down Company B's obligations and to fund transaction fees upon acquisition. Some key assumptions are noted below:

Key Market Data

	Company A	Company B
Price	$12	$6
Shares	250MM	100MM
Options	10MM	20MM
@ Strike Price	$15	$6

(*Continued*)

	Company A	Company B

Balance Sheet Items:
Company A has $125MM debt, $0MM cash, and a book value of $500MM.
Company B has $175MM debt, $0MM cash, and a book value of $700MM.

Income Statement Items:
Company A EBIT is expected to be $100MM.
Company B EBIT is expected to be $20MM.

Key Assumptions:
7% interest on debt
40% tax rate
1% of total EBIT cost savings
Intangible asset allocation is 25% and amortized over 15 years.
Fees 1% of purchase price

43) Company A is looking to acquire Company B through a combination of cash and shares. You have been assigned to determine the accretion or dilution to Company A's earnings. Company B is being acquired for $2 per share and in addition each Company B share will be exchangeable for 0.25× Company A shares. In addition, Company A has no cash on hand; it will raise additional funds in debt to pay down Company B's obligations and to fund transaction fees upon acquisition. Some key assumptions are noted below:

Key Market Data

	Company A	Company B
Price	$8	$2
Shares	100MM	50MM
Options	25MM	10MM
@ Strike Price	$15	$3

Balance Sheet Items:
Company A has $250MM debt and a book value of $500MM.
Company B has $100MM debt and a book value of $150MM.

Income Statement Items:
Company A EBIT is expected to be $250MM.
Company B EBIT is expected to be $50MM.

Key Assumptions:
9% interest on LTD
40% tax rate
3% of total EBIT cost savings
Intangible asset allocation is 25% and amortized over 15 years.
Fees 2% of purchase price

44) Company A is looking to acquire Company B at a 20% premium above Company B's current share price. You have been assigned to determine the accretion or dilution to Company A's earnings. One-third of the uses will be funded in debt. Company's B's net debt will be retired upon acquisition. Some additional key assumptions are noted below:

Key Market Data

	Company A	Company B
Price	$12	$5
Shares	250MM	150MM
Options	15MM	50MM
@ Strike Price	$15	$4

Balance Sheet Items:

Company A has $200MM LTD, $50MM STD, $0MM cash, and a book value of $1.5Bn.

Company B has $150MM LTD, $10MM STD, $5MM cash, and a book value of $800MM.

Income Statement Items:

Company A EBIT is expected to be $200MM.
Company B EBIT is expected to be $50MM.

Key Assumptions:

7% interest on LTD
5% interest on STD
1% interest income on investments
40% tax rate
1% of total EBIT cost savings
Intangible asset allocation is 25% and amortized over 15 years.
Fees 1% of purchase price

45) Company A is looking to acquire Company B at an exchange ratio of 0.75×
Company A shares. You have been assigned to determine the accretion or dilution to Company A's earnings. Company B's debt will *not* be paid down upon
acquisition. Some additional key assumptions are noted below:

Key Market Data

	Company A	Company B
Price	$16	$10
Shares	750MM	250MM
Options	15MM	50MM
@ Strike Price	$20	$11

Balance Sheet Items:

Company A has $100MM LTD, $25MM STD, $0MM cash, and a book value
    of $2Bn.
Company B has $150MM LTD, $50MM STD, $10MM cash, and a book value
    of $750MM.

Income Statement Items:

Company A EBIT is expected to be $600MM.
Company B EBIT is expected to be $250MM.

Key Assumptions:

8% interest on LTD
5% interest on STD
1% interest income on investments
35% tax rate
1% of total EBIT cost savings
Intangible asset allocation is 20% and amortized over 15 years.

46) Company A is looking to acquire Company B at a 15% premium above Company B's current share price. You have been assigned to determine the accretion or dilution to Company A's earnings. One-third of the uses will be funded in debt. Company B's net debt will be retired upon acquisition. Some additional key assumptions are noted below:

Key Market Data (MM)

	Company A	Company B
Price	$40	$20
Shares	135MM	425MM
Options	15MM	75MM
@ Strike Price	$60	$20

Balance Sheet Items:
Company A has $1250MM LTD, $20MM STD, $0MM cash, and a book value of $1.5Bn.
Company B has $50MM LTD, $10MM STD, $5MM cash, and a book value of $800MM.

Income Statement Items:
Company A Revenue is expected to be $900MM
Company B Revenue is expected to be $1,500MM.
Company A COGS is 40% of Revenue and also has $140MM of Operating Expenses
Company B COGS is 35% of Revenue and also has $75MM of Operating Expenses

Key Assumptions:
10% interest on LTD
7% interest on STD
1% interest income on investments
40% tax rate
Cost savings is 2% of total Operating Expenses.
Intangible asset allocation is 25% and amortized over 15 years.
Fees 1% of purchase price

47) A company is being acquired at a purchase price of $250MM. The company has a book value of 150MM. 20% of the purchase price over book can be allocated to intangible assets and amortized over 10 years. What is the value of goodwill, intangible assets, and intangible asset amortization per year?

48) Please draw the appropriate transaction adjustments in this chart:

Uses	Additions (+)	Subtractions (−)
Purchase price	Assets	
Target book value		
Goodwill		
Intangible assets		
Net debt	Liabilities	
Target short-term debt		
Target long-term debt		
(Target cash)		
Transaction fees	Shareholders' Equity	
Sources		
Debt		
Equity		

ANSWERS

11) If $250MM of long-term debt is raised at a 10% interest rate, what is the impact to the income statement, cash flow statement, and balance sheet? Assume a 40% tax rate. Ignore effects of interest income.

Income Statement	Cash Flow	Balance Sheet
Interest Expense −$25	Net Income −$15	Cash +$235
Tax +$10	Long-term Debt +$250	Long-term Debt +$250
Net Income −$15	Cash +$235	Retained Earnings −$15

12) If $250MM of common equity is raised at $10 per share, what is the impact to the income statement, cash flow statement, and balance sheet? Ignore effects of interest income.

Income Statement	Cash Flow	Balance Sheet
New shares 25MM	Common stock +$250	Cash +$250
	Cash +$250	Common stock +$250

13) If $1,750MM of long-term debt is raised at a 7% interest rate, what is the impact to the income statement, cash flow statement, and balance sheet? Assume a 35% tax rate. Ignore effects of interest income.

Income Statement	Cash Flow	Balance Sheet
Interest Expense −$122.5	Net Income −$79.625	Cash +$1,670.375
Tax +$42.875	Long-term Debt +$1,750	Long-term Debt +$1,750
Net Income −$79.625	Cash +$1,670.375	Retained Earnings −$79.625

14) If $1,750MM of common equity is raised at $25 per share, what is the impact to the income statement, cash flow statement, and balance sheet? Ignore effects of interest income.

Income Statement	Cash Flow	Balance Sheet
New shares 70MM	Common stock +$1,750	Cash +$1,750
	Cash +$1,750	Common stock +$1,750

15) If $325MM of long-term debt is raised at a 15% interest rate, what is the impact to the income statement, cash flow statement, and balance sheet? Assume a 40% tax rate. Ignore effects of interest income.

Income Statement	Cash Flow	Balance Sheet
Interest Expense −$48.75	Net Income −$29.25	Cash +$295.75
Tax +$19.5	Long-term Debt +$325	Long-term Debt +$325
Net Income −$29.25	Cash +$295.75	Retained Earnings −$29.25

16) If $325MM of common equity is raised at $25 per share, what is the impact to the income statement, cash flow statement, and balance sheet? Ignore effects of interest income.

Income Statement	Cash Flow	Balance Sheet
New shares 13MM	Common stock +$325	Cash +$325
	Cash +$325	Common stock +$325

17) If an asset is purchased for $500MM, what is the impact to the income statement, cash flow statement, and balance sheet? Assume a 40% tax rate. Ignore effects of depreciation for the time being.

Income Statement	Cash Flow	Balance Sheet
No Change	Net Income $0	Cash −$500
	Asset purchase −$500	PP&E +$500
	Cash −$500	Retained Earnings −$0

18) What is the impact of straight-line depreciation on the $500MM asset to the income statement, cash flow statement, and balance sheet? Assume a 10-year useful life and a 40% tax rate.

Income Statement	Cash Flow	Balance Sheet
Depreciation −$50	Net Income −$30	Cash +$20
Tax +$20	Depreciation +$50	PP&E −$50
Net Income −$30	Cash +$20	Retained Earnings −$30

19) What is the impact of accelerated depreciation on the $500MM asset to the income statement, cash flow statement, and balance sheet? Assume a 25% accelerated rate, a 10-year useful life, and a 40% tax rate.

The impact is actually the deferred tax liability, assuming accelerated depreciation is allowable for tax purposes. At a 25% rate, the accelerated depreciation would be $125MM. To calculate deferred taxes we need to subtract the straight-line depreciation from the accelerated and multiply by the tax rate, or ($125 − 50) × 40% = $30MM.

Income Statement	Cash Flow	Balance Sheet
No change	Net Income +$0	Cash +$30
	Deferred Tax +$30	Deferred Tax +$30
	Cash +$30	

20) If the $500MM asset is sold for $400MM, what would be the impact on the income statement, cash flow statement, and balance sheet? Assume a 40% tax rate on the asset gain (loss).

Income Statement	Cash Flow	Balance Sheet
After tax loss on sale −$60	Net Income −$60	Cash +$440
Net Income −$60	Adjustment: loss on sale +$100	PP&E −$500
	Asset sale +$400	Retained Earnings −$60
	Cash +$440	

21) If an asset was purchased for $1,750MM, what is the impact to the income statement, cash flow statement, and balance sheet? Ignore effects of depreciation for the time being.

Income Statement	Cash Flow	Balance Sheet
No change	Net Income $0 Asset purchase −$1,750 Cash −$1,750	Cash −$1,750 PP&E +$1,750 Retained Earnings $0

22) What is the impact of straight-line depreciation on the $1,750MM asset purchase to the income statement, cash flow statement, and balance sheet? Assume a 25-year useful life and a 35% tax rate.

Income Statement	Cash Flow	Balance Sheet
Depreciation −$70 Tax +$24.5 Net Income −$45.5	Net Income −$45.5 Depreciation +$70 Cash +$24.5	Cash +$24.5 PP&E −$70 Retained Earnings −$45.5

23) What is the impact of *accelerated* depreciation on the $1,750MM asset purchase to the income statement, cash flow statement, and balance sheet? Assume a 20% accelerated rate and a 35% tax rate.

At a 20% rate, the accelerated depreciation would be $350. To calculate deferred taxes we need to subtract the straight-line depreciation from the accelerated and multiply by the tax rate, or ($350 − 70) × 35% = $98.

Income Statement	Cash Flow	Balance Sheet
No change	Net Income +$0 Deferred Tax +$98 Cash +$98	Cash +$98 Deferred Tax +$98

24) If the $1,750MM asset is sold for $2,000MM, what would be the impact on the income statement, cash flow statement, and balance sheet? Assume a 35% tax rate on the asset gain (loss).

Income Statement	Cash Flow	Balance Sheet

After tax gain on sale
  +$162.5
Net Income +$162.5
	Net Income +$162.5
	Adjustment: gain on sale
	  −$250
	Asset sale +$2,000
	Cash +$1,912.5
		Cash +$1,912.5
		PP&E −$1,750
		Retained Earnings
		  +$162.5

25) $175MM is raised to fund the purchase of an asset. $125MM is raised in equity, and $50MM is raised in debt. What is the impact of the *debt raise* to the income statement, cash flow statement, and balance sheet? Assume a 10% interest rate and a 40% tax rate. Ignore effects of interest income.

Income Statement	Cash Flow	Balance Sheet
Interest Expense −$5	Net Income −$3	Cash +$47
Tax +$2	Long-term Debt +$50	Long-term Debt +$50
Net Income −$3	Cash +$47	Retained Earnings −$3

26) If the $125 equity is raised at $10 per share, what is the impact to the income statement, cash flow statement, and balance sheet? Ignore effects of interest income.

Income Statement	Cash Flow	Balance Sheet
New shares 12.5MM	Common stock +$125	Cash +$125
	Cash +$125	Common stock +$125

27) Now, what is the impact of the $175MM asset acquisition to the income statement, cash flow statement, and balance sheet? Assume a 40% tax rate. Ignore effects of depreciation for the time being.

Income Statement	Cash Flow	Balance Sheet
No change	Net Income $0	Cash −$175
	Asset purchase −$175	PP&E +$175
	Cash −$175	Retained Earnings $0

28) What is the impact of straight-line depreciation on the $175MM asset purchase to the income statement, cash flow statement, and balance sheet? Assume a 25-year useful life and a 40% tax rate.

Income Statement	Cash Flow	Balance Sheet
Depreciation −$7	Net Income −$4.2	Cash +$2.8
Tax +$2.8	Depreciation +$7	PP&E −$7
Net Income −$4.2	Cash +$2.8	Retained Earnings −$4.2

29) What is the impact of *accelerated* depreciation on the $175MM asset purchase to the income statement, cash flow statement, and balance sheet? Assume a 20% accelerated rate and a 40% tax rate.

At a 20% rate, the accelerated depreciation would be $35. To calculate deferred taxes we need to subtract the straight-line depreciation from the accelerated and multiply by the tax rate, or ($35 − 7) × 40% = $11.2.

Income Statement	Cash Flow	Balance Sheet
No change	Net Income +$0 Deferred Tax +$11.2 Cash +$11.2	Cash +$11.2 Deferred Tax +$11.2

30) If the $175MM asset is sold for $150MM, what would be the impact on the income statement, cash flow statement, and balance sheet? Assume a 40% tax rate on the asset gain (loss).

Income Statement	Cash Flow	Balance Sheet

After tax loss on sale −$15
Net Income −$15
	Net Income −$15
	Adjustment: loss on sale
	  +$25
	Asset sale +$150
	Cash +$160
		Cash +$160
		PP&E −$175
		Retained Earnings
		  −$15

31) $425MM is raised to fund the purchase of an asset. $275MM is raised in equity, and $150MM is raised in debt. What is the impact of the *debt raise* to the income statement, cash flow statement, and balance sheet? Assume a 5% interest rate and a 40% tax rate. Ignore effects of interest income.

Income Statement	Cash Flow	Balance Sheet
Interest Expense −$7.5 Tax +$3 Net Income −$4.5	Net Income −$4.5 Long-term Debt +$150 Cash +$145.5	Cash +$145.5 Long-term Debt +$150 Retained Earnings −$4.5

32) If the $275 equity is raised at $25 per share, what is the impact to the income statement, cash flow statement, and balance sheet? Ignore effects of interest income.

Income Statement	Cash Flow	Balance Sheet
New shares 11MM	Common stock +$275 Cash +$275	Cash +$275 Common stock +$275

33) Now, what is the impact of the $425MM asset acquisition to the income statement, cash flow statement, and balance sheet? Assume a 40% tax rate. Ignore effects of depreciation for the time being.

Income Statement	Cash Flow	Balance Sheet
No Change	Net Income $0 Asset purchase −$425 Cash −$425	Cash −$425 PP&E +$425 Retained Earnings $0

34) What is the impact of straight-line depreciation on the $425MM asset purchase to the income statement, cash flow statement, and balance sheet? Assume a 25-year useful life and a 40% tax rate.

Income Statement	Cash Flow	Balance Sheet
Depreciation −$17	Net Income −$10.2	Cash +$6.8
Tax +$6.8	Depreciation +$17	PP&E −$17
Net Income −$10.2	Cash +$6.8	Retained Earnings −$10.2

35) What is the impact of *accelerated* depreciation on the $425MM asset purchase to the income statement, cash flow statement, and balance sheet? Assume a 20% accelerated rate and a 40% tax rate.

At a 20% rate, the accelerated depreciation would be $85. To calculate deferred taxes we need to subtract the straight-line depreciation from the accelerated and multiply by the tax rate. Or ($85 − 17) × 40% = $27.2.

Income Statement	Cash Flow	Balance Sheet
No change	Net Income +$0	Cash +$27.2
	Deferred Tax +$27.2	Deferred Tax +$27.2
	Cash +$27.2	

36) If the $425MM asset is sold for $475MM, what would be the impact on the income statement, cash flow statement, and balance sheet? Assume a 40% tax rate on the asset gain (loss).

Income Statement	Cash Flow	Balance Sheet
After tax gain on sale +$30	Net Income +$30	Cash +$455
Net Income +$30	Adjustment: loss on sale −$50	PP&E −$425
	Asset sale +$475	Retained Earnings +$30
	Cash +$455	

37) $3,880MM. The purchase price is $15 × (1 + 25%) × 200MM = $3,750MM. Since this is a public company we need to be responsible for the net debt. It is stated that the net debt cannot carry over to the acquirer, so the acquirer needs to allocate additional funds to pay it down. So we add the additional $125MM in net debt plus the $5MM in transaction fees to get to a purchase price of $3,880MM.

38) $802MM. The purchase price is 8 × $100MM. Since this is based on an EBITDA multiple, this already includes the value of the net debt, so we do not add the $75MM of debt to this. We do, however, add $2MM in transaction fees to get to total uses of $802MM.

39) The purchase price is $600MM. One Company B shareholder would receive $1 plus 0.5× Company A shares. If Company A is trading at $10 per share, then a Company B shareholder would be receiving 0.5 × $10 or $5. So in total each Company B shareholder would be receiving $6 ($5 + $1). With 100MM outstanding shareholders, the total purchase price would be $600MM.

40) $3,250. One Company B shareholder would receive 0.75× Company A shares. If Company A is trading at $16 per share, then a Company B shareholder would be receiving 0.75 × $16 or $12 per share. With 250MM outstanding shareholders, the total purchase price would be $3,000MM ($12 × 250MM). So the transaction fees will be 2% of $3,000MM or $60. With a net debt responsibility of $190MM ($150 + 50 − 10), the total uses will be $3,250 ($3,000 + $60 + $190).

41) $1,720. One Company B shareholder would receive $2 plus 1.5× Company A shares. If Company A is trading at $10 per share, then a Company B shareholder would be receiving 1.5 × $10 or $15 in addition to the $2 in cash for a total of $17. It is stated that Company B has 100MM *basic* shares outstanding. They have an additional 10MM in stock options exercisable at $15 per share. At a $17 per share purchase price, those options are in the money, so we need to use the Treasury Method to create a total diluted share count. If 10MM shares are exercised at the strike price of $15, $150MM in funds will be generated. At the $17 purchase price, there would be approximately 8.82MM shares ($150/$17) less the original 10MM shares exercised, leaving approximately 1.18MM shares, or a total diluted share count of 101.18MM. The total purchase price would be approximately $1,720MM ($17 × 101.18MM). For more information on the Treasury method, please see the book *Financial Modeling and Valuation*.

42) I will explain the answer to this first example and paste the solution. This is an analysis designed to be done on paper with a calculator as opposed to in Excel. You'll be surprised how much more difficult it is to do this on paper when already used to Excel, so this is where practice helps.

Structure is key to these cases, so keep in mind the accretion/dilution process. First we need to determine the purchase price. As per the question, Company B (the target) is being bought out for $1 per share and 0.5× Company A (the acquirer) shares. So each Company B shareholder would receive $1 in cash and one half of a Company A share. Company A's shares are worth $12, so half a share is worth $6. Each Company B shareholder will then receive $7 ($1 + 0.5 × $12).

So we now need to determine how many Company B shareholders exist to get the total purchase price. The table shows 100 Company B shares outstanding, but we need to consider the total diluted share count. Company B has 20 options exercisable at $6. Since the purchase price per share of $7 is above the strike price of the options, the options will dilute upon acquisitions. We use the Treasury method to calculate the diluted shares. I will run through the calculation here. Twenty options exercise at $6 per share (the strike price) to give $120 in capital. The $120 will fund the purchase of shares at $7, resulting in 17.143 options ($120/$7). Twenty original options less 17.143 results in 2.857 shares. So the total diluted share count is 102.857. We multiply this by the acquisition price per share to get the total purchase price: 102.857 × $7 = $720MM.

Note if you are getting slight differences in calculations, it may be due to rounding. Although I'm presenting these numbers in three decimal places, I did not round while calculating the results on a calculator.

With the purchase price we can calculate uses of cash. It was noted in the example that the target's debt will be retired upon acquisition. It was also noted that fees will be calculated at 1% of the purchase price.

Uses	
Purchase Price	$720,000,000
Net Debt	175,000,000
Transaction Fees	$7,200,000
Total Uses	**$902,200,000**

The sources are based on a combination of debt and equity. We know the equity component, as there is a portion of the purchase price exchanged in shares: 0.5× Company A shares to be exact. In the purchase price, we calculated that exchange to have a value of $6 ($12 × 0.5×). We can multiply $6 by the total diluted shares outstanding (102.857MM) to get the value of equity raised by the acquirer of $617.142MM. As it was stated that Company A has no existing cash on hand, the other $1 that made up the purchase price ($1 × 102.857) will be funded in Company A debt. It was also stated in the example the target company's net debt and fees will also be funded in acquirer debt. So the total debt raised by the acquirer is $102.857MM + $175MM + $7.2MM or $285.057MM.

Sources	
Debt	285,057,143
Equity	617,142,857
Cash	0
Total Sources	**902,200,000**

Now that we have the purchase price, sources, and uses, we can move on to analyzing the accretion/(dilution) impact. We first want to assess Company A's stand-alone EPS. EBIT was given in the example. The interest expense is calculated by applying the given 7% interest rated to the $125MM balance of acquirer debt. The EPS is $0.22.

Income Statement	Company A
EBIT	100,000,000
Interest Exp	8,750,000
Interest Income	0
EBT	91,250,000
Tax	36,500,000
Net Income	54,750,000
Shares	250,000,000
EPS	$0.22

We can now begin the pro-forma analysis. Both Company A's and B's EBITs are added together, giving us $120MM. We now need to make adjustments to the EBIT for potential synergies and amortization of identifiable intangible assets. It was given that synergies will be assumed at 1% of combined EBIT, or $1.2MM. Remember, synergies are a reduction in expenses, so they will increase EBIT.

It was also stated that 25% of the purchase price – book value will be allocated to intangible assets and amortized over 15 years. The Company B book value is $700MM. So, the purchase price over book value is $20MM ($720MM – $700MM). 25% of $20MM is $5MM and, amortized over 15 years, gives annual amortization of $0.333MM.

So the adjusted EBIT is $120.867MM ($125 + $1.2 – $0.333).

We now need to work down from EBIT to net income. Since we've paid down the target company debt, there will be no target (Company B) interest. We will simply pull over the Company A interest expense, which we calculated previously as $8.75MM. However, there will be new interest as Company A has raised $285.057MM in debt to fund the acquisition. So at an assumed 7% interest rate, we need to include $19.954 of additional interest expense.

We can now adjust for taxes to get a pro-forma net income of $55.298MM.

Pro Forma

EBIT	120,000,000
Adj: Synergies	−1,200,000
Adj: Amortization	333,333
Interest Expense	8,750,000
Interest Income	0
Adj: New Interest	19,954,000
EBT	92,162,667
Tax	36,865,067
Net Income	55,297,600

Now that we have pro-forma net income we need to calculate the new number of shares to get a pro-forma EPS. Company A had an original share count of 250MM. As per the sources, it has raised $617.142MM of equity to fund the acquisition. We assume Company A will raise shares at its current share price of $12.00. So the company will raise an additional 51.429MM ($617.142/$12) shares to meet the acquisition costs. The additional 51.429 shares will give a pro-forma share count of 301.429MM.

Finally, the new net income divided by new shares will give the final EPS of $0.18, or a dilution of 16.23% to the original acquirer EPS of $0.22 ($0.18/ $0.22 – 1). Again, some of these numbers I've rounded in this writeup, so direct calculator calculations may provide slightly different numbers. If you do not round the calculations, you will get these exact numbers. The Excel tables are extended into the thousands so you can better match the actual calculations.

Shares	250,000,000
Adj: New Shares	51,428,571
Total Shares	301,428,571
New EPS	$0.18
Accretion/(Dilution)	= (16.23%)

43) Answer:
   Purchase Price:

Purchase Price	
Target Basic Shares	50,000,000
Target Options	10,000,000
Option Strike Price	3

Purchase Price	
Options Exercised	30,000,000
Purchase Price per Share	4
Shares Repurchased	7,500,000
Diluted Shares	2,500,000
Total Diluted Shares	52,500,000
Purchase Price	$210,000,000

Sources and Uses:

Uses		Sources	
Purchase Price	$210,000,000	Debt	209,200,000
Net Debt	100,000,000	Equity	105,000,000
Transaction Fees	$4,200,000	Cash	0
Total Uses	**$314,200,000**	**Total Sources**	314,200,000

Company A Financials:

Income Statement	Company A
EBIT	250,000,000
Interest Exp	22,500,000
Interest Income	0
EBT	227,500,000
Tax	91,000,000
Net Income	136,500,000
Shares	100,000,000
EPS	$ 1.37

Pro-Forma Results:

Pro-Forma	
EBIT	300,000,000
Adj: Synergies	−9,000,000
Adj: Amortization	1,000,000
Interest Expense	22,500,000
Interest Income	0
Adj: New Interest	18,828,000
EBT	266,672,000
Tax	106,668,800
Net Income	160,003,200

Pro-Forma	
Shares	100,000,000
Adj: New Shares	13,125,000
Total Shares	113,125,000
New EPS	$1.41
Accretion/(Dilution)	3.62%

44) Answer:

Purchase Price:

Purchase Price	
Target Basic Shares	150,000,000
Target Options	50,000,000
Option Strike Price	4
Options Exercised	200,000,000
Purchase Price per Share	6
Shares Repurchased	33,333,333
Diluted Shares	16,666,667
Total Diluted Shares	166,666,667
Purchase Price	$1,000,000,000

Sources and Uses:

Uses		Sources	
Purchase Price	$1,000,000,000	Debt	388,333,333
Net Debt	155,000,000	Equity	776,666,667
Transaction Fees	$10,000,000	Cash	0
Total Uses	**$1,165,000,000**	**Total Sources**	**1,165,000,000**

Company A Financials:

Income Statement	Company A
EBIT	200,000,000
Interest Exp	16,500,000
Interest Income	0
EBT	183,500,000
Tax	73,400,000
Net Income	110,100,000
Shares	250,000,000
EPS	$0.44

Pro-Forma Results:

Pro-Forma	
EBIT	250,000,000
Adj: Synergies	*−2,500,000*
Adj: Amortization	*3,333,333*
Interest Expense	16,500,000
Interest Income	0
Adj: New Interest	*27,183,333*
EBT	205,483,333
Tax	82,193,333
Net Income	123,290,000
Shares	250,000,000
Adj: New Shares	*64,722,222*
Total Shares	314,722,222
New EPS	$0.39
Accretion/(Dilution)	−11.05%

45) Answer:
Purchase Price:

Purchase Price	
Target Basic Shares	250,000,000
Target Options	50,000,000
Option Strike Price	11
Options Exercised	550,000,000
Purchase Price per Share	12
Shares Repurchased	45,833,333
Diluted Shares	4,166,667
Total Diluted Shares	254,166,667
Purchase Price	$3,050,000,000

Sources and Uses:

Uses		Sources	
Purchase Price	$3,050,000,000	Debt	0
Net Debt	0	Equity	3,050,000,000
Transaction Fees	0	Cash	0
Total Uses	$3,050,000,000	**Total Sources**	3,050,000,000

Company A and Company B Financials: Remember, as Company B's debt will not be paid down, it will be consolidated into the combined entity. As a result, it may make a bit more sense to see Company B's full financials:

Income Statement	Company A	Company B
EBIT	600,000,000	250,000,000
Interest Exp	9,250,000	14,500,000
Interest Income	0	−100,000
EBT	590,750,000	235,600,000
Tax	206,762,500	82,460,000
Net Income	383,987,500	153,140,000
Shares	750,000,000	250,000,000
EPS	$0.51	$0.61

Pro-Forma Results:

Pro-Forma	
EBIT	850,000,000
Adj: Synergies	*−8,500,000*
Adj: Amortization	*30,666,667*
Interest Expense	23,750,000
Interest Income	−100,000
Adj: New Interest	*0*
EBT	804,183,333
Tax	281,464,167
Net Income	522,719,167
Shares	750,000,000
Adj: New Shares	*190,625,000*
Total Shares	940,625,000
New EPS	$0.56
Accretion / (Dilution)	8.54%

46) Answer:
   Purchase Price:

Purchase Price	
Target Basic Shares	425,000,000
Target Options	75,000,000
Option Strike Price	20
Options Exercised	1,500,000,000
Purchase Price per Share	23

Purchase Price	
Shares Repurchased	65,217,391
Diluted Shares	9,782,609
Total Diluted Shares	434,782,609
Purchase Price	$10,000,000,000

Sources and Uses:

Uses		Sources	
Purchase Price	$10,000,000,000	Debt	3,385,000,000
Net Debt	55,000,000	Equity	6,770,000,000
Transaction Fees	$100,000,000	Cash	0
Total Uses	**$10,155,000,000**	**Total Sources**	**10,155,000,000**

Company A Financials:

Income Statement	Company A
Revenue	900,000,000
COGS	360,000,000
(COGS % of Rev)	*40%*
OpEx	140,000,000
EBIT	400,000,000
Interest Exp	126,400,000
Interest Income	0
EBT	273,600,000
Tax	109,440,000
Net Income	164,160,000
Shares	135,000,000
EPS	$1.22

Pro-Forma Results:

Pro-Forma

EBIT	1,300,000,000
Adj: Synergies	*−4,300,000*
Adj: Amortization	*153,333,333*
Interest Expense	126,400,000
Interest Income	0
Adj: New Interest	*338,500,000*
EBT	686,066,667
Tax	274,426,667
Net Income	411,640,000

Pro-Forma

Shares	135,000,000
Adj: New Shares	*169,250,000*
Total Shares	304,250,000
New EPS	$1.35
Accretion/(Dilution)	11.26%

47) A. Goodwill? 80MM_____
    B. Intangible assets? 20MM_____
    C. Intangible asset amortization per year? 2MM_____

48) Answer:

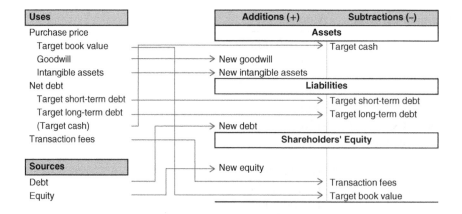

Leveraged Buyouts

A leveraged buyout is an acquisition of an entity using a significant amount of debt to meet the acquisition cost. Leveraged buyouts are typically conducted by private equity funds designed to acquire businesses with the hope that they can exit the business at a later date, making a return on the investment. An understanding of this topic is necessary for those interested in the private equity industry. The technical leveraged buyout modeling is often seen as complex, and so knowledge of leveraged buyouts would set one apart competitively even in an investment banking interview process. In addition, there are some investment banking groups that do leveraged buyout modeling. If you find an interest or need to review leveraged buyouts in more complete detail, read my book, *Leveraged Buyouts*.

CHAPTER 8

Leveraged Buyouts Overview

A leveraged buyout is an acquisition of a company using a significant amount of debt to meet the cost of the acquisition. This allows for the acquisition of a business with less equity (out-of-pocket) capital. Think of a mortgage on a house. If you take out a mortgage to fund the purchase of a house, you can buy a larger house with less out-of-pocket cash (your down payment). Over time, your income will be used to make the required principal (and interest) mortgage payments; as you pay down those principal payments, and as the debt balance reduces, your equity in the house increases. Effectively, the debt is being converted to equity. And maybe you can sell the house for a profit and receive a return. This concept, on the surface, is similar to a leveraged buyout (LBO). Although we use a significant amount of borrowed money to buy a business in an LBO, the cash flows produced by the business will hopefully, over time, pay down the debt. Debt will convert to equity, and we can hope to sell the business for a profit.

There are three core components that contribute to the success of a leveraged buyout:

1. Cash availability, interest, and debt pay-down
2. Operations improvements
3. Multiple expansion

CASH AVAILABILITY, INTEREST, AND DEBT PAY-DOWN

This is the concept illustrated in the chapter's first paragraph. The cash being produced by the business will be used to pay down debt and interest. It is the reduction of debt that will be converted into the equity value of the business.

It is for this reason that a company with high and consistent cash flows makes for a good leveraged buyout investment.

OPERATIONS IMPROVEMENTS

Once we own the business, we plan on making some sort of improvements to increase the operating performance of that business. Increasing the operating performance of the business will ultimately increase cash flows, which will pay down debt faster. But, more important, operating improvements will increase the overall value of the business, which means we can then (we hope) sell it at a higher price. Taking the previous mortgage example, we had hoped to make a profit by selling the house after several years. If we make some renovations and improvements to the house, we can hope to sell it for a higher price. For this reason, investors and funds would look for businesses they can improve as good leveraged buyout investments. Often the particular investor or fund team has expertise in the industry. Maybe they have connections to larger sources of revenue or larger access to distribution channels, based on their experience, where they feel they can grow the business faster. Or, maybe the investor or fund team sees major problems with management they know they can fix. Any of these operation improvements could increase the overall value of the business.

MULTIPLE EXPANSION

Multiple expansion is the expectation that the market value of the business will increase. This would result in an increase in the expected multiple one can sell the business for. We will later see, in a business entity, that we will most likely base a purchase and sale on multiples. We will also conservatively assume the exit multiple used to sell the business will be equal to the purchase multiple (the multiple calculated based on the purchase price of the business). This would certainly enhance the business returns.

WHAT MAKES A GOOD LEVERAGED BUYOUT?

In summary, a good leveraged buyout has strong and consistent cash flows that can be expected to pay down a portion of the debt raised and related interest. Further, the investor or fund sees ways to improve the operating performance of the business. It is hoped that the combination of debt converting into equity and the increase in operating performance would significantly increase the value of the business. This results in an increase in returns to the investor or fund. The next pages of this book step through such an analysis in its entirety and are intended to give you the core understanding of how such an analysis can provide not only benefits to a company, but high returns to an investor. This will also indicate pitfalls many investors face and reasons why many LBOs may not work out as planned.

EXIT OPPORTUNITIES

The financial returns from a leveraged buyout are not truly realized until the business is exited, or sold. There are several common ways to exit a business leveraged buyout:

1. *Strategic sale:* The business can be sold to a strategic buyer, a corporation that may find strategic benefits to owning the business.
2. *Financial sponsor:* Although not too common, the business can be sold to another private equity firm, maybe one with a different focus that can help take the business to the next level.
3. *Initial public offering (IPO):* If the company is at the right stage, and if the markets are right, the company can be sold to the public markets—an IPO.
4. *Dividend recapitalization:* Although not necessarily a sale, a dividend recapitalization is a way for a fund to receive liquidity from their business investments. Think of it like refinancing a mortgage or taking out a second mortgage on your home in order to receive cash. The business will raise debt and distribute the cash raised from the debt to business owners or fund management.

LEVERAGED BUYOUT TECHNICAL ANALYSIS

There are three major steps to conducting an LBO analysis:

Step 1: Obtaining a purchase price

Step 2: Estimating sources and uses of funds

Step 3: Calculating investor rate of return (IRR)

PURCHASE PRICE

In order to conduct a leveraged buyout analysis, we first need to obtain a potential purchase price of the entity. Conducting a valuation analysis on the entity will help us arrive at an approximate current value of the entity. The book *Financial Modeling and Valuation* steps through how to model and value a company. Although a valuation analysis is helpful in providing an indication of what the appropriate value of the entity is today, one will most likely have to consider a control premium. A control premium is the percentage above current market value that one would consider paying to convince the business owner or shareholders to hand over the business or shares.

Public versus Private Company Purchase

It is important to note that for a public company the purchase price is most likely based on a percentage above the current market trading value per share as exemplified in the preceding press release. However, private companies are popular LBO candidates as well. If we are evaluating a private company, we do not have a current market trading value from which to value the business. So, we need to use multiples to establish an estimated purchase price. Multiples of a private company can be based on public company comparables or historical transactions. In other words, to find an appropriate value of a private company, you can look for companies that are similar in product and size to that company: comparable companies. The multiples ranges of these comparable companies can determine the value of the private company. Also, looking at the price paid for historical transactions similar in product and size to the private company as a multiple can help establish an appropriate purchase price.

SHIPCO EXAMPLE

Let's take an example of a local package delivery business—a private company that makes money by delivering packages to consumers. Let's say in 2015 it has produced $20 million in revenue. After cost of goods sold (COGS) and operating expenses, the company produces $5 million in earnings before interest, taxes, depreciation, and amortization (EBITDA). This is a private business, so we can look to public comparable companies (if they exist) to assess a proper value. Or we can look at precedent transactions—other acquisitions of local delivery businesses. The goal of this section is to assess leveraged buyout (LBO) returns, not valuation; so let's assume the comparable company analysis results in a range of

(continued)

4.0× to 6.0× EBITDA, and we found a few historical transactions where buyers paid 4.5× to 5.5× EBITDA for a local delivery business. For this example, we will base a purchase price on a 5.0× EBITDA multiple, as it is the midpoint of both the comparable company analysis and the precedent transaction analysis. That will result in a $25 million estimated purchase price (5 times $5 million EBITDA). Keep this example in mind, as we will use it to illustrate core LBO concepts in this chapter before we get to some practice questions.

SOURCES AND USES OF FUNDS

Once a purchase price has been established, we need to determine the amount of funds we actually need raised to complete the acquisition (uses), and we need to know how we will obtain those funds (sources).

Uses of Funds

The uses of funds represent how much funding we need to complete the acquisition. These uses generally fall into three major categories:

1. Purchase price
2. Net debt
3. Transaction fees

Purchase Price   As discussed previously in this chapter, the purchase price is based either on the current market trading value of the business or on some multiple.

Net Debt   As discussed in Chapter 7, in addition to the purchase price, a buyer is responsible for raising additional funds to pay off the target company's outstanding debt obligations. This can also include other liabilities such as capital lease obligations. The need to pay down such obligations is dependent on several factors, including whether the company is public or private.

In the ShipCo example, we used an EBITDA multiple to arrive at the purchase price. So the $25 million purchase price is effectively an enterprise value, and it includes the effects of debt. Therefore, if we actually purchase the business, the seller is responsible for taking the $25 million and paying down debt. We will receive a debt-free business.

Transaction Fees   Transaction fees are expenses related to the pursuit and close of the transaction. Lawyers and investment bankers need to get paid for their services in helping the deal come together, for example. The buyer needs to allocate additional funds to pay such fees. The fees can run from a small retainer to a percentage of the transaction size.

The amount depends on negotiations and firm-wide policy. See Chapter 7 for more detail on transaction fees.

Let's keep the ShipCo example simple and assume there are no transaction fees. Again, we want to use ShipCo to illustrate the LBO process, so we don't want to complicate the example with distracting details.

Sources of Funds

Now that we know how much we need to raise in total to fund the acquisition, we need to source such funds. Funds are sourced either by raising equity or debt or by using cash on hand. Table 8.1 gives an example of the types of sources one would see in a leveraged buyout. The percentage ranges in the left column represent on average the percentage of total sources raised by each security. The expected returns can vary depending on the market environment. Also note that the expected equity returns of >25% stated in Table 8.1 is the percentage many funds hope to achieve; it is different from what has actually been achieved on average given the recent market environment.

Debt   A company can raise various types of debts in order to obtain funding for an acquisition. Common debts raised exist in several categories.

Bank Debt   Bank debt or a term loan is the most fundamental type of debt. It usually carries 5 percent to 12 percent interest and can be backed by the core assets of the business. Such debt is also typically amortized over the transaction horizon, five to seven years, for example. Bank debts can come from commercial or investment banks, private funds, or investors. It is also possible, but more difficult, to receive multiple loans from different lenders. However, there is almost always a hierarchy where one is subordinate to another. Subordinated debt would be riskier and warrant a higher interest rate.

Note that the purpose of this book is not to educate on all the various debt instruments. The selection is vast and there are other great books out there that focus solely

TABLE 8.1   Example of Leveraged Buyout Capital Structure

Bank Debt (30% to 50%)	▪ Has initial rights on the assets ▪ Lowest-risk security ▪ Expected returns (interest): 5% to 12%
High Yield Debt (0% to 10%)	▪ Junk bonds ▪ Higher-risk security ▪ High interest ▪ Not used as often (mezzanine is more common today) ▪ Expected returns: 12% to 15%
Mezzanine Lending (20% to 30%)	▪ Combination of debt and equity; downside protection (debt) and upside potential (equity) ▪ Also can be considered convertible debt or preferred equity ▪ Helpful in increasing equity returns ▪ Expected returns: 13% to 25%
Equity (20% to 30%)	▪ Financial sponsors ▪ No downside protection ▪ Expected returns: >25%

on debt instruments. This is meant to be a brief overview to better illustrate how various debts are applied to a leveraged buyout analysis.

A private entity can attempt to raise not only standard term debt, but also more aggressive types of debt that would arguably not be doable if the company were public. A public company receiving a significant amount of high-interest debt might send shareholders running. This ability for a private company to access debts that a public market might not allow is key to a leveraged buyout.

High Yield Debt   High yield debt is a more aggressive type of debt borrowed at much higher interest rates to compensate for additional risk of defaulting on such debt. Interest in such debt can be upward of 15 percent, but it varies depending on the situation at hand. We mention in Table 8.1 that 0 percent to 10 percent of high yield debt typically is used in a leveraged buyout transaction because we've seen two schools of thought. Some funds we have spoken to used high yield debt previously but not anymore. Other funds are starting to access high yield debt markets again. If you are the buyer, it really depends on who is willing to lend and at what cost (interest rate).

Seller Notes   Upon purchasing the business, a smart buyer would want to find ways to incentivize the prior owner of the business to help aid in the business transition. In a worst-case scenario, the seller could attempt to build a competing business directly after the sale. To try to prevent such scenarios from happening, and further to encourage the seller of the business to stick around and help transition the business to the new buyer, seller incentives such as a seller note or rollover equity are put in pace. A seller note is a loan from the seller to the buyer paid back in agreed-upon installments. For example, let's say that in the $25 million ShipCo purchase, we agreed on paying the seller $20 million up front and $5 million will be a seller note payable over five years. The seller is now incentivized to help out in the business until he has received his $5 million in full in five years. Such seller notes may or may not incur interest, depending on the agreement between the seller and the buyer. As a side note, sellers often sign "noncompete" agreements, which prevent the seller from starting a new business competitive to the one recently sold. Seller notes are a good way to help enforce such agreements.

Mezzanine   Mezzanine securities are hybrids between debt and equity. Convertible bonds or preferred securities are examples of mezzanine securities. The general concept of a mezzanine security is that it is initially considered debt that will convert to equity after a certain amount of time or after certain hurdles are met. We're being a bit vague here because virtually any combination of debt and equity can be created if there is an investor willing to invest in such a security and if there is a company willing to borrow such a security. As such, convertible markets departments exist in investment banks whose sole purpose is to create unique hybrid structures designed to match a buyer with a seller of a mezzanine security.

The benefit of mezzanine lending to an investor is there is some downside protection (as it is debt for the first specified number of years), but there is upside potential if the security converts into equity. Given the fact that there is an equity component to such securities, and knowing equity is more risky than debt, the effective combined return of a convertible security should be higher than that of debt. In Table 8.1 we suggest that anywhere from 20 percent to 30 percent of the total sources are typically made up of mezzanine securities. Again, this depends on the company and respective markets.

Just a note: Preferred securities can technically be considered equity, although they are also considered mezzanine as they often simulate debt in some form.

Equity A public company can raise shares in the open market in order to obtain funding for an acquisition. A private entity can attempt to raise equity from funds or investors, or they can use their own funds. Typically, in a leveraged buyout, 20 to 30 percent of equity is raised to meet the total amount needed. That number can change depending on the transaction situation and market environment.

Rollover Equity In private companies the seller of the business can also invest some funds back into the business and receive a small equity stake. This is helpful in incentivizing the seller to continue to consult with the business, especially as the seller may be tied to clients and important relationships necessary to sustain or further business growth.

Cash If an entity has adequate cash on hand to meet the total funding needs, raising equity or debt may not be necessary.

■ ■ ■

The sources of funding are totaled and should match the uses of funding.

Sources of Funds = Uses of Funds

Let's say in the ShipCo example we have been able to raise 35 percent in bank debt, 25 percent in high yield debt, and 40 percent in equity. So, 35 percent of the $25 million is $8.75 million, 25 percent of the $25 million is $6.25 million, and $10 million is the equity we will use to purchase the company. We also note that the company has $100,000 in net debt on the business. Because the net debt is effectively included in the purchase price in this case, we separate out the portion of net debt from the purchase price. In other words, of the $25 million we agreed to pay the seller, $100,000 will be used to pay down net debt. (See Table 8.2.) There are other ways to look at this, which we will practice in the next chapter.

IRR ANALYSIS

Once we have our sources and uses of cash, we can now proceed to determine the annualized rate of return for our potential investment (Table 8.2).

TABLE 8.2 ShipCo Sources and Uses

Uses	Amount	Sources	Amount	%
Purchase price	24,900.0	Bank debt	8,750.0	35%
Transaction fees	0.0	High yield debt	6,250.0	25%
Net debt	100.0	Equity	10,000.0	40%
Total	25,000.0	Total	25,000.0	100%

Initial Assumptions

First, we begin with the following assumptions.

Time Horizon   It is first important to consider a time horizon. How long do we expect to own and hold the business before selling it? This time horizon could be dependent on how long we deem it would take to make adequate improvements, or maybe it is based on the timing of investment funds required to be returned to investors. Often the horizon is five, seven, or ten years.

Exit Value Method   Once we know when we will sell the business, we need to determine the exit value—how much we can expect to sell the business for. Since the company is now private, we would most likely base the sale on a multiple at the time of sale, an exit multiple. Here, comparable companies or precedent transactions can help determine a fair exit multiple. But often, we can conservatively use the same multiple as we paid for the business. In other words, if we paid 10× EBITDA for the company, we would hope in five years to sell the business for at least 10× EBITDA. The idea is that we would have most likely improved business performance and increased EBITDA, so although the multiple remains unchanged, the sale value would have increased. Therefore, it is useful to consider in advance, for the analysis, what method we will use to arrive at the exit value; that is, will it be a multiple of EBIT, EBITDA, or some other method? It is most common to use EBIT or EBITDA, as they are unlevered metrics and better represent performance of the business operations (see Chapter 4 on valuation).

> For the ShipCo example, let's use five years as the time horizon. Since we paid 5× EBITDA for the business, let's assume conservatively we will sell the business for 5 times the Year 5 EBITDA.

Steps to Investor Return

Once we have the core assumptions—the purchase price, the uses of funds, the sources of funds, time horizon, and exit value method—we can proceed with the analysis.

Step 1: Unlevered Free Cash Flow Projections   Once we have our core assumptions, we would most likely need five-year projections in order to interpret the exit multiple into an actual exit value. Further, once we have an exit value, we note that this exit value, if calculated based on an enterprise value multiple, will produce an enterprise exit value. If so, we need to convert enterprise value into equity value by removing net debt. It is equity value that reflects our actual return. In other words, when selling the business, we will most likely be responsible for paying down the business debts. Again, the company we are selling is private, and if the sale is based on an EBIT or EBITDA multiple, then the sale value is an enterprise value, and therefore includes the value of debt.

However, in order to predict the level of debt in Year 5, for example, we need to understand not only the impact of interest incurred over the five years, but also the cash produced by the business over the five years. The cash produced can be used to pay down debts. Unlevered free cash flow projections contain both EBIT and EBITDA projections, which can be used for our exit value, and also contain cash projections, which can be used to project cash. So, for a simple IRR analysis it is first recommended to build simple unlevered free cash flow projections.

Unlevered Free Cash Flow   Unlevered free cash flow is cash that is available to all capital providers, including equity holders and lenders. In other words, it is a measure of cash flow before equity holders and lenders have been paid. Further, as valuation is a measure of a company's core operating assets of a business, unlevered free cash flow should represent the cash generated or lost based on the core operations of the business. To clarify, let's take a look at a complete cash flow statement.

To get to an unlevered cash flow amount, we want to remove all cash flows related to the capital structure. So we eliminate dividend payouts, noncontrolling interests, share issuances, share buybacks, debt raises, and debt pay-downs; the entire financing activities section is removed. Further, we want a measure of cash that approaches everyday activity, so nonrecurring and extraordinary items such as acquisitions and divestitures will be removed. In the investing activities section, we are left with capital expenditures. (See Table 8.4.)

Simplifying the leftover cash flows gives us:

Unlevered Free Cash Flow

Net income
+ Depreciation and amortization
+ Deferred taxes
+ Other noncash items
+ Working capital changes
− Capital expenditures

Finally, since we are trying to capture an unlevered measure of cash, we also need to adjust the net income for interest expense. So we need to add one more line item: after-tax net interest expense.

Unlevered Free Cash Flow

Net income
+ Depreciation and amortization
+ Deferred taxes
+ Other noncash items
+ Working capital changes
− Capital expenditures
+ A/T net interest expense
= Total unlevered free cash flow

There's often a lot of confusion as to whether these line items should be added or subtracted. The best rule of thumb is to follow how the cash flow statement is making these

TABLE 8.3 Consolidated Statements of Cash Flows (in US$ millions)

Period Ending January 31	Actuals			Estimates				
	2010A	2011A	2012A	2013E	2014E	2015E	2016E	2017E
Cash flows from operating activities								
Net income	14,883.0	16,993.0	16,387.0	17,192.1	18,030.3	18,665.9	19,066.2	19,215.5
Loss (income) from discontinued operations to net cash	79.0	(1,034.0)	67.0	0.0	0.0	0.0	0.0	0.0
Depreciation and amortization	7,157.0	7,641.0	8,130.0	8,591.7	9,188.6	9,809.4	10,448.9	11,101.1
Deferred income taxes	(504.0)	651.0	1,050.0	715.9	1,003.5	791.0	596.3	411.4
Other operating activities	318.0	1,087.0	398.0	318.0	318.0	318.0	318.0	318.0
Changes in operating working capital								
Changes in accounts receivable	(297.0)	(733.0)	(796.0)	146.5	(289.5)	(243.2)	(189.7)	(130.3)
Changes in inventory	2,213.0	(3,205.0)	(3,727.0)	(148.4)	(2,043.1)	(1,716.2)	(1,338.7)	(919.2)
Changes in prepaid expenses and other	0.0	0.0	0.0	(773.9)	(122.9)	(103.3)	(80.6)	(55.3)
Changes in accounts payable	1,052.0	2,676.0	2,687.0	701.2	1,865.5	1,567.0	1,222.2	839.3
Changes in accrued liabilities	1,348.0	(433.0)	59.0	1,425.7	979.0	822.3	641.4	440.5
Changes in accrued income taxes	0.0	0.0	0.0	(460.7)	34.3	26.0	16.4	6.1
Net changes in operating working capital	4,316.0	(1,695.0)	(1,777.0)	890.4	423.1	352.6	271.2	181.1
Total cash flows from operating activities	26,249.0	23,643.0	24,255.0	27,708.1	28,963.6	29,936.9	30,700.5	31,227.1
Cash flows from investing activities								
Payments for property and equipment (CAPEX)	(12,184.0)	(12,699.0)	(13,510.0)	(14,213.0)	(14,923.7)	(15,520.6)	(15,986.2)	(16,305.9)
CAPEX % of revenue	3.0%	3.0%	3.0%	3.0%	3.0%	3.0%	3.0%	3.0%
Proceeds from disposal of property and equipment	1,002.0	489.0	580.0	0.0	0.0	0.0	0.0	0.0
Investments and business acquisitions, net of cash acquired	0.0	(202.0)	(3,548.0)	0.0	0.0	0.0	0.0	0.0
Other investing activities	(438.0)	219.0	(131.0)	(438.0)	219.0	(131.0)	(438.0)	219.0
Total cash from investing activities	(11,620.0)	(12,193.0)	(16,609.0)	(14,651.0)	(14,704.7)	(15,651.6)	(16,424.2)	(16,086.9)

218

Cash flows from financing activities							
Short-term borrowings (repayments)	(1,033.0)	503.0	3,019.0	0.0	0.0	0.0	0.0	0.0
Long-term borrowings (repayments)	(487.0)	7,316.0	466.0	0.0	0.0	0.0	0.0	0.0
Long-term debt due within one year	0.0	0.0	0.0	0.0	0.0	0.0	0.0	0.0
Capital lease obligations due within one year	0.0	0.0	0.0	0.0	0.0	0.0	0.0	0.0
Dividends paid	(4,217.0)	(4,437.0)	(5,048.0)	(5,344.7)	(5,187.3)	(5,029.9)	(4,872.5)	(4,715.1)
Dividends paid ($/share)			*1.59*	*1.59*	*1.59*	*1.59*	*1.59*	*1.59*
Purchase of common stock [treasury stock]	(7,276.0)	(14,776.0)	(6,298.0)	(7,318.8)	(7,318.8)	(7,318.8)	(7,318.8)	(7,318.8)
Purchase of redeemable noncontrolling interest	(436.0)	0.0	0.0	0.0	0.0	0.0	0.0	0.0
Capital lease obligations	(346.0)	(363.0)	(355.0)	0.0	0.0	0.0	0.0	0.0
Other	(396.0)	(271.0)	(242.0)	0.0	0.0	0.0	0.0	0.0
Total cash from financing activities	(14,191.0)	(12,028.0)	(8,458.0)	(12,663.5)	(12,506.1)	(12,348.7)	(12,191.3)	(12,033.9)
Effect of exchange rate on cash	194.0	66.0	(33.0)	194.0	66.0	(33.0)	194.0	66.0
Total change in cash and cash equivalents	632.0	(512.0)	(845.0)	587.6	1,818.8	1,903.6	2,279.0	3,172.3
SUPPLEMENTAL DATA:								
Cash flow before debt paydown				587.6	1,818.8	1,903.6	2,279.0	3,172.3

TABLE 8.4 Consolidated Statements of Cash Flows—Unlevered and Free

Period Ending January 31	Actuals			Estimates				
	2010A	2011A	2012A	2013E	2014E	2015E	2016E	2017E
Cash flows from operating activities								
Net income	14,883.0	16,993.0	16,387.0	17,192.1	18,030.3	18,665.9	19,066.2	19,215.5
Loss (income) from discontinued operations to net cash	79.0	(1,034.0)	67.0	0.0	0.0	0.0	0.0	0.0
Depreciation and amortization	7,157.0	7,641.0	8,130.0	8,591.7	9,188.6	9,809.4	10,448.9	11,101.1
Deferred income taxes	(504.0)	651.0	1,050.0	715.9	1,003.5	791.0	596.3	411.4
Other operating activities	318.0	1,087.0	398.0	318.0	318.0	318.0	318.0	318.0
Changes in operating working capital								
Changes in accounts receivable	(297.0)	(733.0)	(796.0)	146.5	(289.5)	(243.2)	(189.7)	(130.3)
Changes in inventory	2,213.0	(3,205.0)	(3,727.0)	(148.4)	(2,043.1)	(1,716.2)	(1,338.7)	(919.2)
Changes in prepaid expenses and other	0.0	0.0	0.0	(773.9)	(122.9)	(103.3)	(80.6)	(55.3)
Changes in accounts payable	1,052.0	2,676.0	2,687.0	701.2	1,865.5	1,567.0	1,222.2	839.3
Changes in accrued liabilities	1,348.0	(433.0)	59.0	1,425.7	979.0	822.3	641.4	440.5
Changes in accrued income taxes	0.0	0.0	0.0	(460.7)	34.3	26.0	16.4	6.1
Net changes in operating working capital	4,316.0	(1,695.0)	(1,777.0)	890.4	423.1	352.6	271.2	181.1
Total cash flows from operating activities	26,249.0	23,643.0	24,255.0	27,708.1	28,963.6	29,936.9	30,700.5	31,227.1
Cash flows from investing activities								
Payments for property and equipment (CAPEX)	(12,184.0)	(12,699.0)	(13,510.0)	(14,213.0)	(14,923.7)	(15,520.6)	(15,986.2)	(16,305.9)
CAPEX % of revenue	3.0%	3.0%	3.0%	3.0%	3.0%	3.0%	3.0%	3.0%
Proceeds from disposal of property and equipment	1,002.0	489.0	580.0	0.0	0.0	0.0	0.0	0.0
Investments and business acquisitions, net of cash acquired	0.0	(202.0)	(3,548.0)	0.0	0.0	0.0	0.0	0.0
Other investing activities	(438.0)	219.0	(131.0)	(438.0)	219.0	(131.0)	(438.0)	219.0
Total cash from investing activities	(11,620.0)	(12,193.0)	(16,609.0)	(14,651.0)	(14,704.7)	(15,651.6)	(16,424.2)	(16,086.9)

Cash flows from financing activities

~~Short-term borrowings (repayments)~~	~~(1,033.0)~~	~~503.0~~	~~3,019.0~~	~~0.0~~	~~0.0~~	~~0.0~~	~~0.0~~	~~0.0~~
~~Long-term borrowings (repayments)~~	~~(487.0)~~	~~7,316.0~~	~~466.0~~	~~0.0~~	~~0.0~~	~~0.0~~	~~0.0~~	~~0.0~~
~~Long-term debt due within one year~~	~~0.0~~	~~0.0~~	~~0.0~~	~~0.0~~	~~0.0~~	~~0.0~~	~~0.0~~	~~0.0~~
~~Capital lease obligations due within one year~~	~~(4,217.0)~~	~~(4,437.0)~~	~~(5,048.0)~~	~~0.0~~	~~0.0~~	~~0.0~~	~~0.0~~	~~0.0~~
~~Dividends paid~~	~~(4,217.0)~~	~~(4,437.0)~~	~~(5,048.0)~~	~~(5,344.7)~~	~~(5,187.3)~~	~~(5,029.9)~~	~~(4,872.5)~~	~~(4,715.1)~~
~~Dividends paid ($/share)~~				~~1.59~~	~~1.59~~	~~1.59~~	~~1.59~~	~~1.59~~
~~Purchase of common stock (treasury stock)~~	~~(7,276.0)~~	~~(14,776.0)~~	~~(6,298.0)~~	~~(7,318.8)~~	~~(7,318.8)~~	~~(7,318.8)~~	~~(7,318.8)~~	~~(7,318.8)~~
~~Purchase of redeemable noncontrolling interest~~	~~(436.0)~~	~~0.0~~	~~0.0~~	~~0.0~~	~~0.0~~	~~0.0~~	~~0.0~~	~~0.0~~
~~Capital lease obligations~~	~~(346.0)~~	~~(363.0)~~	~~(355.0)~~	~~0.0~~	~~0.0~~	~~0.0~~	~~0.0~~	~~0.0~~
~~Other~~	~~(396.0)~~	~~(271.0)~~	~~(242.0)~~	~~0.0~~	~~0.0~~	~~0.0~~	~~0.0~~	~~0.0~~
~~Total cash from financing activities~~	~~(14,191.0)~~	~~(12,028.0)~~	~~(8,458.0)~~	~~(12,662.5)~~	~~(12,506.1)~~	~~(12,348.7)~~	~~(12,191.3)~~	~~(12,033.9)~~
~~Effect of exchange rate on cash~~	~~194.0~~	~~66.0~~	~~(33.0)~~	~~194.0~~	~~66.0~~	~~(33.0)~~	~~194.0~~	~~66.0~~
Total change in cash and cash equivalents	632.0	(512.0)	(845.0)	587.6	1,818.8	1,903.6	2,279.0	3,172.3

SUPPLEMENTAL DATA:

Cash flow before debt paydown				587.6	1,818.8	1,903.6	2,279.0	3,172.3

adjustments. We are trying to replicate a form of cash flow, so if the cash flow statement is adding the item, we should also add it; if the cash flow statement is subtracting the item, we should subtract. According to a standard cash flow statement, the flow should be:

Net Income + D&A + Deferred Taxes + Other Noncash Items
+ Working Capital Changes − CAPEX + A/T Net Interest Expense

Yes, it is plus working capital changes, because the cash flow statement adds working capital changes to the net income to get to cash from operations. Many textbooks suggest subtracting working capital, but they are actually referring to subtracting the balance sheet working capital changes. In other words, if accounts receivable increased from $0 to $1, 000, or if the balance sheet change is $1,000, then we know the cash flow change is −$1,000, because an increase in an asset reflects a cash outflow. However, if we take the actual working capital number directly from the cash flow statement, which is already represented as a negative (−$1,000), we just add it.

It is crucial to note that there can be items in the investing activities other than capital expenditures (CAPEX) that could arguably be attributable to everyday operations. Although it's not explicitly defined in the unlevered free cash flow formula, the point of the entire analysis is to get to a number that reflects the cash we expect to be generated from the future operations of the business. Further, in the operating activities, there may be other adjustments that are not categorized within the standard unlevered free cash flow definition. It is important to step back and think about how these line items are affecting net income to decide if they should also be adjusted in the unlevered free cash flow. In other words, if these line items are actually noncash items that need to be adjusted to net income in order to get to a closer measure of cash from net income, then they should be included in the analysis. However, if these are truly nonrecurring events, and if we have already pulled them out of net income on the income statement, adjusting them here may not be correct. This is one example of how important it is to understand fully where unlevered free cash flow is coming from and why it is being used as opposed to just taking and using the formula as printed.

Now, the previous definition is not the most standard definition of unlevered free cash flow. Typically, we use EBIT as a starting point, not net income. It is easier to project an income statement from revenue down to EBIT only, rather than all the way down to net income, especially since we are adding back so many items anyway. However, both ways will get you the same results. So if we had EBIT as a starting point, we still have to make the same core adjustments:

Unlevered Free Cash Flow	Unlevered Free Cash Flow
Net income	EBIT
+ Depreciation and amortization	+ Depreciation and amortization
+ Deferred taxes	+ Deferred taxes
+ Other noncash items	+ Other noncash items
+ Working capital changes	+ Working capital changes
− Capital expenditures	− Capital expenditures
+ A/T net interest expense	
= Total unlevered free cash flow	

Note here we have to double-check once again which line items we are (or are not) including as other noncash items, and for a different reason: If the particular noncash item was a net income adjustment for a line item that was below the EBIT line, which we didn't even include anyway, adjusting it here would be incorrect.

We still have to make one more adjustment: taxes. We do not need to adjust for interest expense, as EBIT is already before interest expense. But EBIT is also before taxes. So in order to adjust for taxes, we need to take EBIT × Tax Rate. It is important to note we do not take the taxes figure from the income statement, as that number includes the effects of interest.

Unlevered Free Cash Flow	Unlevered Free Cash Flow
Net income	EBIT
+ Depreciation and amortization	+ Depreciation and amortization
+ Deferred taxes	+ Deferred taxes
+ Other noncash items	+ Other noncash items
+ Working capital changes	+ Working capital changes
− Capital expenditures	− Capital expenditures
+ A/ T net interest expense	− Taxes (EBIT × Tax %)
= Total unlevered free cash flow	= Total unlevered free cash flow

For ShipCo, we have in Table 8.5 simple unlevered free cash flow projections. We have assumed EBIT will grow at 5 percent per year. We have kept the depreciation and amortization (D&A) expense, CAPEX, and working capital constant each year—this is just for simplification and illustration. We have also assumed a 40 percent tax rate. We will use these cash flows to determine the investor rate of return (IRR) for ShipCo.

It is important to note here the importance of understanding the derivation of unlevered free cash flow. In this ever-changing market environment with new and evolving business models, the standard textbook definition of unlevered free cash flow may need

TABLE 8.5 ShipCo Unlevered Free Cash Flow

	Projected Free Cash Flow					
	2012A	2013E	2014E	2015E	2016E	2017E
EBIT	5,000.0	5,250.0	5,512.5	5,788.1	6,077.5	6,381.4
EBIT growth rate		5.0%	5.0%	5.0%	5.0%	5.0%
D&A	400.0	400.0	400.0	400.0	400.0	400.0
CAPEX	(1,000.0)	(1,000.0)	(1,000.0)	(1,000.0)	(1,000.0)	(1,000.0)
Changes in working capital	(100.0)	(100.0)	(100.0)	(100.0)	(100.0)	(100.0)
Taxes (40%)		(2,100.0)	(2,205.0)	(2,315.3)	(2,431.0)	(2,552.6)
Unlevered free cash flow		2,450.0	2,607.5	2,772.9	2,946.5	3,128.8

to be adjusted to be a true measure of value for a particular entity. Understanding the purpose of unlevered free cash flow as a measure of value will help us to create our own adjustments to get to the true value of an entity.

Step 2: Calculation of Exit Enterprise Value Unlevered free cash flows contain EBIT and EBITDA. So, assuming we have used an EBIT or EBITDA multiple as our exit value method, we can apply that multiple to the exit year metric found in the unlevered free cash flow projections.

Note that this gives us enterprise value. To calculate our return, we need equity value, so we need to remove the effects of debt.

> Looking at Table 8.5 we note the 2017E EBITDA is $6,381.4 + $400.0 (EBIT + D&A). So 5 times $6,781.4 gives us the exit value of $33,907.0.

Step 3: Calculation of Exit Debt Now that we have an exit value, we need to subtract Year 5 net debt to determine that actual value returned to us as investors. In order to calculate exit year debt, we need to take several things into consideration:

- We always begin with the amount of debt raised upon initial acquisition.
- We need to calculate interest incurred each year we own the business.
- Cash generated (unlevered free cash flow) can be used to pay down debt and interest.

So, the beginning value of debt raised upon initial acquisition (beginning debt) plus the interest incurred each year less cash generated is the exit debt, or:

$$\text{Beginning Debt} + \text{Total Interest} - \text{Total Cash} = \text{Exit Debt}$$

Total interest can be calculated by applying an interest rate to the amount of debt raised, multiplied by the number of years we have held the business, and multiplied by (1 − Tax %).

Or:

$$\text{Beginning Debt} \times \text{Interest Rate \%} \times \text{Years} \times (1 - \text{Tax \%})$$

Should the company have more than one type of debt with different interest rates, interest should be calculated for each type of debt, then added together. Note that this is a quick analysis and is not designed to handle the fact that interest expense can be reduced if debt is paid down year after year. We are conservatively assuming the interest expense is held constant. We will see later that the ability to handle a more dynamic debt and interest pay-down schedule is a benefit of a full-scale leveraged buyout analysis.

Total cash is the sum of the unlevered free cash flows for the projected years.

Explanation of Adjusting Interest by (1 − Tax %) We often get questions on why we multiply the interest expense by (1 − Tax %). Interest is tax deductible. We will clarify with this example.

Net income including interest:

Interest × (1 − Tax %)	
EBIT	$5,000
Interest	1,000
EBT	4,000
Tax (40%)	1,600
Net income	2,400

This demonstrates net income of $2,400 and contains the effects of $1,000 in interest. If we remove $1,000 in interest expense, we also need to adjust taxes.

Net income excluding interest:

Interest × (1 − Tax %)	
EBIT	$5,000
Interest	0
EBT	5,000
Tax (40%)	2,000
Net income	3,000

You can see that once the $1,000 interest is removed, the net income has increased from the $2,400 to $3,000. Notice that the increase was $600, not $1,000. This is because although interest expense is removed, taxes associated with that interest expense are also removed.

In other words, once that interest expense is removed, the EBT has in fact increased by $1,000 (from $4,000 to $5,000). Higher EBT means higher taxes. Consequently, the taxes have increased from $1,600 to $2,000. So, the real changes are: (1) an interest expense reduction of $1,000 and (2) tax expense increase of $400, or $1,000 − $400; this is the $600 net effect to net income.

Now the $1,000 is interest less the $400 (interest times the tax rate). So,

$$\text{Interest} - (\text{Interest} \times \text{Tax \%})$$

Using algebra, we can pull out interest so the formula will read:

$$\text{Interest} \times (1 - \text{Tax \%})$$

Step 4: Calculation of IRR   Once we have the exit enterprise value and the exit debt, we simply subtract to get exit equity value. This is the value returned to us as investors. With this value, we can calculate the IRR.

$$\text{IRR} = (\text{Exit Equity Value}/\text{Equity Invested})^{\wedge}(1/\text{Years}) - 1$$

where the equity invested is the value of equity the investors originally invested in the business (found in the sources of cash), and the years is the amount of time that we held the business.

Looking at Table 8.2 (sources of cash), we notice we have raised $8,750.0 of bank debt and $6,250.0 of high yield debt. Let's assume the interest rates are 10 percent for the bank debt and 15 percent for the high yield debt. Note again that we are making oversimplifications to illustrate the LBO process; don't take these assumptions as being realistic.

We now calculate total interest for each. With the formula we can plug in the assumptions to get bank debt and high yield debt, totaling $5,437.5 in interest expense.

To calculate total cash, we just need to add up the cash flows from 2013E to 2017E from Table 8.5: $2,450.0 + $2,607.5 + $2,772.9 + $2,946.5 + $3,128.8 = $13,905.7.

$$\text{Exit Debt} = \text{Beginning Debt} + \text{Total Interest} - \text{Cash}$$

or

$$\$8,750.0 + \$6,250.0 + \$5,437.5 - \$13,905.7 = \$6,531.8$$

So, with an exit enterprise value of $33,907.0 and $6,531.8 of final debt, the exit equity value is $27,375.2 ($33,907.0 − $6,531.8). This is basically the net amount returned to us. We compare this with our initial investment to calculate the IRR. Our original equity investment is $10 million. This is found in the sources of cash (Table 8.2). So to calculate IRR, ($27,375.2/$10,000) ^ (1/5) − 1 = 22.3%.

That's it! This is the simple version of a leveraged buyout IRR analysis.

Although 22.3 percent is not too bad a yearly return, some funds have minimum return requirements, such as 25 percent.

To strengthen your understanding of such an analysis, it is important to highlight some key variables affecting the IRR:

- *Purchase price.* Of course the purchase price plays a major role in determining the IRR. The higher the purchase price, the more costly the investment may be to the investor, and therefore the lower the IRR. A couple of exceptions here: We are assuming that a higher purchase price would mean the investor would have to put more equity into the initial investment. Also, a higher purchase price can be offset by a higher sale value, and if so, the IRR may not be affected.
- *Sources of cash.* The amount of debt that can be raised to make such an investment will also affect the IRR. The more debt we can raise, the less equity we have to put in, and so the higher our expected returns will be.
- *Interest rate.* A lower interest rate would lower our costs, which would increase our cash, which would allow us to pay down debt faster and increase the IRR.
- *Time frame.* Typically, a shorter time frame would produce a higher IRR. But be careful not to get fooled, as this is a compounded percentage. In other words, a 25 percent annual return over five years does not give us as high an overall return as 20 percent annually over 10 years. Take a $1,000 investment, for example:

$$\$1,000 \times (1 + 25\%)^5 = \$3,051.76$$

or
$$\$1,000 \times (1 + 20\%)\char`^10 = \$6,191.74$$

Which would you prefer? Although the first example is showing a higher return of 25 percent, the overall exit value is only half of the second example.

- *Operations performance (EBITDA projections).* The more we can improve EBITDA, the higher our potential sale value, which would increase IRR. Also, a higher EBITDA would improve our cash flow.
- *Cash flow (UFCF projections).* Improved cash flow performance will allow us to pay down debt faster and will improve our IRR.
- *Exit multiple.* The higher our exit multiple (exit value), the higher our return.

These are the major variables that affect an IRR analysis. Although such analyses are used as a quick estimate of investor return, there are several major flaws with such a brief analysis:

- *Lack of income statement.* We have no record of net income, and we may have overlooked some crucial expenses below the EBIT line that could potentially hinder business performance.
- *Lack of complete cash flow statement.* Although unlevered free cash flow as discussed earlier is a good measure of cash, without a complete cash flow statement we may overlook some other crucial cash flow line items that can hinder cash generation.
- *Lack of balance sheet.* Without a balance sheet we really don't know how much debt the business can take on. A complete model will help us better determine debt capacity.
- *Interest expense.* In this example we calculated interest expense by multiplying the interest rate by the amount of debt initially raised. We then multiplied the interest expense by the number of years we owned the business. In doing so, we are assuming the interest expense is held flat each year. However, in reality debt could be paid down each year, thus reducing interest expense. Although keeping the interest expense the same each year can be seen as conservative, the ability to capture interest savings each year by paying down debt is a crucial component to a leveraged buyout analysis.
- *Goodwill/intangible assets.* We have not assumed benefits of amortizing intangible assets related to paying a premium above book value for the business.
- *Synergies.* We did not account for the effects of synergies or cost savings. Although we could have done this in the unlevered free cash flow analysis, it is better to project synergies directly in the income statement.

These are some of the many reasons why a full-scale leveraged buyout analysis provides a more accurate estimation of an effective investor return. However, such a quick analysis is helpful in highlighting the major concepts and drivers to a leveraged buyout analysis. In the book *Leveraged Buyouts* we evaluate a complete analysis as done on Wall Street. However for interview preparation purposes the concepts and the high level LBO analysis discussed herein are key. Let's practice some questions in the next chapter.

CHAPTER 9

Leveraged Buyouts Questions

1) What is a leveraged buyout?

   A leveraged buyout is an acquisition of a company using a significant amount of debt to meet the cost of the acquisition.

2) Name three core components that contribute to the success of a leveraged buyout.

   1. Cash availability, interest, and debt pay-down
   2. Operation (EBITDA) improvements
   3. Multiple expansion

3) Name four exit strategies to a leveraged buyout.

   1. Strategic sale
   2. Sale to another financial sponsor
   3. IPO
   4. Dividend recapitalization

4) What are some characteristics of a company that make a good LBO candidate?

   1. Steady cash flows
   2. Opportunities for earnings growth or cost reductions
   3. A high asset base—collateral to raise more debt

5) What are the three main steps to conducting a leveraged buyout analysis?

   Step 1: Obtaining a purchase price
   Step 2: Estimating sources and uses of funds
   Step 3: Calculating investor rate of return (IRR)

6) What is the purpose of a leveraged buyout analysis?

   A leveraged buyout analysis helps determine the annualized returns (IRRs) of an investor's equity investment in a business after a specific time horizon.

7) Walk me through a leveraged buyout analysis.

   In order to determine the IRR of a particular investment after a certain number of years, one first needs to establish the purchase price of the business. After estimating purchase price, one needs to determine the entire uses of funds (purchase price, net debt, and transaction fees) and the sources used to fund the acquisition (some combination of term loans, high yield debts, mezzanine, and equity). One can then construct a simple unlevered free cash flow analysis that will provide a projected EBITDA for estimating an exit and total cash produced for paying down debt. The projected EBITDA is multiplied by a multiple to get an estimated exit value. Often the purchase multiple is used as an estimated exit multiple. In order to establish return, one needs to calculate the final debt. The original debt raised to fund the acquisition plus the total interest incurred is calculated. One can estimate total interest by taking each annual interest expense multiplied by the number of years and multiplied by 1 – tax%. The sum of the original debt raised and the total interest expense less the sum of the unlevered free cash flow is the final debt balance. The return is the exit value (from the EBITDA times the multiple) less this final debt number. One can then compare the return with the equity originally invested in the business to calculate the IRR.

8) What are some major differences between a basic LBO analysis and full-scale LBO model?

There are many differences between a basic and full-scale LBO model. One major difference is that simple analysis would just contain a simple cash flow build-up, whereas a full-scale model would contain complete projections. This would include the income statement, cash flow statement, balance sheet, as well as the supporting schedules. A full-scale analysis would also include balance sheet adjustments—a more detailed look at the balance sheet post-transaction adjustments. Another major difference to highlight is the simple analysis estimates interest in one year and multiplies by the number of transaction years to estimate total interest obligations. In reality, if a company is paying down debt each year, the interest expense should also be reducing. Because a full-scale model contains a debt schedule, it will more properly associate declining interest in line with debt paydown.

9) What are some common types of debts raised in a leveraged buyout?

Although there is a vast range of possible securities utilized in funding a particular LBO transaction, they can come in several major categories: bank debt, high yield debt, and mezzanine debt. Bank debt, or a term loan, is the most fundamental type of debt. It usually carries 5 percent to 12 percent interest and can be backed by the core assets of the business. Such debt can be a revolving line of credit, a term loan, and other subordinated loans or notes.

High yield debt is a more aggressive type of debt borrowed at much higher interest rates to compensate for additional risk of defaulting on such debts. Interest in such debt can be upwards of 15 percent, but it varies depending on the situation at hand.

Mezzanine (or convertible) lending is a hybrid between debt and equity. The general concept of a mezzanine security is that it is initially considered debt that will convert to equity after a certain amount of time or after certain hurdles are met.

10) What are the most common variables in an LBO analysis?

a. *Purchase price.* The higher the purchase price, the more costly the investment may be to the investor, and therefore the lower the IRR.

b. *Sources of cash.* The amount of debt that can be raised to make such an investment will also affect the IRR. The more debt we can raise, the less equity we have to put in, and so the higher our expected returns will be.

c. *Interest rate.* A lower interest rate would lower our costs, which would increase our cash, which would allow us to pay down debt faster and increase the IRR.

d. *Time frame.* Typically, a shorter time frame would produce a higher IRR.

e. *Operations performance (EBITDA projections).* The more we can improve EBITDA, the higher our potential sale value, which would increase IRR. Also, a higher EBITDA would improve our cash flow.

f. *Cash flow (UFCF projections).* Improved cash flow performance will allow us to pay down debt faster and will improve our IRR.

g. *Exit multiple.* The higher our exit multiple (exit value), the higher our return.

11) Name four sources of funds in a leveraged buyout from least to most risky.

1. Bank debt (term loan, notes)
2. High-yield debt
3. Mezzanine funding (convertible securities)
4. Equity

12) Name the three methods of acquiring a business.

1. Asset acquisition
2. Stock acquisition
3. 338(h)10 election

13) Name the core uses of funds categories.

1. Purchase price
2. Net debt
3. Transaction fees

14) What is one way to conservatively estimate an exit multiple?

Often, one can conservatively assume the purchase multiple will be the exit multiple.

15) Name one way to calculate IRR.

IRR can be calculated as: (Exit Equity Value/Equity Invested) $\wedge$ (1/Years) $-$ 1

16) What are the major variables to an LBO analysis? Name at least four.

1. Purchase price
2. Sources of cash
3. Interest rate
4. Time frame
5. Operations performance (EBITDA projections)
6. Cash flow (UFCF projections)
7. Exit multiple

17) What are some advantages of LBO financing?

a. The more debt used to make the purchase, the less equity needed, which can maximize potential returns.
b. Interest payments on debt are tax deductible.

18) What is the advantage to using leverage when making an acquisition?

The more leverage used to fund an acquisition, the less equity needed. Less equity invested will maximize your return.

19) How can one determine the amount of debt raised?

One can use debt multiples as comparable metrics to other similar leveraged buyouts.

20) Would you rather have an extra dollar of debt paydown or an extra dollar of EBITDA?

You would rather have the extra dollar of EBITDA because of the multiple. At exit, the sale price is dependent on the EBITDA times the exit multiple. So, an extra dollar of debt paydown increases your equity value by only one dollar; an extra dollar of EBITDA is multiplied by the exit multiple.

21) Name several strategies to maximize returns in an LBO.

1. Minimize equity invested (this can be done by increasing the debt used).
2. Reduce the purchase price.
3. Increase the sale price (exit).
4. Increase EBITDA (cutting costs or boosting revenue).
5. Maximize cash flow.

22) What is a dividend recapitalization?

In a dividend recap, the company re-levers (raises debt on) the balance sheet. The new money raised is often paid out as a dividend.

23) What is the advantage of performing a dividend recap?

A dividend recap could have several advantages in maximizing returns. One common advantage is to extend the holding period of the company while still raising cash to expend for the fund's needs. If the market environment is not the best for target company exit, a dividend recap would allow the fund more time to look for the right exit opportunity.

24) What cost of equity discount rate would you use to value a target company in a leveraged buyout using a discounted cash flow analysis?

You would often use a rate that reflects the expected equity return of the fund. If the fund is expecting a 25% return, this could be the rate to use.

25) What is a PIK security?

A PIK security is a paid-in-kind security. The periodic interest obligations are satisfied "in kind," meaning in something other than currency. Typically, when the interest obligation comes due, more debt is raised to meet that obligation. This results in interest-on-interest, which can get costly. On the other hand, it reserves cash for other beneficial uses.

26) What is the purpose of a seller note in a leveraged buyout?

A seller note is a loan to the purchased business from the seller. If a certain purchase price is negotiated in an acquisition, a certain amount is of course paid immediately, and the rest can be deferred as a seller note payable in certain terms. This can be used to prevent the seller from starting a competing business or can incentivize the seller to continue to support the business.

PRACTICE QUESTIONS

Use the space available to answer the following examples. The answers are at the end of the chapter.

27) We have evaluated and would like to acquire a public company. The company is trading at $12 per share and has a total of 150 million diluted shares outstanding. We have negotiated a 25 percent purchase premium. The company has an LTM EBITDA of $50 million, $100 million of net debt outstanding. We will also assume $5 million of transaction fees. The net debt cannot carry over. What are the total uses of funds?

28) We have evaluated and would like to acquire a private business, so we look to public comparable companies (if they exist) to assess a proper value. We assume the comparable company analysis results in a range of 4.0× to 6.0× EBITDA. The company has an LTM EBITDA of $15 million and $7MM of net debt outstanding. If we assume $1 million of transaction fees and a 5.0× EBITDA purchase price, what are the total uses of funds?

29) You would like to invest in a company that has an LTM EBITDA of $25 million. The entry multiple is 8×; leverage is 5×. At time of exit, you have generated cash flow after interest payments of $100 million, which will go toward debt paydown. You generate a 4× return, but 25 percent of the business is given to management. At what price must you sell the business?

30) Which is the better investment opportunity based on this information? Assume everything about the companies is the same except for what is given in the information, and assume the exit multiple is the same as the entrance multiple.

Company A:

    EBITDA: $100 million
    Projected annual revenue growth: 5 percent for the next five years
    Purchase price: 6× EBITDA/5× Debt

Company B:

    EBITDA: $100 million
    Projected annual revenue growth: 10 percent for the next five years
    Purchase price: 7× EBITDA/5× Debt

31) A company has $250MM of EBITDA. It grows to $400MM in five years. Each year you paid down $50MM of debt. Let's say you bought the company for 8.0× and sold it for 9.0×. How much equity value did you create? How much is attributed to each strategy of creating equity value?

PRACTICE CASES

These next few examples are designed to be 45-minute cases and answered on paper. I have provided blank pages to work out answers on your own. The solutions are provided at the end of the chapter.

32) You are an analyst at a private equity firm. You have been tasked with analyzing a leveraged buyout opportunity of a retail company. Does this look like a good investment for the fund?

Key Assumptions:

The fund expects to hold the company for five years.

Comparable analysis puts the company value at 5× EBITDA.

We have been able to negotiate a Term A loan at 3.0× LTM EBITDA (5 percent interest rate).

We have also been able to negotiate a high-yield loan for 0.5× LTM EBITDA at a 10 percent interest rate.

Assume no transaction fees.

Company Assumptions:

The company has an LTM EBITDA of $5 million.

Management expects the company to grow at 5 percent per year.

The company has a $20 million asset that will be evenly depreciated over 20 years.

The company's working capital is steadily increasing at $100k per year (resulting in a $100k cash flow decrease).

The company will maintain CAPEX spend at $1MM per year and will be depreciated over 20 years.

The tax rate is 40 percent.

33) What is the IRR of the following leveraged buyout investment?

Key Assumptions:

The fund expects to hold the company for five years.

Comparable analysis puts the company value at 4× EBITDA.

We have been able to negotiate a Term A loan at 2.5× LTM EBITDA (10% interest rate).

We have also been able to negotiate a Term B loan at 15% of the total uses of funds (12% interest rate).

Assume transaction fees to be 1% of the purchase price enterprise value.

Company Assumptions:

The company has an LTM EBITDA of $7 million.

The company has 100k of existing net debt on its balance sheet.

Management expects the EBITDA to grow at 10 percent per year.

The company has a $20 million asset that will be evenly depreciated over 20 years.

The company will maintain CAPEX spend at $1.25MM per year, and it will be depreciated over 20 years.

Assume the company's working capital is projected at 30 days on EBITDA.

The tax rate is 40 percent.

34) You are an analyst at a private equity firm. You have been tasked with analyzing the following leveraged buyout opportunity. What is the expected IRR?

Key Assumptions:

The fund expects to hold the company for five years.

Comparable analysis puts the company value at 5× EBITDA.

We have been able to negotiate a Term A loan at 3.5× LTM EBITDA (10 percent interest rate).

We have also been able to negotiate a high-yield loan for 0.5× LTM EBITDA at a 15 percent interest rate.

Transaction fees are assumed to be 0.5% of the purchase price.

Company Assumptions:

The company has an LTM EBITDA of $10 million.

Management expects the company's EBITDA to grow at 5 percent per year.

The company has 250k of net debt on its balance sheet.

The company has a $40 million asset that will be evenly depreciated over 10 years.

The company will maintain CAPEX spend at $1.1MM per year and will be depreciated over 10 years.

The company's working capital is projected at 15 days off of EBITDA.

The tax rate is 40 percent.

35) An investor is looking into buying out the following business. What is the expected IRR given the following scenario?

Key Assumptions:

The fund expects to hold the company for five years.

Comparable analysis puts the company value at 6× EBITDA.

The investor has been able to negotiate a Term A loan at 25% of the total uses (10 percent interest rate).

He has also been able to negotiate a Term B loan at 2× EBITDA (12 percent interest rate) and a high-yield loan for 1× LTM EBITDA at a 15 percent interest rate.

Transaction fees are assumed to be 1% of the purchase price.

Company Assumptions:

The company has revenue of $10 million.

Management expects the company's revenue to grow at 2 percent per year.

The company is projecting total operating expenses at 30% of revenue each year.

The company has a $50 million asset that will be evenly depreciated over 20 years.

The company will maintain CAPEX spend at $1MM per year, and it will be depreciated over 10 years.

The company's working capital consists of accounts receivable (projected at 30 days) and accrued expenses (projected at 10 days).

The tax rate is 40 percent.

36) You are an associate assigned to assessing the potential IRR of the following company. Please calculate the IRR.

Key Assumptions:

The fund expects to hold the company for five years.

Comparable analysis puts the company value at 7× EBITDA.

The investor has been able to negotiate a Term A loan at 3.5× EBITDA (10 percent interest rate).

He has also been able to negotiate a Term B loan at 1.5× EBITDA (12 percent interest rate) and a high-yield loan for 0.5× EBITDA at a 15 percent interest rate.

Transaction fees are assumed to be 2% of the purchase price.

Company Assumptions:

The company has revenue of $12 million.

Management expects the company's revenue to grow at 7 percent per year.

The company is projecting total operating expenses at 25% of revenue each year.

The company has a $50 million asset that will be evenly depreciated over 20 years.

The company will maintain CAPEX spend at $0.5MM per year and that will be depreciated over 20 years.

The company's working capital consists of accounts receivable (projected at 35 days) and accrued expenses (projected at 15 days).

The tax rate is 40 percent.

ANSWERS

27) $2,355 million: The purchase price is $12 × (1 + 25%) × 150MM = $2,250MM. Because this is a public company, we need to be responsible for the net debt. It is stated that the net debt cannot carry over to the acquirer (us), so we need to pay it down. So, we add the additional $100 in net debt plus the $5 million in transaction fees to get to a purchase price of $2,355 million.

28) $76MM: The purchase price is 5.0 × $15MM, or $75MM). Since this is based on an EBITDA multiple, this already includes the value of the net debt, so we do not add the $7 million of debt to this. We do, however, add $1 million in transaction fees to get to total uses of $76 million.

29) To make a 4× return based on the financial parameters, you must sell the business at $425 million. Let's start with calculating the purchase price, which is $25 million × 8× EBITDA, or $200 million. We know 5× EBITDA (leverage) is debt raised to fund the acquisition, so 5 × $25 is $125 million in debt raised. So of the $200 million purchase price, $125 million is funded with debt, which means $75 million (or $200 million – $125 million) is funded with equity. So, if you want a 4× return on equity you need to make 4 × $75, or $300 million. However, the question is what you need to sell the company for. After selling the company you still need to pay down the remaining debt and give 25 percent of the business value to management. So, we back-calculate: $300/(1 – 25%) is $400 million. We then have to increase this value further by the exit net debt, which is $25 million (the $125 million raised less the $100 million cash generated after making interest payments). So the sale price should be $425 million. To look at this another way, if we sell the company for $425 million, we need to pay down the net debt, which is $25 million. This gets us to $400 million. Then, 25 percent goes to management, or $100 million. This leaves us with $300 million—a 4× return on our original investment of $75 million.

30) The answer is Company B. Hint: If you do not have access to a calculator to compound the interest, you can ignore compounding. You will still be able to get an understanding of what the potential investment opportunity is. So, assuming constant EBITDA margins, EBITDA for Company A in Year 5 will be about $125 million = $100 million * [1 + (5% * 5)], and Company B will be $150 million = $100 million * [1 + (10% * 5)]. If the purchase price was 6× EBITDA for Company A, and 5× of that was leverage, then 1× EBITDA was the equity invested. So $100 million (1 × $100 million) was the equity invested in Company A, and $125 million (1 × $125 million) was the expected equity returned in Company A. The equity investment in Company B is 2× EBITDA. So, $200 million (2 × $200 million) was the equity invested in Company B, and $300 million (2 × $150 million) was the expected equity returned in Company B. So the expected return in Company A is 125/100 or 1.25× versus 300/200 or 1.50×. Notice the question specifically states to assume everything is the same, which includes the debt and equity structure at purchase and at exit. We also did not factor in debt paydown. But given that Company B is producing more EBITDA, and presumably more cash flow, adding debt paydown into the analysis would make Company B look even better. So either way Company B is the better investment opportunity.

31) Remember, the three ways value is created are (1) EBITDA growth, (2) debt paydown, and (3) multiple expansion. The purchase price is $2,000MM ($250MM * 8.0×). The exit value is $3,600MM ($400MM × 9.0×). This is a profit of $1,600 MM, plus you paid down debt of $250MM ($50 × 5), so your total equity value increased by $1,850MM ($1,600MM + $250MM). $250MM of the total equity value is of course due to debt paydown. The EBITDA growth value is determined by assuming an 8.0× exit (no multiple expansion). So, 8.0 × $400MM ($3,200MM) less the $2,000MM is the value increase based on EBITDA growth, or $1,200MM. The remaining is based on multiple expansion. So (9.0× − 8.0×) × $400MM is the value based on the multiple expansion. $250 + $1,200 + $400 = $1,850MM.

32) Answer:
I will go through this one step by step. Remember the first important task is to calculate the purchase price. A 5MM EBITDA at a 5× multiple gives us a $25MM purchase price. Next, we need to calculate sources and uses of funds. The uses are made up of the purchase price, target net debt, and transaction fees. No fees were assumed, so we can leave that at $0. There was also no mention of target net debt, but it's important to remember that even if the company did have target net debt, it is assumed in the purchase price, as the purchase price of $25MM is effectively an enterprise value. So the total uses of funds are simply $25MM. Now the sources are made up of debt and some equity investment. It is mentioned there will be a Term A loan raised at 3× EBITDA, or $15MM (3 × $5MM). And there will also be a high yield loan at 0.5× EBITDA, or $2.5M. Since there are no more debt assumptions, we assume the remainder is equity, or $25MM − $15MM − $2.5MM = $7.5MM.

Uses		Sources	
Purchase Price	$25,000,000	Term A	$15,000,000
Net Debt	$0	High Yield	$2,500,000
Transaction Fees	$0	Equity	$7,500,000
Total Uses	**$25,000,000**	**Total Sources**	**$25,000,000**

Now that we have the purchase price, sources, and uses of funds, we can proceed to the transaction at hand. The two key items needed are exit value (based on final year EBITDA) and the final debt determined to calculate our return. Both of these items depend on a simple cash flow analysis. So we first have to build an unlevered free cash flow for the estimated five years. Starting with the given EBITDA of 5MM at Year 0, we can use the 5% EBITDA growth assumption to project out five years.

Unlevered Free Cash Flow	Year 0	Year 1	Year 2	Year 3	Year 4	Year 5
EBITDA	5,000,000	5,250,000	5,512,500	5,788,125	6,077,531	6,381,408
D&A						
EBIT						
Deferred Tax						
WC						
CAPEX						
Taxes						
Total UFCF						

We now need to fill out the rest of this UFCF table starting with D&A. As with any standard D&A table, we have PP&E and CAPEX to depreciate. The assumptions suggest 20MM in PP&E and 1MM in CAPEX, both with depreciation on a straight-line basis over 20 years.

Depreciation St Line	Year 1	Year 2	Year 3	Year 4	Year 5
PP&E	$20,000,000				
CAPEX	$1,000,000	$1,000,000	$1,000,000	$1,000,000	$1,000,000
Years	20	20	20	20	20
Year 0	$1,000,000	$1,000,000	$1,000,000	$1,000,000	$1,000,000
Year 1	$50,000	$50,000	$50,000	$50,000	$50,000
Year 2		$50,000	$50,000	$50,000	$50,000
Year 3			$50,000	$50,000	$50,000
Year 4				$50,000	$50,000
Year 5					$50,000
Total	$1,050,000	$1,100,000	$1,150,000	$1,200,000	$1,250,000

Notice we didn't bother with Year 0. We only need to know the cash flow from Years 1 to 5, as these are the years the business was actually held by the fund. We can now plug the depreciation into the UFCF and subtract to get EBIT. We need EBIT in order to calculate taxes. Remember, in an UFCF, taxes are EBIT × tax%.

Unlevered Free Cash Flow	Year 0	Year 1	Year 2	Year 3	Year 4	Year 5
EBITDA	5,000,000	5,250,000	5,512,500	5,788,125	6,077,531	6,381,408
D&A		1,050,000	1,100,000	1,150,000	1,200,000	1,250,000
EBIT		4,200,000	4,412,500	4,638,125	4,877,531	5,131,408
Deferred Tax						
WC						
CAPEX		(1,000,000)	(1,000,000)	(1,000,000)	(1,000,000)	(1,000,000)
Taxes		(1,680,000)	(1,765,000)	(1,855,250)	(1,951,013)	(2,052,563)
Total UFCF						

There were no assumptions for deferred taxes. The example also mentions working capital is increasing at 100k per year. So a working capital increase results in a cash outflow. This completes our UFCF analysis.

Unlevered Free Cash Flow	Year 0	Year 1	Year 2	Year 3	Year 4	Year 5
EBITDA	5,000,000	5,250,000	5,512,500	5,788,125	6,077,531	6,381,408
D&A		1,050,000	1,100,000	1,150,000	1,200,000	1,250,000
EBIT		4,200,000	4,412,500	4,638,125	4,877,531	5,131,408
Deferred Tax		0	0	0	0	0
WC		(100,000)	(100,000)	(100,000)	(100,000)	(100,000)
CAPEX		(1,000,000)	(1,000,000)	(1,000,000)	(1,000,000)	(1,000,000)
Taxes		(1,680,000)	(1,765,000)	(1,855,250)	(1,951,013)	(2,052,563)
Total UFCF		2,470,000	2,647,500	2,832,875	3,026,519	3,228,845

Now that we have UFCF, we can proceed with calculating our exit. Assuming no multiple expansion, we can apply the 5× purchase multiple to the Year 5 projected EBITDA to get our exit value, giving us $31,907,039 (5 × $6,381,308). This is our exit value but it's not the money the investor receives as a return. We need to figure out how much debt is left at Year 5 and subtract from the exit value to get our return. To calculate final debt, we take the debt raised to fund the acquisition and add in five years of after-tax interest. We then use all the cash generated during the five years to pay down as much debt and interest as possible. So based on our sources, we've raised 15MM in Term A loans and 2.5MM in high yield. We need to calculate the interest on each and multiply by 1 – tax% and the number of years to get the total interest incurred. So for Term A:

$$15,000,000 \times 5\% \times (1 - 40\%) \times 5 \text{ Years} = 2,250,000$$

And for the high yield:

$$2,500,000 \times 10\% \times (1 - 40\%) \times 5 \text{ Years} = 750,000$$

So there's a total of 3,000,000 in interest incurred (2,250,000 + 750,000).

We can add the total interest to the debt raised to get total obligations 15,000,000 + 2,500,000 + 3,000,000 = 20,500,000.

We can now add up the five years of cash calculated in the UFCF analysis, giving us $14,205,738. This cash will be used to pay down all obligations.

So, $20,500,000 – $14,205,738 = $6,294,262. This is the final debt. So, subtracting the final debt from the exit gives us our return:

$$\$31,907,039 - \$6,294,262 = \$25,612,777$$

We can now calculate our IRR:

$$(\$25,612,777 / \$7,500,000) \hat{} (1/5) - 1 = 27.84\%$$

33) Answer:

The purchase price should be straightforward at $28,000,000 (4 × $7,000,000). Now for the sources and uses. Remember, although the example suggests 100k target company net debt, we do *not* add this net debt to the uses of cash. As the purchase price is an enterprise value, it already included the assumption of net debt. We do, however, need to take 1% of the purchase price for transaction fees.

Uses	
PP	$28,000,000
Debt	0
Fees	$280,000
Total	**$28,280,000**

Notice the Term B loan in the sources is estimated at 15% of the total uses of funds. The remainder is Equity (Total Uses less Term A less Term B).

Sources	
Term A	$17,500,000
Term B	$4,242,000
Equity	$6,538,000
Total	$28,280,000

Next we can start to lay out the unlevered free cash flow. Most components are straightforward.

Unlevered Free Cash Flow	Year 0	Year 1	Year 2	Year 3	Year 4	Year 5
EBITDA	7,000,000	7,700,000	8,470,000	9,317,000	10,248,700	11,273,570
D&A		1,062,500	1,125,000	1,187,500	1,250,000	1,312,500
EBIT		6,637,500	7,345,000	8,129,500	8,998,700	9,961,070
Deferred Tax		0	0	0	0	0
Working Capital						
CAPEX		(1,250,000)	(1,250,000)	(1,250,000)	(1,250,000)	(1,250,000)
Taxes		(2,655,000)	(2,938,000)	(3,251,800)	(3,599,480)	(3,984,428)
Total UFCF						

The example suggests to estimate total working capital at 30 days on EBITDA. So we can use the working capital formula (30/360 × EBITDA) to make our annual working capital estimates. We then need to calculate the year-over-year changes for our cash flow.

Working Capital	Year 0	Year 1	Year 2	Year 3	Year 4	Year 5
EBITDA	7,000,000	7,700,000	8,470,000	9,317,000	10,248,700	11,273,570
Days	*30*	*30*	*30*	*30*	*30*	*30*
Total Working Capital	583,333	641,667	705,833	776,417	854,058	939,464
Changes in Working Capital		(58,333)	(64,167)	(70,583)	(77,642)	(85,406)

We can now use these changes in our UCFC and calculate the total.

Unlevered Free Cash Flow	Year 0	Year 1	Year 2	Year 3	Year 4	Year 5
EBITDA	7,000,000	7,700,000	8,470,000	9,317,000	10,248,700	11,273,570
D&A		1,062,500	1,125,000	1,187,500	1,250,000	1,312,500
EBIT		6,637,500	7,345,000	8,129,500	8,998,700	9,961,070
Deferred Tax		0	0	0	0	0
Working Capital		(58,333)	(64,167)	(70,583)	(77,642)	(85,406)
CAPEX		(1,250,000)	(1,250,000)	(1,250,000)	(1,250,000)	(1,250,000)
Taxes		(2,655,000)	(2,938,000)	(3,251,800)	(3,599,480)	(3,984,428)
Total UFCF		3,736,667	4,217,833	4,744,617	5,321,578	5,953,736

With this information we can calculate our exit and return. Final EBITDA times 4 gives us an exit of $45,094,280. Applying interest to the Term A and B loans multiplied by 5 years and then multiplied by (1 − tax%) give us:

$$\text{Term A} = \$17,500,000 \times 10\% \times 5 \times (1 - 40\%) = \$5,250,000$$

$$\text{Term B} = \$4,242,000 \times 12\% \times 5 \times (1 - 40\%) = \$1,527,120$$

Total obligations are $28,519,120 ($17,500,000 + $4,242,000 + $5,250,000 + $1,527,120).

The total cash generated is $23,974,431. Reducing the obligations with cash leaves us with $4,544,689 in final debt.

So the return is the exit less final debt, or $40,549,591. Applying the IRR formula (($40,549,591/$6,538,000) ^ (1/5) −1) gives a return of 44.05%.

34) Answer:
The purchase price, sources, and uses should be straightforward.

Uses		Sources	
PP	$50,000,000	Term A	$35,000,000
Debt	$0	Term B	$5,000,000
Fees	$250,000	Equity	$10,250,000
Total	$50,250,000	Total	$50,250,000

Next we can start to lay out the unlevered free cash flow. Most components are straightforward.

Unlevered Free Cash Flow	Year 0	Year 1	Year 2	Year 3	Year 4	Year 5
EBITDA	10,000,000	10,500,000	11,025,000	11,576,250	12,155,063	12,762,816
D&A		4,110,000	4,220,000	4,330,000	4,440,000	4,550,000
EBIT		6,390,000	6,805,000	7,246,250	7,715,063	8,212,816
Deferred Tax		0	0	0	0	0
Working Capital						
CAPEX		(1,100,000)	(1,100,000)	(1,100,000)	(1,100,000)	(1,100,000)
Taxes		(2,556,000)	(2,722,000)	(2,898,500)	(3,086,025)	(3,285,126)
Total UFCF						

The example suggests to estimate total working capital at 15 days on EBITDA. So we can use the working capital formula (30/360 × EBITDA) to make our annual working capital estimates. We then need to calculate the year-over-year changes for our cash flow.

Working Capital	Year 0	Year 1	Year 2	Year 3	Year 4	Year 5
EBITDA	10,000,000	10,500,000	11,025,000	11,576,250	12,155,063	12,762,816
Days	*15*	*15*	*15*	*15*	*15*	*15*
Total Working Capital	416,667	437,500	459,375	482,344	506,461	531,784
Changes in Working Capital		(20,833)	(21,875)	(22,969)	(24,117)	(25,323)

We can now use these changes in our UCFC and calculate the total.

Unlevered Free Cash Flow	Year 0	Year 1	Year 2	Year 3	Year 4	Year 5
EBITDA	10,000,000	10,500,000	11,025,000	11,576,250	12,155,063	12,762,816
D&A		4,110,000	4,220,000	4,330,000	4,440,000	4,550,000
EBIT		6,390,000	6,805,000	7,246,250	7,715,063	8,212,816
Deferred Tax		0	0	0	0	0
Working Capital		(20,833)	(21,875)	(22,969)	(24,117)	(25,323)
CAPEX		(1,100,000)	(1,100,000)	(1,100,000)	(1,100,000)	(1,100,000)
Taxes		(2,556,000)	(2,722,000)	(2,898,500)	(3,086,025)	(3,285,126)
Total UFCF		6,823,167	7,181,125	7,554,781	7,944,920	8,352,366

With this information we can calculate our exit and return. Final EBITDA times 5 gives us an exit of $63,814,078. Applying interest to the Term A and B loans multiplied by 5 years and then multiplied by (1 − tax%) give us:

$$\text{Term A} = \$35,000,000 \times 10\% \times 5 \times (1 - 40\%) = \$10,500,000$$

$$\text{Term B} = \$5,000,000 \times 15\% \times 5 \times (1 - 40\%) = \$2,250,000$$

Total obligations are $52,750,000 ($10,500,000 + $2,250,000 + $35,000,000 + $5,000,000).

The total cash generated is $37,856,360. Reducing the obligations with cash leaves us with $14,893,640 in final debt.

So the return is the exit less final debt, or $48,920,438. Applying the IRR formula (($48,920,438/$10,250,000) ^ (1/5) − 1) gives a return of 36.7%.

35) Answer:

The purchase price is based on EBITDA, which needs to be calculated from revenue and costs. Costs are projected at 30% of the $10MM revenue, so EBITDA is $7MM ($10MM − $3MM). This gives us a $42MM purchase price ($7MM × 6). From here, sources and uses should be straightforward. Note the Term A loan assumption at 25% of the total uses.

Uses		Sources	
Purchase Price	$42,000,000	Term A	$10,605,000
Debt	0	Term B	$14,000,000
Fees	$420,000	High Yield	$7,000,000
Total	$42,420,000	Equity	$10,815,000
		Total	$42,420,000

Next we can start to lay out the unlevered free cash flow.

Unlevered Free Cash Flow	Year 0	Year 1	Year 2	Year 3	Year 4	Year 5
Revenue	10,000,000	10,200,000	10,404,000	10,612,080	10,824,322	11,040,808
Operating Expenses	3,000,000	3,060,000	3,121,200	3,183,624	3,247,296	3,312,242
EBITDA	7,000,000	7,140,000	7,282,800	7,428,456	7,577,025	7,728,566
D&A		2,600,000	2,700,000	2,800,000	2,900,000	3,000,000
EBIT		4,540,000	4,582,800	4,628,456	4,677,025	4,728,566
Deferred Tax		0	0	0	0	0
Working Capital						
CAPEX		(1,000,000)	(1,000,000)	(1,000,000)	(1,000,000)	(1,000,000)
Taxes		(1,816,000)	(1,833,120)	(1,851,382)	(1,870,810)	(1,891,426)
Total UFCF						

For working capital, the example provides guidance on accounts receivable and accrued expenses. These items should be based on revenue and operating expenses, respectively. So we can use the working capital formula, 30/360 × revenue, to make our annual accounts receivable estimates, and the formula, 10/360 × expenses, for the accrued expenses estimates. We then need to subtract assets less liabilities and calculate the year-over-year changes for our cash flow.

Working Capital	Year 0	Year 1	Year 2	Year 3	Year 4	Year 5
Accounts Receivable	833,333	850,000	867,000	884,340	902,027	920,067
Days	*30*	*30*	*30*	*30*	*30*	*30*
Accrued Expenses	83,333	85,000	86,700	88,434	90,203	92,007
Days	*10*	*10*	*10*	*10*	*10*	*10*
Total Working Capital	750,000	765,000	780,300	795,906	811,824	828,061
Changes in Working Capital		(15,000)	(15,300)	(15,606)	(15,918)	(16,236)

We can now use these changes in our UCFC and calculate the total.

Unlevered Free Cash Flow	Year 0	Year 1	Year 2	Year 3	Year 4	Year 5
Revenue	10,000,000	10,200,000	10,404,000	10,612,080	10,824,322	11,040,808
Operating Expenses	3,000,000	3,060,000	3,121,200	3,183,624	3,247,296	3,312,242
EBITDA	7,000,000	7,140,000	7,282,800	7,428,456	7,577,025	7,728,566
D&A		2,600,000	2,700,000	2,800,000	2,900,000	3,000,000
EBIT		4,540,000	4,582,800	4,628,456	4,677,025	4,728,566
Deferred Tax		0	0	0	0	0
Working Capital		(15,000)	(15,300)	(15,606)	(15,918)	(16,236)
CAPEX		(1,000,000)	(1,000,000)	(1,000,000)	(1,000,000)	(1,000,000)
Taxes		(1,816,000)	(1,833,120)	(1,851,382)	(1,870,810)	(1,891,426)
Total UFCF		4,309,000	4,434,380	4,561,468	4,690,297	4,820,903

With this information we can calculate our exit and return. Final EBITDA times 6 gives us an exit of $46,371,394. Applying interest to the loans multiplied by 5 years and then multiplied by $(1 - \text{tax}\%)$ gives us:

$$\text{Term A} = \$10,605,000 \times 10\% \times 5 \times (1 - 40\%) = \$3,181,500$$

$$\text{Term B} = \$14,000,000 \times 12\% \times 5 \times (1 - 40\%) = \$5,040,000$$

$$\text{High Yield} = \$7,000,000 \times 15\% \times 5 \times (1 - 40\%) = \$3,150,000$$

Total obligations are $42,976,500 ($10,605,000 + $14,000,000 + $7,000,000 + $3,181,500 + $5,040,000 + $3,150,000).

The total cash generated is $22,816,047. Reducing the obligations with cash leaves us with $20,160,453 in final debt.

So the return is the exit less final debt, or $26,210,941. Applying the IRR formula $((\$26,210,941/\$10,815,000) \wedge (1/5) - 1)$ gives a return of 19.4%.

36) Answer:
The purchase price is based on EBITDA, which needs to be calculated from revenue and costs. Costs are projected at 25% of the $12MM revenue, so EBITDA is $9MM ($12MM – $3MM). This gives us a $63MM purchase price ($9MM × 7). From here, sources and uses should be straightforward.

Uses		Sources	
PP	$63,000,000	Term A	$31,500,000
Debt	0	Term B	$13,500,000
Fees	$1,260,000	HY	$4,500,000
Total	$64,260,000	Equity	$14,760,000
		Total	$64,260,000

Next we can start to layout the unlevered free cash flow.

Unlevered Free Cash Flow	Year 0	Year 1	Year 2	Year 3	Year 4	Year 5
Revenue	12,000,000	12,840,000	13,738,800	14,700,516	15,729,552	16,830,621
Operating Expenses	3,000,000	3,210,000	3,434,700	3,675,129	3,932,388	4,207,655
EBITDA	9,000,000	9,630,000	10,304,100	11,025,387	11,797,164	12,622,966
D&A		2,525,000	2,550,000	2,575,000	2,600,000	2,625,000
EBIT		7,105,000	7,754,100	8,450,387	9,197,164	9,997,966
Deferred Tax		0	0	0	0	0
Working Capital						
CAPEX		(500,000)	(500,000)	(500,000)	(500,000)	(500,000)
Taxes		(2,842,000)	(3,101,640)	(3,380,155)	(3,678,866)	(3,999,186)
Total UFCF						

For working capital, the example provides guidance on accounts receivable and accrued expenses. We then need to subtract assets less liabilities and calculate the year-over-year changes for our cash flow.

Working Capital	Year 0	Year 1	Year 2	Year 3	Year 4	Year 5
Accounts Receivable	1,166,667	1,248,333	1,335,717	1,429,217	1,529,262	1,636,310
Days	*35*	*35*	*35*	*35*	*35*	*35*
Accrued Expenses	125,000	133,750	143,113	153,130	163,850	175,319
Days	*15*	*15*	*15*	*15*	*15*	*15*
Total Working Capital	1,041,667	1,114,583	1,192,604	1,276,086	1,365,413	1,460,991
Changes in Working Capital		(72,917)	(78,021)	(83,482)	(89,326)	(95,579)

We can now use these changes in our UCFC and calculate the total.

Unlevered Free Cash Flow	Year 0	Year 1	Year 2	Year 3	Year 4	Year 5
Revenue	12,000,000	12,840,000	13,738,800	14,700,516	15,729,552	16,830,621
Operating Expenses	3,000,000	3,210,000	3,434,700	3,675,129	3,932,388	4,207,655
EBITDA	9,000,000	9,630,000	10,304,100	11,025,387	11,797,164	12,622,966
D&A		2,525,000	2,550,000	2,575,000	2,600,000	2,625,000
EBIT		7,105,000	7,754,100	8,450,387	9,197,164	9,997,966
Deferred Tax		0	0	0	0	0
Working Capital		(72,917)	(78,021)	(83,482)	(89,326)	(95,579)
CAPEX		(500,000)	(500,000)	(500,000)	(500,000)	(500,000)
Taxes		(2,842,000)	(3,101,640)	(3,380,155)	(3,678,866)	(3,999,186)
Total UFCF		6,215,083	6,624,439	7,061,750	7,528,972	8,028,200

With this information we can calculate our exit and return. Final EBITDA times 7 gives us an exit of $88,360,759. Applying interest to the loans multiplied by 5 years and then multiplied by (1 − tax%) gives us:

$$\text{Term A} = \$31,500,000 \times 10\% \times 5 \times (1 - 40\%) = \$9,450,000$$

$$\text{Term B} = \$13,500,000 \times 12\% \times 5 \times (1 - 40\%) = \$4,860,000$$

$$\text{High Yield} = \$4,500,000 \times 15\% \times 5 \times (1 - 40\%) = \$2,025,000$$

Total obligations are $65,835,000.

The total cash generated is $35,458,445. Reducing the obligations with cash leaves us with $30,376,555 in final debt.

So the return is the exit less final debt, or $57,984,204. Applying the IRR formula (($57,984,204/$14,760,000) ^ (1/5) − 1) gives a return of 31.5%.

CONCLUSION

As mentioned in the beginning, this book was designed to allow practice of technical questions and exercises representing the knowledge one would require in an investment banking interview. Of course, the technical aspect is one of several required to be a strong interview candidate. The ability to communicate these questions effectively, to present oneself effectively, in addition to behavior and fit are among the attributes assessed in an interview. I hope this book proves to be one of many useful tools in helping achieve your investment banking career goals.

About the Companion Website

This book includes a companion website, which can be found at www.wiley.com/go/interviewguide. Enter the password: pignataro17. This website includes the following Excel templates:

Valuation Case 1.xls

Valuation Case 2.xls

Index

Page references followed by f indicate an illustrated figure; followed by t indicate a table.

Printed and bound by CPI Group (UK) Ltd, Croydon, CR0 4YY

16/04/2025

14658467-0004